Women in the House

A Study of Women Members of Parliament

Women
in the House

A Study of
Women Members of Parliament

by

ELIZABETH VALLANCE

LONDON
THE ATHLONE PRESS
1979

Published by
THE ATHLONE PRESS
at 4 Gower Street London WC1

Distributed by Tiptree Book Services Ltd
Tiptree, Essex

USA and Canada
Humanities Press Inc
New Jersey

© *Elizabeth Vallance* 1979

British Library Cataloguing in Publication Data
Vallance, Elizabeth
    Women in the House.
    1. Great Britain. Parliament. House of Commons
    2. Legislators—Great Britain
    3. Women in politics—Great Britain
    I. Title
    301.5'92   JN673
    ISBN 0 485 11186 1

Printed in Great Britain by
WESTERN PRINTING SERVICES LTD
Bristol

To
Iain, Rachel and Edmund

Author's Note

This book is essentially the result of research done prior to the election of May 1979. Most of the women and many of the men in Parliament from 1974 to 1979 were interviewed, as were a large number of the earlier women M.P.s. Although the results of the 1979 election did not change but rather confirmed the pattern of women's political representation as outlined in this study, I thought it was appropriate to include them in a Postscript and to up-date the relevant appendices accordingly. The main text, however, has been left unchanged.

May 1979   E.M.V.

Acknowledgements

I am grateful to many people for their cooperation and support in the researching and writing of this book. The women in the Commons gave me their time in interviews and many of them patiently answered repeated enquiries and elucidated points of detail for me.

I would like too to thank my colleagues in the Department of Political Studies at Queen Mary College for their interest, in particular Trevor Smith who was unfailingly helpful and encouraging.

During 1977–8, I was fortunate enough to have a Leverhulme Research Fellowship which helped enormously in financing the project and for this I am extremely grateful to the Trustees. I am also grateful to Judith Perry for her research help and to Carole Mann of the House of Commons Library for her advice. Evelyn Lockington has cheerfully typed seemingly endless drafts and chapters, deciphering my crabbed script. No one else could have done it.

Finally my thanks to my husband and to my children who had to endure with me the process of writing. The book is for them.

E.M.V.

Contents

Introduction

This book is a study of the women members of Parliament. It is also an attempt to explain their very small numbers, both historically and at present. For although women have been in the Commons now for sixty years, they are still a tiny minority of the membership. Further, and perhaps surprisingly, the influence of the women's movement in the late sixties and seventies seems to have had no impact at all on that representation. In 1945, nearly 4% of the House was female; in the election of October, 1974, that figure was still only 4.3%. And only once in the intervening period was this bettered when in 1964 4.6% of candidates returned were women. Never then in the history of women's involvement in national politics have the dizzy heights of a 5% parliamentary representation been achieved, and this in a country where more than 50% of the electorate are women.

Part of the explanation for this is to be sought in the general position of women in British society, in attitudes to them, particularly to their wielding of power, and in their own self-perceptions. Many of the factors involved here will affect all women aspiring to succeed in the typically male-dominated professions, and some of the problems which women M.P.s face are those with which all such women have to deal. But there appear also to be special difficulties in the case of a political career—from the clear contradiction of the most deeply engraved images of the eternal feminine implicit in the combative and opinionated world of politics, to quite mundane problems of exclusion from the professional gossip of the male world of the smoking room.

To begin at the beginning is to look at the way parliamentary candidates are selected and here women do seem often to lose out. Whether this is a result of discrimination on the part of selectors—male and female—is uncertain, but it seems clear that women do end up with the weaker seats and proportionately many more of them than men never make it. There exists a whole mythology on the electoral appeal, general suitability, and political efficacy of women most of which is, to say the least, questionable and probably empirically untestable. Yet these beliefs, often trenchantly held by selection conferences, may very directly affect the chances of women at this early stage.

Those who do get to the House are often surrounded by further assumptions of one kind or another about how women M.P.s behave— for example that they are predominantly concerned, or that they ought to be concerned, with 'women's issues' and that they therefore have no real competence beyond consumerism, social services and education. To some extent this belief is bolstered by the fact that women have held so few of the major offices of state. No woman has ever been Chancellor, Foreign or Home Secretary and of the seven women who have achieved Cabinet rank, four have been Ministers of Education. And yet their participation and achievements in the House have been much wider than this would suggest and on very few occasions have they ranged themselves as a united group, far less as one simply concerned with women's ideology.

The attitudes of successful women—political or otherwise—to other women is one which sociologists sometimes characterise as at the least unhelpful if not hostile, and it is worth exploring how far this might be the case with the women in Parliament, who are apparently presented with a dual constituency, their elected territorial one, and that of all women. How far women M.P.s acknowledge their representation of women, whether they would favour any sort of women's group in Parliament and to what extent their views are influenced here by their generational outlook was discussed with almost all the women currently in the Commons.

Although many men were also consulted in the process of this research, a study of this kind, predominantly preoccupied with the attitudes and values of the women, might still be open to charges of female tendentiousness and bias. In the interest of balance therefore, it seemed important to look at the views of the largely male House and parties to women, as revealed in debates, party literature and manifestoes. In this context, the continuities of attitude from 1918 to the 1970s are often as revealing as the changes.

One of the original impulses for this study was the realisation that although women are not well represented in national politics in most of Western Europe (although we in Britain do come very near the bottom of the league) this was not the case in other parts of the world. In the Scandinavian countries for example, women make up from 17% to over 23% of national elected representatives and while the perils of cross-cultural comparison must be appreciated, it seems clear that their electoral processes and not simply their social attitudes play a large part in achieving this difference. Our first-past-the-post electoral system is acknowledged to discriminate against minorities and in terms of the accepted conventions and mores of society, women have the characteristics of a minority. There is no reason, in a first-past-the-post system, why a selection conference should choose any minority candidate—whether black, gay or female—and there is every reason for them to opt for the standard product—a middle-class, middle-aged man. In a proportional representation (PR) system, there is every incentive for a party to present a 'balanced' list to make as wide an electoral appeal as possible. In an electorate over 50% of which is female it is inconceivable, in these post-Greer days, that an appropriate number of women would not be included.

At any rate, it seems clear that no amount of tinkering with the services or hours of the House—providing crèches or ladies' hairdressers—will affect the situation, but only quite fundamental levels of technical and constitutional change will bring more women to Westminster.

CHAPTER I

Why so Few?

'What seems to be the right means of training girls so that they may best perform that subordinate part in the world to which I believe they have been called?' Miss Dorothea Beale

'Educate women like men and the more they resemble our sex, the less power they will have over us.' Rousseau

It is perhaps surprising that, in the era of the women's movement, of equal opportunity, anti-discrimination and equal pay, when women with equal political rights compose rather more than 50% of the electorate, 96% of the members of the central institution of our democratic process, the House of Commons, are male. Of the six hundred and thirty-five M.P.s returned to Westminster in the October 1974 general election, only twenty-seven were women (i.e. some 4%). A by-election in July 1976[1] brought the number up to twenty-eight.

Women have now been in Parliament for the best part of sixty years yet in many ways they appear never really to have found their feet there. Of course individual women have achieved a great deal, but their success has not been cumulative. By this I mean that there is very little continuity which can be traced either in terms of rising numbers or even in breaking into areas of government or parliamentary life where women had not been accepted before. The first woman member was not rapidly followed by an ever-increasing number of women M.P.s; the first woman Cabinet Minister retained her position of solitary splendour for a great many years; the first woman to sit in the Speaker's Chair is so far also the last; and the first woman Chancellor or Foreign Secretary has still to be. In many other areas of professional life, the pioneer women who fought to be doctors and barristers and academics seemed to achieve rather more in the way of solid gains and real acceptance for women in their professions. Women in Parliament on the other hand, always appear rather to be there on sufferance. The odd talented individual is given recognition, but this does not necessarily appear to accrue to the breed as a whole. After all this time, as Edith Summerskill says, 'Parliament with its conventions and protocol, [seems] a little like a boys' school which has decided to take a few girls.'[2]

Yet whether women have in fact done so much worse in politics than in other areas of professional life is perhaps rather contentious. There is, it is true, a smaller percentage of women M.P.s (about 4%) than of women doctors (22%), barristers (7%), academics (11%) or dentists (14%). Yet for all these unfavourable comparisons, there are others which make the representation of women in Parliament seem much more solid. In 1974, for example, only just over 4% of architects were women and only 1% of the 1975 membership of the Institute of Directors was female. Equally, in 1974 only 4% of solicitors were women and although the numbers of women in medicine and in the universities seem fairly substantial, when it comes to the higher reaches of these professions, they are less so. Only 12% of consultants (in 1975) were women,[3] and only 1.7% of university professors, and the percentage of readers and senior lecturers actually went down between 1966 and 1974.

Just as the evidence for women being particularly under-represented in political life compared with their numbers elsewhere is rather ambivalent, so equally is the evidence for British women being particularly backward in this sphere. Cross-cultural comparison is always a dubious enterprise in that the comparison may be of the incomparable. What appears to be 'the same' institution or attitude or idea in two or more cultures may in fact have little in common to justify their posited 'sameness'. Thus to look at women in national parties in other countries and to compare their positions with women in this country is to be liable to a charge of manipulation of the evidence where it does not directly and obviously relate to similar conditions—or at best of a culpable naivety.

Certainly there are special conditions which appear, if not to explain, at least to make less puzzling the existence of women heads of government in other (mainly 'underdeveloped') parts of the world, well before such an idea was being contemplated here. Their experience is thus not directly comparable to our own. Equally, the rather different systems of representation, election and appointment make direct comparisons of women in Cabinet positions in Britain with say, France or America, inappropriate. Yet when differences in social and institutional factors have been recognised, some points of comparison may well be instructive. In most of Western Europe, for example, the numbers of women in national politics are low and have in some cases, until recently, even been falling.

In the United States, there were in 1977 no women in the Senate and only a handful in the House of Representatives. In Norway, Sweden and Denmark, on the other hand, the percentages of women representatives are significantly higher than elsewhere, and seem to be rising. (The Norwegian Storting has about 22% female representation, for example, while in Sweden the figure is 21% and in Denmark 17%.) While accepting the problems of comparing societies in this kind of way, if it appears that we can isolate certain factors as having a significant influence on female representation in national politics in the Scandinavian countries, and these factors are not to be found in our own experience, it may be that these factors have a particular importance in explaining the disparity between their situation and ours in this context.

What then are the factors which seem likely to influence the numbers of women choosing a career in national politics? Many of them, as already stated, are of significance for women in professional life generally and all of them limit in one way or another the numbers of such women. Perhaps it is best to acknowlege at the beginning that in stating that there are very few women in politics, it is not being suggested that all women are potential M.P.s, any more than all men are such. Being an M.P., like being a brain surgeon or a gardener, is not everybody's life's ambition. But it does not at all explain the problem to say that only some people, male or female,—the suggestion is that the gender issue is a red herring—will want to get involved in this way of life, and indeed will have the requisite combination of capabilities and qualities, education and luck to make it possible to do so. For one is still left with the problem of explaining why it is, in an apparently otherwise democratic society, that 96% of the people who do so are men. One is not suggesting that vast numbers of women somehow must come forward in pursuance of the life of politics, only that it is at least problematic that so few of them in fact do.

The obvious reasons for women being less inclined to get involved in any job outside the home are physiological and biological. Women have babies; they tend to want to look after those babies and it is their mates, rather than they, who work outside the home to provide for the nuclear family thus formed. Even when a woman does return to work after her family has grown up, it tends to be in the belief that her job is less important, both financially and in terms of status (and the two are often related) than her husband's.[4] And whether she likes it or not, she is still years behind her male counterpart in the promotion league, having had these years at home with her children.

Yet over 40% of married women do work, and indeed 62%[5] of all employed women are married, the great majority of these with family commitments. And the number of married women working is on the increase (in 1931, only 10% worked). More and more women are therefore either not stopping work at all after their children are born, or stopping only for a relatively short time. The pressures for this are probably largely financial. The economic situation of most families has become more uncertain, at least when compared with the halcyon days of the late 50s and 60s when rising expectations, economic stability and minimal inflation meant women could choose more easily to remain at home, and that conversely their outside work could be thought of as a luxury, a social enjoyment rather than a financial necessity. This is no longer the case and social attitudes to the employment of women have changed accordingly.

It is sometimes suggested that women don't go into public life, and don't make the contribution that might be expected of them in the professions, largely because they have domestic commitments and that in the absence of, for instance, nursery schools and flexible working hours (for both sexes), there is nothing they can do but stay at home, thus risking the loss of both their social and professional confidence. However true this may be at the middle-class professional level, it should not be forgotten that the huge increase in the number of ordinary working women has taken place without the provision of extensive nursery school places. Although there may be some force in the argument that the provision of nursery school places for the children of all mothers who want them would release a whole area of the population from their homes, it is not the case that there is a total congruence here; for women, when they have needed to (either for financial or other reasons) have found ways of having their children cared for, with or without nurseries, and equally women who could have their children taken care of, choose to stay at home and care for them themselves.

This seems to point to two things. One is that the relations of women within the family, to husbands, to children and to society, are much more complicated than they at first appear. And the second is that the real toll of domestic duties on women is altogether too diffuse to be alleviated by any single organisational or institutional change. On the first point it is simplistic to suppose that the provision of nursery places for all children of working mothers would of itself and overnight change attitudes and values or women's self-image. There is, at the least, often a considerable time-lag between changes in institutions and social arrangements and changes in the attitudes which are associated with them. Very often a few opinion-formers, or simply those with political power, make changes in our legal or institutional arrangements and it is only when this is a fait accompli that people have the chance to come to terms with it. In the present social climate, it seems very unlikely that providing nursery places for pre-school children would immediately convince the great majority of women that they need not look after their own children, far less ought not to. Socialisation since the hour of their birth has seen to that, and to suggest that an isolated institutional change will successfully reverse the conditioning of a lifetime is perhaps unrealistic.[6]

The second point is that one should not underestimate the importance of domestic responsibility in keeping women either inside the home, or often under-achieving in jobs outside it. Women do not, it would seem, give the same commitment to their jobs as men do. They are unwilling to take on extra responsibility; they are not prepared in general to do overtime; they are not active in the formation of strategy within their work-places, or within their trade unions. Statistically, many of these points seem incontestable,[7] yet the reasons are a good deal more complicated than simple apathy on the part of women workers. Gone are the days when women worked—or believed they worked—largely for lipstick and tights money. Now, as May Hobbs, militant leader of the London cleaners says, they work for little luxuries like food for the family, clothes for the children and money for the rent. They do not pass up chances of overtime and more money out of a perverse lack of interest in their own welfare, and by extension that of their families. Rather their involvement with their families is often at the root of their apparent lack of commitment at work. Overtime is seldom convenient for a woman with school-age children: union meetings are often evening or after-work affairs and again domestic involvements intervene. And over and above those specific commitments is the diffuse and often enervating responsibility for the quite mundane but necessary running of the household, the cleaning, the shopping, the cooking, or just being around with the children. Women of all classes generally now run their own homes and families with minimal if any domestic help. Thus even before they go to work they may have to arrange breakfast, do household chores, get children ready and off to school and a husband out to work. Before she starts on a job outside, a woman has generally done a job inside the house. And after work, or in the lunch hour, she is shopping and planning meals ready for the evening. It is this diffusion of energy as much as anything that is the important legacy of domesticity for women.[8] More than any single factor—like child-care itself, or housework—it is the general organisation of the life of a family that takes up a major part of most women's energy. In this respect, professional women, and putative political women, are equally disadvantaged. They do not and cannot have—if they are family women—the single-mindedness of a man, even a family man. The operation of what might be called the Law of the Conservation of Energy ensures that men typically walk out of the house in the morning with no further sense of responsibility for its running, no channelling of energy into speculation about provision of meals or care of children.

What applies to women in general in these respects applies obviously to women aspiring to a political career. It is clearly necessary for an M.P. to be able to give his or her whole-hearted attention to the job. It was in this context that one of the early women M.P.s remarked that a wife is the most valuable asset in politics.[9] And a wife is just what a woman doesn't have.

Against this background, other more specific problems for women clearly emerge. To begin with, getting elected to Parliament can be a long-term and uncertain business. To put one's name forward, or allow it to go forward for selection, may only be the beginning of an extended process of short-listings, selection conferences, fighting of hopeless or marginal seats in by-elections or general elections, and 'nursing' of constituencies on the chance of election come the next round. It is quite possible that a woman may convince herself that it is acceptable to continue with an already established career, that she must go on with the work for which she is trained and which she thinks of as a very important part of herself. A woman doctor, lawyer or academic has an identifiable and, to most people, legitimate aspiration in the pursuit of her career. But the pursuit of a political ambition is much less clear-cut. To have your children cared for while you use your acquired abilities to minister to the sick or impart knowledge to the student may now be socially acceptable: to do so when your aim is the off-chance of a parliamentary seat, involving probably much travel and time away from home, may be much less so. So a whole section of the female population of the requisite age and background tends to be excluded even from the serious consideration of entering national politics. Thus, as one would expect, young women with children are simply not represented in any numbers in the House. In the Parliament elected in 1974, although most of the women are married (16 out of 27), and many have children (15), only two have children under ten. This is a case of one social change being off-set by another. The original female M.P.s were middle and upper class almost to a woman. They had, therefore, staff to run their houses and care for their children. Many of them did in fact have young children (Lady Astor came to Parliament first when her youngest child was less than two years old) but this did not constrain them as it does today's women, partly because they were not so physically tied to the home, but partly too because of social attitudes. They belonged to a time and class which accepted both that women—particularly of the upper classes—did have social functions, performed 'good works', sat on committees etc., all of which extended quite easily into politics, and also that they did not personally bring up their children. They 'oversaw' a nursery, chose nannies and governesses, or finally sent their children off to school. They did not feel guilty about this process, however personally sad it may have made some of them. But one of the spin-offs of the relatively new middle-class idea of bringing up children personally within the small family unit is that this job, having been devolved largely on women, has proved the most potent social as well as practical constraint on women's mobility. It is not only the contemporary lack of servants (or any of the possible 'servant surrogates' in this area like pre-school nurseries) that ties many women so securely to their children and inhibits their development into extra-familial pursuits, but their own strongly maintained belief that children's upbringing is much too important to be left to others.

There is perhaps one more quite practical problem—or group of problems—based in the domestic framework of the average family—which limits the possibility of serious consideration being given to a political career by most women. This is the reorganisation of family life which would have to accompany a woman's election to Parliament. Parliament meets in London, while most constituencies are far from London and many M.P.s have their homes in their constituencies with wife and children remaining there during the week and the member going home on Thursday night or Friday for the weekend. This is complicated enough, but it assumes that the wife is either static, or at least able to organise family life and children during the working week. If a woman is elected, does the family move to London? What about the husband's job? If they don't move, who looks after the family during the week? The kind of three-cornered arrangement—London/ constituency/place of husband's job and home—that might develop here is clearly complicated, and probably for most people too involved to be seriously contemplated. Even before this stage, there is the quite clear financial problem of a woman nursing a constituency perhaps hundreds of miles from her home and family. She must make herself known there, which means travelling there frequently and almost certainly at her own expense. The vast majority of women in a position to afford this are professional women with salaries of their own, yet professional women are by definition involved in their professions and not in finding Parliamentary seats. It may be said that the same is true of men and to some extent this is so. But there are many more men in the Labour Party at any rate who are sponsored by trade unions or Labour organisations,[10] and again, if a woman is married and has children, all the problems of domestic arrangements repeat themselves.

To dwell at some length, as I have done, on the practical and domestic constraints of most women's experience is not to suggest that this need be the only reason (or even perhaps the major one) for their under-representation in politics. Yet it is important not only in the quite practical sense of being time-consuming, but also in consuming a large part of most women's need for identity. To be a 'good wife and mother' just does seem more important to most women than being a member of Parliament (or a heart surgeon or professor of Greek, for that matter). And this in a way in which being a 'good husband and father' does not at all completely fulfil the aspirations or self-consciousness of most men. Socialisation then, seems crucial in any understanding of women's attitudes (and indeed men's) in this respect. Women are socialised both positively and negatively in ways which conspire to dampen both their general aspirations of achievement and the specific political abilities which they might develop.

Positively, girls are brought up to believe that their role is different from that of boys (separate but equal, so the story goes). They have a role as wife and mother to look forward to and their education, although formally often similar to that of their brothers, is to this end. They are encouraged therefore to see their goals as different from those of boys. This need no longer take the overtly inegalitarian form of seeking an education for girls which, in the words of Miss Beale, the great Victorian educationalist, would allow them to 'best perform that subordinate part in the world to which I believe they have been called', yet implicit in our educational standards is an image of the eternal feminine. As a recent Department of Employment paper has it, 'boys are trained to be achieving, independent, competitive and self-sufficient, . . . girls are trained to be comforting, dependent, co-operative and group-orientated'.[11] Positively girls are encouraged, not just in school, in formal education, but in the attitudes they take from home, the media etc., to aspire and conform to certain standards of passivity, softness, domesticity and above all perhaps, maternal feelings, the dispensation of care and comfort. Negatively, the encouragement to femininity means the discouragement of the masculine virtues. Girls who are too self-opinionated or articulate are 'brash'; those who flaunt their logicality are 'cold'; those who have qualities of leadership are 'hard', or just generically 'lacking in feminity'. Again, there is discouragement of the woman who looks outside the traditional maternal role for her fulfilment. A whole generation, for example, were brought up in the Bowlby dogma of 'maternal deprivation'[12] which suggested that for a mother to be absent from her child for any time at all would cause irreparable damage to that child's emotional development. The inevitable conclusion was that any woman who would risk the danger of emotionally crippling her child in this way by leaving him while she amused herself outside the home was criminally selfish. Even Bowlby's later modification of his theories (which had been the product of his work with children in institutions and children's homes where no distinction could be made between partial and complete separation) did little to reverse the impression already made on women in the 1950s, and has only recently been challenged and rethought. Bowlby's was a theory which fitted very well with the post-war desires for a return to 'normality', which meant in this area the return of women from the factory or forces to the home. Women had looked after families as well as holding down jobs during the war crisis, and had been provided with child-care facilities to do it when it was in the national interest. Later however, it was presumably in the national interest for them to become once again the providers of care and comfort within a regularised family situation. And it was for this reversal that Bowlby provided the theoretical justification.

In general, too, girls are brought up not to be too competitive and not to see personal achievement, at least in educational or professional terms, as primarily important. This is clear in the educational progress of girls and boys in the subjects they choose and in their final educational achievements. Although girls do at least as well as boys in primary school, by the onset of adolescence, the boys begin to pull ahead and by the time they sit A-levels the boys are in the majority (1972 figures show that 6.6% of girls leave school with three or more A-Levels, compared with 9.1% of boys, when at the O-Level stage rather more girls than boys leave school with five or more O-Levels). The reasons for this decline are many but not hard to find. Girls themselves cease to compete when they realise that beating him in Chemistry exams is not the way to a boy's heart and girls' schools sometimes do not encourage their pupils to do the 'tougher' intellectual disciplines such as mathematics and sciences, often because they do not have adequate staffing or equipment. And so a vicious circle develops where girls are not generally encouraged to aspire to high academic achievement and so there is not the demand from them for this kind of education (e.g. grammar school education as it used to be understood) and so this kind of education is not provided in the way that it is for boys. For example, it emerged during the Tameside Council's dispute with the Secretary of State for Education and Science in 1976, that only one third of the grammar school places were allocated to girls, the remaining two thirds being for boys. This was justified on the grounds that a much smaller proportion of girls than boys applied for grammar school.

The differing patterns of education of boys and girls means not only that women are not in our society, in general, as formally educated as men, but that they do not acquire many of the peripheral attributes of wider educational experience. Formal education is obviously not a necessary requirement of membership of the House of Commons, but the women members more than their male counterparts have tended to be highly educated, most with higher education, and increasing numbers with university degrees. Clearly, women, who are generally socialised to avoid so many of the characteristics which are advantageous in political life (being aggressive, for example, or opinionated, competitive and articulate), have more chance of acquiring the necessary confidence the more their education has been like that of men. And this not just because they have the formal knowledge which this kind of education provides, but because they have already acquired an awareness of their own worth and ability in the undiscriminated and egalitarian world of the college or university. The way in which women's upbringing impedes or at least initially inhibits their political development is I think underlined by at least two points mentioned to me independently by several women M.P.s. Firstly, they are very much aware of having to get through a confidence barrier which allows them to stick their necks out without crippling inhibitions. Nobody, male or female, likes to make a fool of himself, but women are particularly fearful of even being outstanding and they have to overcome this sensitivity before they can be effective politically. They also have to learn quite literally to talk. Politics is the articulate profession par excellence and oratory and debate are its very centre. Women are not generally articulate, nor are they normally encouraged to take pleasure in the cut and thrust of debate. Again they are particularly sensitive about looking foolish or pretentious in what they have been brought up to believe is the male world of politics. Consequently women do not typically put themselves forward politically, do not ask questions at public meetings, do not appear to have any kind of grasp of, or even interest in, the issues. Several of the women members have emphasised to me that while men will dominate the question and answer sessions of public meetings, women will consistently come up afterwards to ask of the M.P. (another woman, which presumably in this context makes it easier to do) a question which is more intelligent and to the point than any that have been asked in open forum. (And several M.P.s made the comment that the questioner would often begin with 'I hope this isn't too stupid/obvious/irrelevant a question . . .'). Mrs Judith Hart says she has become so aware of this problem among women that she has actively encouraged sessions in the women's sections of the Labour Party where women simply practised asking questions—and she adds, 'not just asking them, but shouting them!'

I have so far ignored the theory that women, regardless of their education and general socialisation, are simply in some ways genetically different from men and that it is this difference which really lies at the root of what is called their 'under-achievement' in certain areas of life. They under-achieve that is, because they are not made, either physiologically, or psychologically to achieve in these areas. In a recent book,[13] Steven Goldberg an American sociologist, has claimed that there are differences in the endocrine structures of men and women which impel men to dominance-seeking behaviour to a much greater extent than women. These behavioural differences are innate and not socially acquired. Socialisation, says Goldberg, is 'the process by which society utilises the reality of differentiated tendencies'. Even if this were the case (and Goldberg himself admits the uncertainty of his conclusions if not of his physiological premises), it is still unlikely that innate differences alone are such as to make women's attempted involvement in certain areas inevitably unsuccessful. It is much more likely that the social backup—if indeed that is all it is—of education etc., is sufficiently strong to be the determining factor in women's under-performance and indeed under-involvement, in the so-called male areas. After all, if as Goldberg argues, it is all a question of hormones, why are the hormones of otherwise apparently normal females, most of them wives and mothers, so inefficient as to allow them to believe that they want to achieve the genetically unachievable? The weakness of the argument is not so much that it is provably false (in fact, of course, it is neither provably false, nor provably true) as that the other sociological, educational and domestic explanations of women's relatively poor performance in the areas in question are better documented and more compelling. And Barbara Castle and Margaret Thatcher, not to mention Lady Astor, seem to be the proof that, for example, the political virtues of competitiveness and toughness and determination are either not the innate preserves of the male, or are at least acquirable by the diligent female aspirant. Even the suggestion of the 'sociobiologists', people like Wilson[14] in America and Dawkins[15] in Britain, that genes dictate social behaviour and that the feminine urge is largely domestic and maternal, is significant not in that it is a counsel of despair for aspiring female politicians (and indeed all women who do not see their total fulfilment in breeding and nurturing offspring), but in that it brings into sharp focus the social attitudes and claims which have developed in this area. There is no way at the moment—if ever—of proving such theories empirically one way or the other. How, after all, can it be shown exactly where nature stops and nurture takes over? In this sense, feminists who argue aggressively for the proposition that there is no difference between men and women are on uncertain ground, in that some of the evidence at least (educational and professional achievement for example) is all against them. Further, the theory of genetic inheritance in other areas is well-established—if we can inherit blue eyes and a straight nose from our ancestors why not also a programme of learned reactions? The question then becomes, what are we going to do about it? It is clearly not the case that a 'female genetic programme' utterly voids any educational or social efforts to give women a fairer crack at the extra-domestic whip. When given it, some women do take and always have taken, the chance to enter the external, male world. To give more women that chance is largely what the claim for equality in this context is about. It is about overcoming, as far as possible, the dis-abilities whether natural (genetic, endocrinal or whatever) or social (cultural, educational etc.), or whatever combination of the two, which may hamper women's ability to opt for that external world. We may not be able to change the genes (if they are indeed critical factors), but we can change the social and cultural and educational environment in which they operate. We can, in short, over time, change the way women are taught to think about themselves. And on the way there, and as an integral part of that goal, we can make things easier not harder for the women who choose to go outside their homes and families. This argument rests on no claims of spurious egalitarianism, but on a simple plea of justice for those who are, in this context, disadvantaged.

When physiological, sociological and practical domestic consider-ations have been assessed as contributors to women's sparse rep-resentation in the political ranks, there remains still the possibility of male conspiracy. The world, it is claimed, is man-made, and that has meant the exclusion of women from many areas particularly of public and professional life and their relegation to the home where they can do no harm and present no challenge. In spite of the changes which have taken place in the status of women over the past few years, it is argued that men are still irredeemably chauvinistic. They have built their empire and like all imperialists they will fight hard to re-tain it, for they stand to lose both their status and their servants in the reorganisation. What we have now, this argument continues, is the breakdown of imperialism with all the uncertainties and inconsis-tencies which this entails. And even if men are not aware of their discrimination against women, it is there in their attitudes and values, in their condescension and their lordly patronage of the women who aspire to be their colleagues. Even their chivalry or politeness can be construed as sexism.

The social and sexual uncertainty of the moment, when rigid codes of behaviour and clearly defined mores seem to have given way to a kind of moral laissez-faire and social free-for-all, has allowed women to make their demands for equality and left them, at least temporarily, confused about their own aspirations. It has also left men confused. The clearest equality to come out of the social and sexual revolution of the women's movement has been the equality of uncertainty for men and women which the rejection of clear-cut values and ends has involved. Against this background, it becomes obvious that the relationship between women's under-participation in politics and other male preserves and men's attitudes to that participation is far from simple. The women M.P.s are themselves intuitively aware of this. They will not, in general, claim to be aware of discrimination against them as women. Most of them said they had never been aware of discrimination against themselves, either as established M.P.s, or even (which perhaps is more surprising) at the constituency selection level. Many of them were aware of what they saw as sexist rather than discriminatory attitudes among their male colleagues. One young female M.P., talking about the way men tend to patronise the women, particularly the younger women, said 'they either pat you on the head or the bottom'. It is not intended to be patronising, far less denigratory, but it does as it were set the parties concerned in a certain relationship which rather precludes the equality of colleagues. And perhaps this is what the men intuitively seek to do. They have been used in the past to establishing the parameters of female involvement, even to defining the 'women's issues' which they encouraged women to pursue. The change in the past few years seems to have been that women are now much more self-assured and much more secure in their own value—as women—and therefore less inclined to take the male perspective as the only possible one.[16]

The extent of actual discrimination—at the selection stage, say—is almost impossible to establish. The women M.P.s do not complain of it, but then they are the successful products of the system. They made it, so it can't be totally discriminatory. Yet women do much worse than men when it comes to getting the safe seats, and although the major parties have in the past few years been doing all they can to attract women candidates, there is a difference between passing a generalised resolution at party conference to the effect that more women ought to be attracted into the party at all levels, including the parliamentary, and actually ensuring that individual constituency parties and selection committees in the end are willing to consider women sympathetically. And ironically the situation may have become harder for women within the Conservative Party at any rate since its selection procedure was 'democratised'.[17]

Discrimination then, is at least a factor to be considered in this analysis of women in Parliament, but it is not a case of straightforward male chauvinism. Many men are indeed ambivalent about the entry of women into public life but this ambivalence may as often work for women as against them. They have, after all, scarcity value and this may be a deciding factor in certain situations: they are memorable again simply in virtue of their limited numbers and they may have a great deal in their favour if they are able to reveal and overcome male prejudice.[18] They don't have to be just as direct as Lady Astor who, when treated by one man to a violent and foul-mouthed attack on her lack of feminine passivity ending by his triumphantly proclaiming, 'Anyway I didn't vote for you!', called back imperiously, 'Thank heavens for that!'[19] Dr Oonagh McDonald was equally successful in turning the tables when asked at a selection conference how she would cope if a crowd of hefty dockers 'turned nasty' on her. Tiny Dr McDonald replied that she would 'try not to be too violent!'

The discrimination of men against women may be only a part, and it's sometimes said the gentler part, of discrimination when compared with women's discrimination against other women. Just how significant this is is as hard to determine as with the male variety, and perhaps as ambiguous. In its bald form, the argument goes that women do not like to see other women in public life, either through a sense of its being 'unseemly', or through jealousy. Older women may have the feeling that it is inappropriate for a woman to be leading this kind of life and not at home minding her family, and younger women may subconsciously feel resentful precisely that they *are* stuck at home minding the family. Either way women stand to lose the support of their sisters and it used to be claimed that a woman candidate at an election was bound to lose the Party votes. Whether this ever was the case or not, there seems little evidence for it now.[20]

Women seem, in the past few years, not only to have ceased to want a 'father-figure' male M.P., as they often in the past sought the 'competence' of a male doctor or lawyer or dentist, but positively to support other women. For example a Gallup Poll appearing in the *Daily Telegraph* in 1975 showed that although most voters did not then think Mrs Thatcher would make a good party leader, the majority of women voters supported her. Similarly, an Opinion Research Centre Poll for Independent Television's 'News at Ten' showed one in two women voters more likely to vote Tory with Mrs Thatcher as leader (and nearly one third of Labour women supporters held this view).

Once inside the House, women's problems are not over. However they are treated by their male colleagues (and none of the women M.P.s present or past with whom I talked had any complaints about the equality of the House), and however successful or otherwise they are in making their way, they do have to contend with the lack of facilities of the House itself. Not only have M.P.s seldom got a room, they have often to fight for a desk. The women have only over time acquired, by use and wont, a couple of rooms (the 'Room on the Terrace' and one other) which they can use as sitting-rooms. There is no shopping precinct like that which the delegates to the European Parliament enjoy at Strasbourg, no crèche for the use of those with children, and not even a ladies' hairdresser (although there is of course a barber). Until quite recently women were discouraged from using the bar or the smoking room—unless accompanied by a man. Perhaps most inhibiting of all, the hours of business are horrendous—starting in the middle of the afternoon and going on, if need be, into the middle of the night. But then, there are four times as many lawyers in Parliament as there are women, and the Parliamentary day is geared to the average lawyer rather than the average woman. In recent times much has been made of this particular disadvantage of the M.P.'s life, the complainants being not only M.P.s themselves (who are perhaps characteristically split on this issue) but their wives. Mrs Radice, wife of Giles Radice the M.P. for Chester-le-Street, has campaigned for less unsocial hours, morning sittings for example, and if not a nine until five existence at least a ten until seven or eight one.[21] Inside the House too, Mrs Renee Short has always supported the idea of changes in the hours of the House but has not always had the support of all the members, or even of all the women, some of whom simply accept philosophically that erratic hours go with this particular job. Indeed some of the men who live in London during the week, travelling home to families only at weekends, are known to respond to the idea of shutting up shop in the early evening with anguished cries of 'What will we do during the week if the House isn't sitting in the evening?' The idea, of course, is not to shut down the facilities of the House, the bars and restaurant and smoking room. Says Mrs Short, 'They can still have their club'.

Yet changes in this area, the provision of better facilities, be they rooms for interviewing constituents (at present mostly done in corridors or the Central Lobby) or a supermarket or hairdresser, are hardly going to make the difference between women staying out of national politics and their coming in in droves. Even a change in the hours of the House, although it might be more convenient for the women and men already there, is hardly likely to be a determinant to women who are seriously contemplating entering politics. Anyone at that stage already realises that the work is time-consuming and the hours demanding and even if the hours when physical presence in the Palace of Westminster was demanded were cut, the job itself is essentially open-ended; there is always someone to see, something to read. It is just not a nine-to-five job.

That so many members of the House are professionally involved elsewhere and come to Westminster in the later afternoon and evening points to another factor which may effect the representation of women there. Very many M.P.s come from a fairly narrow professional spectrum. They are members of the 'articulate professions'—teachers, lecturers, lawyers, and members of the media greatly outnumber all the other professions and backgrounds in Parliament. And the women members reflect this same over-all bias. But there clearly aren't nearly so many women in these professions (with the possible exception of teaching and then at the primary level) as there are men. Fewer women therefore get the professional experience which may be an advantage in pursuing a Parliamentary ambition, and most women are for longish periods of their lives involved in looking after home and children which hardly extends their knowledge of economic policy or sharpens their debating techniques. Yet there is precisely this kind of experience to be gained in some of the professions, where there exists what has been termed 'professional convergence',[22] i.e. two professions converging when they have common role requirements—like law and politics where the lawyer has experience in arguing a case, in representing others etc. The roles of housewife and M.P. on the other hand, it might be argued, are not complementary in the same way.

There is always the possibility that women simply do not want to get into Parliament and there's an end to it. They do not want to get in because they do not like that kind of life; they get their satisfaction, even their political satisfaction, from other involvements. On the face of it, it does seem quite possible that the ritual and ceremonial of the House, its slow, ponderous processes, its interminable committees and talk rather than action, should not appeal to women whose experience is largely practical, pragmatic and here and now. Could it be that even politically interested women are more likely to get involved in say, local government, than in national politics? In some ways, this may be so. There are clearly more women in local politics than there are in the national variety (even so, the numbers are not high—or rising very fast).[23] Still it does seem that women do often want to be involved in organising their local facilities by being councillors or mayors or magistrates. Such people often show no personal interest in national politics beyond supporting their local party. This may be partly because they do not have the self-confidence for the national arena and can only see themselves as a big fish in a little pool, but it may also be because some of them can see no appeal in the formalism of the Commons. As Ruth Dalton told Ramsey MacDonald in explaining her decision to leave national politics and return to her work on the L.C.C., 'There we do things, here it seems to be all talk'.

Yet the appeals of national politics remain for many people—women as well as men. Indeed several of the younger women M.P.s have quite self-consciously avoided local politics, disliking its 'parish-pump' image. There is in any case no direct connection between the two, although local politics is and always has been for many, a proving ground for Westminster.

All of these factors may to some extent and in some cases inhibit the greater participation of women in national politics. Yet there is no single, simple explanation of why there are so few of them, or why those few do decide to pursue a political career. What is sought in the following chapters is a wider understanding of the backgrounds and roles of women M.P.s, which may go some way to explaining both why they are and have always been such a select band, and what motivates them in the pursuit of the political life.

CHAPTER II

An Historical Account

'I find a woman's intrusion into the House of Commons as
embarrassing as if she burst into my bathroom when I had
nothing with which to defend myself, not even a sponge.'
Winston Churchill

On 1 December 1919, soon after three o'clock in the afternoon the
first woman member of Parliament took her seat in the House of
Commons. Lady Astor, wearing the dark tailored suit and tricorne hat
which were to become her parliamentary uniform, was introduced into
the House by her sponsors, the Prime Minister, David Lloyd George,
and the President of the Council and Leader of the Conservative Party,
A. J. Balfour. It was in many ways both an end and a beginning. It
marked the culmination of women's fight for political representation
and the start of the battle for equality within the sphere of national
politics itself. To be admitted into the holy of holies, the Palace of Westminster was not at all the same thing as being accepted on an equal
footing. Lady Astor herself later recorded that many members were
unwelcoming to say the least, and not all of these were political
opponents or even unknown to her. 'Men whom I had known for years
would not speak to me if they passed me in the corridor.'[1] The hope
of at least some entrenched opinion was that she was if not a nine-day,
then a six-month wonder, and that was as long as she would last. In
fact of course she lasted for twenty-six years, but more importantly
the trend which she represented—the involvement of women in
parliamentary politics—has never been reversed.

Lady Astor was the first woman to take her seat in Parliament. But
she was neither the first woman elected to a parliament, nor indeed
the first woman elected to the House of Commons. In Finland, where
women had the vote in 1906, the election of 1907 brought nineteen
women to Parliament, making up 9.5 % of the total, a figure which is
twice as high as women in Britain have ever achieved. In this country,
women did not have the vote until 1918[2] and their right to stand for

Parliament was not confirmed until the November of that year when a general election had been announced for the December.

In spite of this rather compressed time scale, there were women ready to stand. There had, in the fight for the vote, been the development of a political consciousness among at least some women who were only too keen to take the active part in political life which was the logical extension of the freedom for which they had fought. The 1918 election involved 1623 candidates in contesting 707 parliamentary seats. Only seventeen, or rather more than 1% of these candidates were women. In one respect, this number was perhaps not as paltry as it might sound. The Bill allowing women candidates had after all been rushed through the House virtually at the last minute (the day Parliament was prorogued, 21 November 1918, it was announced that the Bill was law). Yet women had been actively involved in one way or another in politics for some time and in much greater numbers than this first election showed. Only four women stood as Labour candidates, for example, when this had been the party traditionally associated with support for the suffrage movement. And indeed three of these women, Mrs Pethick Lawrence, Mrs Charlotte Despard, and Mrs MacKenzie had been well-known in the suffrage movement. To get women chosen by local parties seems to have been a problem from the start. The beginnings of the myth of women's lack of support for other women can be found at this time too, as can the reverse fear that women would quickly install other women for their own and not the general good! A newspaper report of the time suggests in support of the former belief that 'it is one thing to give women votes and quite another to induce them to plump for a woman candidate',[3] while Miss Garland, a Liberal candidate with a reputedly strong female following was feared as an example of the latter.

But perhaps the main reason why relatively few women stood for Parliament in the first election was that women's main political and politicising experience to date had been the fight for the vote which was at bottom a non-party political activity. In fact, many of the leaders of the suffrage movement were suspicious of party politics and advocated a Women's Party, on the basis that only by keeping women's particular interests and concerns represented directly, could a sell-out by the politicians be avoided. It is no accident, therefore, that of the seventeen women standing eight stood as independents of one kind or another. Christabel Pankhurst, Mrs Emmeline Pankhurst's

daughter, stood in the election as representative of the Women's
Party which grew directly out of the Women's Social and Political
Union, her mother's women's suffrage foundation. The Women's
Party itself never got off the ground. It met with mixed support and
antagonism among women and it was of course the continuation of the
militant feminism which many men—and a significant number of
M.P.s—had always feared. In any case, the stage was set for women
to make their parliamentary debut in quite another way: not as
aggressive proselytisers for the female cause (most of the rights for
which they had fought had been won), but as aliens, who, having
been given citizenship, now felt they had to prove their loyalty. Not
that the first women in the House were silent, ineffectual creatures.
But they were aware of playing according to rules which were not of
their own making and which they had to acquire and internalise before
anything else. They took over the men's game rather than, as Christabel
Pankhurst would have had it, trying to institute a new one. In any
case, in 1918 the question was academic. All but one (Countess
Markievicz) of the seventeen women who stood were defeated.

It is in this context perhaps not so ironic and surprising as it might
have been that when the first woman member of Parliament took her
seat in a by-election of 1919, she was neither a suffragette nor a
political activist. Yet how strange it must have seemed to the veteran
suffragettes to be faced with Lady Astor. They had doubtless assumed
that the first woman M.P. would very likely be one of themselves—
middle class, dedicated, politically and socially radical. Instead she
was rich, aristocratic, almost dilettante (in the way in which only the
very rich can be)—and American born! They can scarcely have
recognised themselves in the small, neatly-tailored figure who took
her seat that December day in 1919. Although it was not, of course,
the case that Lady Astor was simply a puppet, or lacked all political
sense, yet her political involvement was quite different from theirs.
She came to Parliament taking over the seat which had been her
husband's when he inherited (much to his chagrin, for he was set on
making a name for himself in the Commons) his father's viscountcy
and went to the Lords. She was not then, one of the new women,
making her way on her own account. And yet that is exactly what she
did in her parliamentary career, but because she was erratic and
spontaneous and eccentric in the way of the self-assured, unself-
consciously arrogant upper classes, not because she felt passionately

committed to a cause or even totally involved in the destiny of a party. (She was a notoriously bad 'Party Woman'—the reason why, perhaps, in spite of her dynamism and clear ability, she was never given office.)

It is well-known that Lady Astor was not the first woman to stand for Parliament; what is less well-known is that neither was she the first to be elected. The one successful candidate in the 1918 election did not take her seat. She was Constance Markievicz (née Constance Gore-Booth) who came of an Anglo-Irish family and was married to a Polish Count—a most romantic background. To add to the romance, she was at the time of the election in Holloway prison on a charge of suspected conspiracy with Germany during the war. There seems to be little evidence that she was in fact guilty, but since she had been sentenced to death for her participation in the Easter Rising, a sentence later commuted to penal servitude, the authorities were obviously taking no chances with Countess Markievicz. She clearly saw the election as a bit of a lark 'like Alice in Wonderland or a Gilbert and Sullivan Opera'.[4] Yet she was returned for the St Patrick's division of Dublin. She never took her seat on her release from prison, although she received a letter, signed by Lloyd George (and now in the National Museum in Dublin) summoning her to the opening of Parliament.

The women who had stood for Parliament by 1919 then were all personally politically active before becoming candidates. The women who first entered Parliament were not. The first women candidates were mainly Socialists, whether standing for the Labour Party itself, or as Independents. The first three women in the House were two Conservatives and a Liberal. The first women candidates were all in politics by personal choice and commitment. The three who made it by 1923 were there largely by accident. Lady Astor was joined in 1921 by Mrs Wintringham whose husband, Tom Wintringham, had died while sitting Liberal member for Louth in Lincolnshire. Mrs Wintringham was herself well-known in the constituency for her public work and was persuaded to stand. She won by 791 votes and took her seat in October 1921.

In 1922, the general election of that year produced no new women members, although thirty-three women stood. But in May 1923, Mrs Hilton Philipson took her seat as Conservative member for Berwick-on-Tweed. She was already well-known as Mabel Russell, a musical comedy actress. Her second husband, Captain Hilton Philipson, had been returned in 1922 as the National Liberal member for Berwick-on-Tweed but was unseated because of the fraudulent practices of his agent and debarred from standing for Parliament for seven years. Mrs Hilton Philipson was persuaded to stand in his place. Again, like Mrs Wintringham, she had a good reputation and was well-known in the constituency. She would agree to stand, however, not as a Liberal, but only as the Conservative candidate. This was arranged and so it was that by early in 1923, three women were members of the House. All of them had taken over seats already held by their husbands and this cannot be coincidental. The idea of a woman political representative was after all very new. The fear of most people, men and women, was that these women would be too radical, brash, feministic and iconoclastic. They would not have wanted to be represented by such individuals. These women, on the other hand, had not pushed themselves politically. They had in each case loyally helped their husbands and in so doing had won the affection and acknowledgement of the constituency. They had not sinned against the female virtue of modesty. Their candidacy was the extension of their acceptable roles as wives, and in the case of Lady Astor and Mrs Hilton Philipson, mothers. Their husbands had, as it were, legitimised their political aspirations and this 'halo effect' of male acceptibility was perhaps at the time, essential. And not only did they take over the standing and legitimacy of their male relatives, but quite practically, they also inherited viable seats. Most of the women who stood in these early years laboured under the twin disadvantages of unknown pedigree and unwinnable or at best very marginal seats. Understanding this combination of winnable seats and male acceptance which Lady Astor, Mrs Wintringham and Mrs Hilton Philipson had in common makes it much less problematic how they, and not the much publicised and committed feminists, should have been first to achieve the political honours.

It is worth remembering too in this context that the method of candidate selection in these early years was rather different from now. Historically, in the Labour Party there had always been an attempt to consult the constituency party members on drawing up the short-list and agreeing on the prospective candidate. But in the Conservative Party and the Liberal Party at that time, the selection of the candidate was much more a matter of the agreement of a relatively few important individuals in the local, and occasionally national, party. Thus could

Lady Astor be 'offered the seat' and Mrs Wintringham and Mrs Hilton Philipson 'persuaded to stand'. There was no question in any case that a constituency party would not accept the decision or that a selection conference should be held on the basis of a short-list of candidates which they would be asked to join. This kind of selection procedure, which continued in the Tory Party at least until well after the Second World War clearly favoured those who were known to the influential members of the local party. This point was suggested to me by Lady Davidson (Baroness Northchurch) who said that when she was offered her husband's safe seat at Hemel Hempstead on his elevation to the Lords, the local party refused to look at any other candidate. The women who were known in this way—the wives of the retiring or deceased M.P.s—had already won their spurs in the local party. It was more important that they were admired and accepted in the constituency than that they were women. And the fact that they were admired and accepted for their supportive public works suggested that they were not the sort of women—the feminist harridans of the Left—who would be politically and socially unacceptable.

There have continued to be a number of women coming into Parliament to represent a seat held previously by a male relative. Lady Davidson and Mrs Lena Jeger are more recent examples. But increasingly, the 'legitimisation' process has had less and less significance, the fact of being known in the constituency being the important point in favour of a wife.

The process could of course be, and was on at least one occasion, reversed. When the Countess of Iveagh decided in 1935 not to stand again as Conservative candidate for Southend, the safe seat she had held since 1927 (when she took it over from her husband), she was succeeded by her son-in-law.

While still on the question of family relationships in the House of Commons, it is perhaps worth mentioning the husband and wife teams which have flourished there, if only because the first two of these at least highlight attitudes of women and to women which would nowadays be unlikely to develop. The first married couple to sit together in the House were Walter and Hilda Runciman. Mrs Runciman arrived at Westminster in April 1928. They were soon joined (in February 1929) by Ruth Dalton who with her husband Hugh made the second married couple in the House. Both women had agreed to fight by-elections in constituencies which were more favourable for their husbands than those they already held and for which they had been accepted as prospective candidates at the next general election. Their purpose therefore, rather than to be M.P.s in their own right, was simply to act as 'warming-pans' to keep the constituencies in the family until a general election when their respective husbands could take over. Again, attitudes and values have changed and later par- liamentary couples (e.g. John and Gwyneth Dunwoody) did not have any such joint aspirations. But it is worth remembering that Hilda Runciman and Ruth Dalton were in most respects anything but straw women. Mrs Runciman was a Cambridge History graduate and one of the first women magistrates, while Mrs Dalton had a degree from the London School of Economics and was a member of the L.C.C. Their withdrawal from politics when their husbands took over the seats they had kept warm was their own choice and illustrates clearly the fact that not all politically-involved women (both Mrs Runciman and Mrs Dalton were involved in one way or another in working for the community) are interested in a career in national politics. Ruth Dalton's professed preference for the L.C.C., referred to in Chapter I, is indicative of an attitude which is still to be found among some women (and no doubt some men), that national politics is mainly shadow-boxing, concerned with talking and posturing rather than the taking of practical decisions of real consequence. It may be that women are in general more practical by nature and experience and prefer the more immediate and direct involvement of local politics. It is certainly the case that many M.P.s themselves find the interminable talk and committees and grindingly slow processes of the House extremely frustrating. This is not to suggest that women are necessarily more at home in local politics, but that the greater number of them at this level is only partly explained by the greater suitability of local involvements for wives and mothers and may be the outcome also of an intuitive preference for involvement in what directly affects them, their neighbourhood and their children. There often is, in fact, a connection between local and national political involvement. Many M.P.s do get their first political experience in local government.[5] Yet the attitudes and mentalities of the two sets of participants are on the whole far from identical, local councillors seeing Westminster as remote and abstract, while parliamentarians often dismiss local politics as the 'parish-pump' variety. An M.P. like the late Mrs Millie Miller, for example, whose political background was almost exclusively in local government (she had been Mayor of Stoke Newington and Leader of the Camden Council), admitted to finding Westminster frustrating in just this sort of way.[6] She felt that she had more satisfaction out of her time in Camden than out of her career as an M.P. Perhaps significantly she said she had no political ambition, in parliamentary terms at any rate and felt she had at least as much power as Leader of the Council as she had as a backbench M.P. The distinct attitudes of the local and national political figures is underlined too from the other side by the belief of many of the women M.P.s that local government is parochial and introspective while they are on the whole concerned with national strategy. The conscious rejection of local government involvement is particularly clear among the younger women M.P.s and they are the most specifically committed to a national and strategic understanding of political problems, rather than an individual, episodic or local approach.

By the time of the 1922 election, thirty-three women were accepted as candidates, nearly double the number for 1918, but again none were returned with the exception of Lady Astor and Mrs Wintringham who were already in the House (Mrs Hilton Philipson did not join them until the by-election in 1923, her husband having won the 1922 election and been returned to Westminster before his agent's fraud became known). It was not until the 1923 general election that women came into the House in any numbers (there were then eight of them—three Conservative, three Labour and two Liberal) and it was at this time too that the first women came in who had not inherited seats from their menfolk; Lady Terrington, Miss Susan Lawrence, Miss Margaret Bondfield, and Miss Dorothy Jewson.

The latter three must have seemed to the male members of the House just the kind of terrifyingly committed and competent ladies they had expected and feared ever since 1918. They were there on the approval of no man but by dint of their own political conviction and hard work. Susan Lawrence, whose result in East Ham North (which she took narrowly by 416 votes) was announced first, is technically the first Labour woman member of Parliament and she typified the middle class, female, intellectual socialist of the time. She had taken the mathematics Tripos at Cambridge, made few concessions to femininity and her severely cropped hair and total lack of interest in clothes seemed to confirm the men's fears. Ellen Wilkinson, in *Peeps at Politicians*, describes her as 'tall, cold, severe, plainly dressed, at first when she rose to speak, the House prepared for the worst, then they glimpsed the real Susan, the woman of delicate humour, of a merciless wit, of a logic they had believed was only masculine, of a mind which drank in facts as some men drink whisky' (p. 2). She was however not just a formidable brain, but a sympathetic constituency M.P. held in affectionate regard as 'our Susan' by the electors.

Where Dorothy Jewson had much the same kind of social and intellectual background as Susan Lawrence, Margaret Bondfield was from a class and type so far quite unrepresented among the women in Parliament. Lacking formal education—having left school at thirteen —she had been a shop assistant, first in her native Chard, and then in London. She joined the Shop Assistant's Union and rose to become its Assistant Secretary. She finally became Chief Women's Officer of the National Union of General and Municipal Workers and at the time of her election at the age of fifty was the Chairman of the General Council of the T.U.C. Soon after she made her maiden speech in the House, the Baldwin Government resigned and Ramsay MacDonald took office. Margaret Bondfield was asked to be Parliamentary Under-Secretary of State at the Ministry of Labour (Tom Shaw was the Minister) thus becoming the first woman Minister. It was not to be her only 'first'.

Soon afterwards, Susan Lawrence was appointed Parliamentary Private Secretary to the President of the Board of Education, Charles Trevelyan.

In the general election of 1924, the Labour Party was resoundingly defeated and only one new woman, Ellen Wilkinson, was elected to the House. It is interesting to find that even at this time the beginnings of what might be called the 'statutory woman syndrome' became evident. Since the last Labour Government had appointed women to office, the Baldwin Government felt constrained to do likewise. There were, however, only three women to choose from and it was at this point that Lady Astor's name was most seriously considered for office. However, she had many detractors and Baldwin finally left her on the backbenches and asked the Duchess of Atholl to become Parliamentary Under-Secretary of State to the Board of Education. She thus became the first Conservative woman to hold office.

By 1929, ten women sat in the Commons, several having come in on by-elections in the course of the Parliament, and the so-called Flapper Election of that year caused some excitement. If women had hardly so far swept the boards in elections, it was thought now, with votes at twenty-one for all, the 'flappers', the liberated ladies of the 20s, would add their weight to the cause of women. About seven million new female voters were added to the electoral roll and this and the high percentage of women in the population compared with men (partly as a result of male casualties in the war) was expected to give women their great parliamentary break-through. Indeed sixty-nine female candidates did stand (as compared with forty-one in 1924), but only fourteen were elected. Margaret Bondfield was made Minister of Labour, thus becoming the first woman to hold Cabinet office, and to be made a Privy Councillor.

In 1931, for the first time, the number of women standing in a general election fell; yet the number of women returned was the highest ever—thirteen Conservatives, one Liberal and one Independent. The swing to the Conservatives was so unexpectedly large that several of the younger women, who were contesting what were regarded as hopeless seats, were returned. Irene Ward, for example, took Wallsend from Margaret Bondfield having had almost no competition from aspiring male candidates to fight the seat, such was its reputation. This exemplifies a tendency which seems very much to have continued to the present day, that of giving women the weaker constituencies. Most of the women in Parliament have been aware at one time or another of being used as election fodder in constituencies where the party feels obliged to present a candidate, but where the chances of being elected are negligible. Able women are often expected to win their spurs by standing again and again before finally being rewarded with a 'possible' seat. (A woman of the calibre of Shirley Williams for example had to stand four times before she was elected and even then her majority was low.) It would be tendentious to suggest that only women are in this position, yet a review of the majorities of the women M.P.s shows they do not, even eventually, pick up the 20,000 majority constituencies. Only two women in the 1974 Parliament have majorities of 16,000 or more and the lowest majority in the House is a woman's (the 22 votes by which Margaret Bain won Dunbartonshire East for the Scottish Nationalists). At the same time and presumably for the same reason, men stand a statistically significantly better chance of being elected once adopted (i.e. women find it harder to be adopted for safe seats). In October 1974, for example, 52% of the Labour men candidates were returned, but only

36% of the women. Austin Ranney,[7] after looking at Labour candidates between 1955 and 1965, concludes that women are given less desirable constituencies than men and it is this belief that leads Pamela Brookes to suggest at the end of her book that 'the real hurdle is to get adopted for a winnable seat . . . This is illustrated by the fact that the majority of women members of all three parties first reached Parliament either by winning over constituencies held by their opponents, or by standing for newly created divisions . . .'[8] Between 1919 and 1966 she shows that the total number of women first elected to a constituency held by the candidate's party at the previous election was only fifteen. The number first elected after winning either a newly created division or one previously held by opponents was fifty-two. It also seems to be true that when a party is in the doldrums or politically ineffectual either temporarily or permanently, it is more likely to accept a greater number of women candidates, presumably because it cannot offer much in the way of safe seats. It was not until the Liberal Party, for example, was very much beginning to feel the pinch electorally that it fielded female candidates in any great numbers. In 1950 it put up more women candidates than either of the two major parties and since then until recently has had proportionately more women on its lists than they have. In October 1974, for example, forty-nine Liberal women stood compared with thirty Conservatives and fifty Labour—where the Liberals overall contested rather fewer seats than the other two parties. It may be an indication of the greater aspirations of the Liberal Party as a political force—in the uncertain political climate since 1974—that the lists, admittedly incomplete, for candidate selection as of October 1977 show a significant fall in the number of women both available for selection and already selected as candidates.[9] The Scottish Nationalist Party too drew many of its candidates from among women until the middle 1960s when it ceased to be regarded as part of the lunatic fringe and started to have some substantial electoral success. Since then the percentage of women candidates has fallen substantially.[10]

The general election of 1935 was to be the last until after the war and so it was perhaps unfortunate for women that the Parliament included so few of them. The nine women returned were six Conservatives, one Labour (Ellen Wilkinson), one Liberal (Megan Lloyd George) and one Independent (Eleanor Rathbone). In 1936, Florence Horsbrugh was honoured by being selected to move the Address in

Reply to the Speech from the Throne (the only such speech as it turned out that the then King Edward VIII was to make). Miss Horsbrugh was the first woman to move the address in which she made a moving plea for peace, balanced by a warning that if war should come the forces must be properly equipped. She also referred to her own 'first' by commenting that 'whatever else may be said about me in the future, from henceforward, I am historic'.[11] Throughout the period leading up to the outbreak of war the women M.P.s were actively involved in the whole debate on appeasement. By 1937, Ellen Wilkinson was calling for the formation of a Popular Front with the Communists and the I.L.P., but this was rejected by the rest of the executive of the Labour Party. In 1938, Eleanor Rathbone published her book *War can be averted* in which she argued that this would only be the case if the members of the League of Nations were prepared to stand up to aggression, if necessary by military action. Also in that year, with the threat of European war approaching ever nearer, the Duchess of Atholl, who had been in Parliament since 1923, espoused the cause of Republican Spain and as a direct result of this her constituency party decided to select a new candidate. After Munich and the development of a full-blown appeasement policy, the House became utterly divided in support of either Chamberlain or Churchill and the by-election which the Duchess decided to fight in the winter of 1938 became symbolic of the wider issues of war and peace. There were only two candidates, the Duchess, a supporter of Churchill, and the official new Conservative candidate for Chamberlain. There in microcosm, was the position of the country as a whole—poised on the brink of war yet longing for peace, however precarious it might turn out to be. For almost the last time, appeasement won. The Duchess lost the by-election, never to return to the House.

At the outbreak of war, there were twelve women in the Commons; six Conservatives, four Labour, one Liberal and one Independent. The attitudes and contribution of these women during the war years will be discussed in more detail in Chapter VII. The normal electoral process was suspended and the Labour and Conservative parties agreed to the filling of any seat which might become vacant by the party in possession of it at the time. During the war however, both inside Parliament and without, women did useful work and most probably expected that, as they had come of age electorally after, and as a result of, their involvement in the First World War, so they would come of age politically after their even more direct and active participation in the second war. After all, social attitudes as well as political ones had been changed by the war. Women had been forced to see themselves in a new way, as competent, equal comrades with men and this new self-awareness and self-confidence, it was thought, must be reflected in many more women at last coming out into public life. The women's organisations confidently expected that the flood-gates of female participation in politics would at last be opened.

They were wrong. Although eighty-seven women contested the 1945 election—the greatest number ever—the number was much smaller than might have been expected. They were not all new blood either, for thirty-five of the eighty-seven had fought elections before. In the event, twenty-four women were elected. A sharp move to the left (Labour had an overall majority of 152) had meant, as in 1929, an increase in the number of women M.P.s. Most of the women had in fact been there before, and most of them were of middle-age. The expected entry of younger women, supposedly emancipated by war experience, never materialised. Probably this was at least partly due to the general desire for a return to normality after the exceptional conditions of the war. And 'normality' for most people meant a nuclear family where the man was the breadwinner and the woman was the home-maker.

And the very significant increase in the birthrate at the end of the war and for a year or two afterwards was perhaps another factor in keeping women once again physically tied in the home. For with the end of the war went the end of the provision of the crèches and nurseries which had been there to allow women with children to do their patriotic duty in the factory or wherever, and the so-called 'servant situation' which had made it almost impossible to get domestic help during the war never got back to its pre-war equilibrium. Working-class girls no longer wanted to go into service and middle-class women were increasingly expected to look after their own houses and mind their own children. It is an ironic fact that when women were less politically sophisticated, in the 1920s and 30s, the middle classes at least were still able to avail themselves of the freedom which servants brought. Middle and upper class women could indulge their outside interests without worrying about the every-day running of a household and care of a family. Yet at that stage relatively few were politically engaged, most preferring to involve themselves in good works of a more directly philanthropic kind. As political maturity developed however, and the likelihood of more women wanting to be active politically increased, so the practical possibilities of political participation, at least at the national level decreased. Women without staff were politically neutered almost as surely as if they had been without the vote.

And in a sense the disappointment of the women's showing in 1945 has set the tone of the post-war years. The numbers have tended to increase a little, and then go down again (the high of all time being a rather unimpressive twenty-nine in 1964). But there has been no break-through; no cumulative effect as far as numbers are concerned. The women are and always have been a very tiny minority. The number rose again in 1959 to twenty-five and then to twenty-nine in 1964. In 1966 and 1970 it remained at the slightly lower level of twenty-six and in February 1974, twenty-three women were returned. It was up again to twenty-seven in the October election of 1974 and a by-election then made it twenty-eight.[12]

The record of women in office too—if not just as disappointing is at least equivocal. It is true that as time has gone on, they have increasingly won recognition at all levels in the House—from Parliamentary Private Secretaries and Assistant Whips to Cabinet Ministers, but this is a very recent innovation and many Labour women members put it down largely to the influence of one man, Harold Wilson. It was he who brought women into Government, they claim, in more than 'statutory woman' proportions—and since about 1965, the sight of a woman Cabinet Minister has become if not common at least not uncommon, and it is impossible to imagine the kind of problems ensuing now which developed when Margaret Bondfield became Minister of Labour. Such was the uncertainty about the technical acceptability of femaleness that a 'memo on the gender of the Minister' was produced which suggested that while the feminine gender might be used in the recitals of documents, the masculine should still be the rule in the operative parts—and if this was too complicated (as it clearly was) perhaps the Minister wouldn't mind being referred to as 'he' throughout![13] In the intervening years then, such little uncertainties have been removed, some of them involving important points of principle, and some of them quite trivial aspects of parliamentary ritual and tradition (if such a ritualistic institution as Parliament can ever accept any change in or modification to its framework as 'trivial').

There was initial uncertainty, for example, about how Lady Astor should be addressed by her parliamentary colleagues, whether she should be greeted by the Speaker rising to shake hands with her (in the event, he did not break with custom), or whether she should wear a hat in the Chamber and, if so, should she remove it, as did the men, when speaking? This latter detail was obviously of some interest to the House for although the Speaker appeared to have ruled unequivocally and sensibly at the time, that women could wear hats or not as they pleased, when later Ellen Wilkinson rose to speak 'uncovered', the Speaker was once again called upon to rule on this putative breach of the House rules. Equally, the facilities of the House, not of the best even for men, had little by little to be explored by women. When Lady Astor entered Parliament, she was given a room, overlooking the Terrace, to be used as a Lady Members' Room and the cloakrooms were now labelled 'Lady Members' and 'Members' respectively. It was assumed by most of the men that the 'Club' facilities of the House, the smoking room and bars would remain sacrosanct, and for a long time they did so. Even the Strangers' Dining Room was at the time closed to women—and remained so for many years, and no ladies were allowed into the Distinguished Strangers' Gallery. Gradually these impediments were removed, but it is only in very recent times that women have entered the Smoking Room, for a long time accepting the men's desire for one last male sanctuary where, although no official prohibition existed, women did not go unless invited by a male colleague. This convention had a professional disadvantage for women in that one of the reasons given by Ministers for so infrequently choosing women as P.P.S.s (Parliamentary Private Secretary—often the first step on the way to ministerial appointment) was that a main function of a P.P.S. is to keep the Minister up to date on the professional gossip of the House and that since much of this takes place in the Smoking Room, which women did not frequent, women were less useful in this capacity.

It is perhaps worthwhile reflecting briefly at this stage on the kind of women who have come into the House, and whether they have changed over time. The first women were predominantly upper and middle class, women who, as already mentioned, had been 'legitimised' in the eyes of the electorate by their male relatives and who had the domestic staff to make their involvement outside their homes practically possible. Even when the first factor became less significant the second was still of critical importance and so the few working-class women, who early on made their way into national politics—Margaret Bondfield was the earliest example—were unmarried and/or childless. There was almost no chance at all of a woman without servants being able to run a home and a parliamentary career. And this is still largely the case. The House has always had a high proportion both of un-married women and of older women, whose family responsibilities are less onerous once their children are grown-up. Again, the edu-cational background of the women has tended to be fairly constant. They have increasingly, it is true, had a higher level of formal edu-cation, degrees and professional qualifications, as this became more the norm in society as a whole and among women in particular. But they have always been more highly educated than was usual for their time and this is increasingly the case among the younger women members today, a very high proportion of whom, for example, have university degrees. This whole professional and educational back-ground means that the women members have always been predomi-nantly middle class, even more so in recent times than their male counterparts. This is probably partly a result of the fact that women often need the confidence of formal qualifications before they feel capable of launching into public life, whereas men are socialised to greater self-assurance, and partly of the quite practical fact of women's lack of trade union involvement at the official level, which explains the almost total absence of women from, for example, the Labour Party's A-list of candidates for selection.[14] This effectively bars working-class women from an important point of entry to politics which is available to working-class men.

The attitudes of the House (predominantly, of course, male) to women, too, have perhaps changed less than might be expected in nearly sixty years. Women were from the very beginning accepted and treated, on the whole, with courtesy as equal colleagues. But as women's attitudes to themselves have changed, so have male responses. Inevitably, women who are self-confident about their own role will elicit different reactions from those who are more tentative and uncer-tain. The evolution of this consciousness and its effects for both men and women members will be dealt with later. For the moment, a limited example might be seen in the question of dress in the House. Lady Astor, clearly quite intentionally, kept to her unobtrusive 'uniform' for all the years she served in Parliament. She probably rightly felt that she was making enough of an impact on that venerable institution simply by her presence, without in any way underlining her femininity. Women had not been in the House for long however, before Lady Terrington (elected in 1923) expressed her contempt for 'a dull little frock with a Quakerish collar' and said she intended to wear her best clothes. Yet, perhaps, she could only afford the luxury of being ostentatiously feminine because the women had established their credibility sufficiently in the early years to be taken seriously regardless of what they wore. (Even without this recognition, her covert reference to Lady Astor was at the least ungenerous.) Many of the women have genuinely had no interest in clothes. Margaret Bondfield, for example, recalled going to kiss hands at Windsor after her Cabinet appointment, in the same hat and coat she had worn for the election campaign. There is the story, which seems to be so much in character that it is unlikely to be apocryphal, of Susan Lawrence's method of choosing her wardrobe—sending round to Barkers for half a dozen inexpensive dresses to be sent to the Ministry and when they were brought to her room, indicating her preference by simply raising her head for a minute from her papers and pointing with a pencil! Most of the women however have had a normal interest in their dress and appearance and some have become well-known for their sartorial elegance. Barbara Castle, for example, has always been clothes-conscious, Mrs Patricia McLauchlin reputedly took weeks to arrange her parliamentary wardrobe as an advertisement for the work of her Ulster constituents, and Elaine Burton's (now Baroness Burton) hats became legendary. But dress has been used perhaps subconsciously by the men to keep the women aware that they, the men, set the parameters and define the rules of parliamentary form. Women have quite frequently been unnerved by being greeted by cheers or whistles as they rose to speak in an eye-catching outfit. Ellen Wilkinson, attired in vivid green, was once treated to such a performance and Jean Mann swore she would never again appear in the brown velvet ensemble which caused some members to whisper (so she says) 'Dressed like a bride'. And not to respond to this blatant—albeit perhaps unselfconscious—sexism takes a degree of self-assurance and an ability to command the House's absolute attention and respect which until recently women have not felt able to take for granted. It is perhaps some indication of how far women have come in this sphere that Bernadette Devlin, never a lady to stand on ceremony but one with a sure mastery of the debating techniques and rituals of the House, could by the 1970s, command this attention dressed in blue jeans.

Another aspect of the consciousness of the women in the House which should perhaps be mentioned is that briefly referred to in recounting the views of many of the early women candidates, particularly Christabel Pankhurst—the idea of a Women's Party. It was originally feared by many people that women would act together in the Commons as a bloc and would in this way disrupt the neatness of party lines. This was never in fact to be the case. The parliamentary women have almost without exception seen themselves as M.P.s who happen to be women and not as women M.P.s. They have particularly repudiated the notion of a Women's Party for their party political loyalties have in the vast majority of cases been far too strong. The best-known exception is probably Lady Astor, herself not reputed for her strict partisanship. Mary Agnes Hamilton recalls how the new women members in 1929 were summoned (there was, she says, no other word for it) to lunch with Lady Astor and invited to form a feminine phalanx.[15] By this time Margaret Bondfield was in the Cabinet and Susan Lawrence was a junior minister with Ellen Wilkinson as her P.P.S. They were much too committed to trying to implement Socialist policies to become involved in any such frivolity. Lady Astor's argument was that women united could support the things women stood for—which would mean not only a better deal for women, but a better quality of life for everybody. For a Conservative, that sounds suspiciously like a Marxist interpretation of the electoral position. Women are a class (Marx would say) but not yet a class-conscious class. They are not aware of their power, but once they become so, the potential for change is enormous. Women compose more than half the electorate. If they voted for women to represent them, they could, to all intents and purposes, control the political arrangements of the country. Yet few of the women in politics, past or present, would agree with this suggestion. Perhaps their reasons are best summed up by Eleanor Rathbone's riposte: 'You cannot have a Women's Party because of politics'. The women in the House have in fact acted together effectively on many occasions. During the war, for example, when they thought that womanpower was being under-utilised they pressed for and got a debate on this topic. Indeed throughout the war, they pursued pretty well united the interests and involvements of women in the particularly harrowing circumstances of the time. Again in the later 60s, they pressed—almost united and ultimately led by Barbara Castle—for an Equal Pay Act which finally became law in 1970. The anti-discrimination legislation of 1975 is a slightly more complicated example of women's efforts on their own behalf, for many of the women M.P.s opposed it, fearing its purely 'window-dressing' quality and the complacency it might produce. But this will be dealt with more fully elsewhere along with the Abortion debates of the 1970s where the women, largely united, pursued what they considered to be a basic freedom of individual women.[16]

What then briefly, is the score towards the end of these first sixty years? Women have established their own right to full political and electoral equality. They have joined the men in Parliament, albeit in far from equal numbers, and they are treated equally as members of that body with the use now of all its facilities (including the Smoking Room!) and the responsibilities—for attendance, committee work and the running of the House—which that involves. They have been Whips and Parliamentary Private Secretaries, Junior Ministers and Cabinet Ministers. They have been Chairmen of Committees—even Committees of the whole House, and sat in the Speaker's Chair. One of them has become a Party Leader. But there has still never been a woman Chancellor, or Home Secretary, or Foreign Secretary, nor have there been more than a couple of them in any one Cabinet.

Yet in their capacity as historically mainly backbench, but increasingly governmental instruments, they have taken their share in the work of the House. And this is intended neither simply as a meaningless cliché, nor to damn with faint praise. They have introduced a reputably long list of Private Members' Bills since the first by Lady Astor in 1923. They have been involved, and often instrumental, in the introduction of much of the major domestic legislation since the 1920s, from Lady Astor and Ellen Wilkinson's united front to try to force the Baldwin Government to give votes to women at the age of twenty-one, to Eleanor Rathbone's finally successful crusade for family allowances; from the Welfare State legislation of the post-war Labour Government to Barbara Castle's Equal Pay Act.

And yet their contribution is overwhelmingly of a supportive, secondary nature. They have seldom initiated legislation; they have only very infrequently been the leaders in theoretical discussions on practical revisions within their parties. And perhaps most surprisingly, almost without exception they seem not even to have exploited the one great advantage they have, their very small number, to become personally known to the electorate. Even the moderately politically informed normally find difficulty in naming any of the current women M.P.s, with the exception of Mrs Thatcher, Mrs Castle and Mrs Williams. Of course it may be responded that few people could name many backbench men either. There is however a built-in anonymity in being one of six hundred which is not naturally there for one of twenty-eight. It is almost as if the women wanted to pass unnoticed, as if they strove to be worthy but unremarkable, like good junior prefects who daren't put a foot wrong. But to what extent this rather harsh assessment is true must be the enquiry of a later chapter.[17]

CHAPTER III

Pathways to Parliament

'The farmers' wives won't vote for you.' Selection Committee Chairman

'Perhaps we should get rid of the House of Lords, and make the Second Chamber all-female.' Willie Hamilton, M.P.

One hundred and sixty-one women fought the general election of October 1974, of whom twenty-seven were elected members of Parliament. This was the highest number of women ever to stand, but not the highest number elected at a general election. In 1964 this was achieved when ninety women stood and twenty-nine were returned to Parliament. In 1966, eighty stood for a return of twenty-six and, in 1970, ninety-nine returned the same number. The trend since the mid-6os therefore seems to be towards a higher number standing to keep the number of women M.P.s about the same. Since 1955 the number returned at elections has never been more than twenty-nine or less than twenty-four, and since the war, only on two occasions has it gone slightly below this. Thus even while the figure for women candidates is rising (by almost 43% in February 1974 over the 1970 figures, and again, only a few months later, in October 1974, by a further 13%), the number actually elected is almost static. It would not be surprising if women in this situation began to get the Alice in Wonderland feeling of running very hard to stand still. Why then is this the case, and what are the factors which may affect women's chances of selection and election?

Before they get the chance to meet the electorate in a general election or a by-election candidates have to get through a qualifying round of more or less arduous tests of one sort or another and it is this preliminary stage—the selection process—which initially determines their parliamentary chances. There is no system of 'primaries' in this country whereby the electorate can choose not only a member to represent them, but also the candidates who will run in the election contest itself, and so the process of candidate selection is in the hands of the constituency party. Furthermore, the constituency party as such does not really choose the candidate either. There is often no mass meeting and general discussion. Rather the general management committee or executive committee of the local party may meet to consider potential candidates in a preliminary way, but it is very likely that the actual process of selection (the selection conference itself) will be in the hands of a relatively few senior members of the local party, including the chairman and main office-holders. The decision made by them may then be referred back to the general management committee, but it is more likely to be simply presented to a meeting of the local party for formal endorsement.

So it is not simply or perhaps most importantly the electorates' views of candidates, and of women candidates in particular, which are at issue in trying to determine the reasons for women's poor showing in election statistics, but the attitudes and opinions of the so-called 'selectorate'. In the light of this, it is perhaps worth looking at the processes of selection of the major parties to determine in general how these take place.

In the case of the Labour Party, a short-list of candidates will be drawn up from those who have come, in any of a number of ways, to the attention of the local management committee. Transport House, for example, will supply a central list of candidates who have put themselves up for selection (the so-called 'B' list) and also a list of trade union sponsored candidates (the 'A' list). Constituencies are not of course bound to choose a candidate thus approved by Party Headquarters and it rather depends on the quality of the candidates from other sources whether they look at the central list very carefully. In the meantime, the various organisations affiliated to the party will be putting forward their own candidate suggestions—the various wards in the constituency, as well as the Co-op, the Young Socialists, the women's sections, the Fabians and so on. Some candidates may be put forward by a number of different groups, but this is not a pre-requisite of final inclusion on the short list. The management board of the local party may then agree on the short-list and these candidates are asked to appear before the selection conference.[1] Short-lists generally are short—about four or five candidates who are asked to speak for ten minutes or a quarter of an hour and then questioned for about the same length of time. The final choice is then made and the party has a new candidate to fight the coming general election or by-election.

In the case of the Conservative Party, the process is not dissimilar. Conservative Party Central Office keeps one list which is brought up to date from time to time by the Vice-Chairman of Candidates (and there is a Standing Advisory Committee on Candidates). The process, as perhaps befits a party committed to individual effort and personal reward, is at all points more self-selective than that of the Labour Party. An aspiring Conservative candidate has to put his or her name forward, sponsored by two Conservative M.P.s or peers. If the application is successful, the name then appears on the list. As opposed to this, it is possible in the Labour Party to be put forward or to let one's name go forward without quite the degree of personal choice or forethought that the Conservative process involves. It may be that there is a marginal disadvantage to women in the Conservative method in that they tend to be uncertain about putting themselves up for any kind of office and it seems to be the case that some women have been put forward initially by other people, say in their constituency party, and have gained from this display of confidence a personal self-assurance which allowed them to pursue their candidacy further. The aspiring Conservative candidate is circulated with the details of constituencies as these become available and it is then up to him or her to decide whether to ask to be considered. Again, the candidate has a personal choice here: it is not really possible to get into the process and to cease thereafter positively to reassert one's involvement. Indeed candidates who for one reason or another are not deemed to be suitable for retention on the list (either presumably because they have not been sufficiently active in pursuance of a constituency, or because they have not been sufficiently successful) are removed from it. Candidates therefore within the Conservative framework have to be very much self-starters, which is what few women are. The Labour process, on the other hand, seems to allow for more of a 'drift' into politics, where a woman who had been faithful and efficient in the local party or trade union or women's group might well find herself asked to accept sponsorship and in so doing get over an initial lack of confidence. Jean Mann for example claimed that 'Like most women in public life, I owe all the positions I occupied to men. They pushed me into it from the start [and] kept offering me seats to contest . . .'.[2]

If an approved Conservative candidate from the central list expresses an interest in a constituency, then his or her name goes forward to the constituency general management committee who will be drawing up the short-list. They need not, of course, put any of the central list candidates on their short-list and they again will have suggestions from all levels of the party and from affiliated organisations. In the past few years it seems that the women's sections of the major parties have tended to put forward women candidates for consideration and although they are only one interest group among many in the process, they are often a significant one and in the present social climate unlikely to be disregarded by the management committee. It seems likely in any case that at this stage, there is a strong possibility of a woman's being included in the short-list, if only so that the proper impression of balance can be given. It is impossible to establish this accurately as the figures for women putting themselves forward for selection are not generally available, nor are short-lists, but my impression gained from talking to party organisations and to short-listed candidates is that this is the general picture. As Marcus Fox (Conservative Vice-Chairman) remarks, there is no way in which Central Office can put pressure on individual constituencies to adopt women. And the same is true in the Labour Party.

Again, the selection process for Liberal candidates is not very different. Aspiring candidates who put their names forward are usually interviewed by regional interview committees and if acceptable are put on to the central list which is then available to constituency parties who may be looking for candidates. According to Liberal Party Headquarters, very few women come forward, and those who do, stand a very good chance of getting on to the list. The Liberal Party might be more embarrassed by its lack of female representation in Parliament[3] if it were not so preoccupied with its lack of any very significant representation there at all.

All the major parties agree that very few women come forward for selection and those who do have a certain advantage in virtue of their scarcity value. They are all aware of the importance of being seen to encourage women into politics and it is comforting to be able to refute any charges of male conspiracy by pointing to the presence of a woman on any short-list of candidates. Most of the M.P.s and candidates I spoke to agreed that it is initially at least no handicap to be a woman, both in that selection committees are probably looking for at least one female and in that there are not so many to choose from.

Once the short list has been drawn up, however, the advantages of femininity, if they do exist, become far less obvious. Indeed although a woman may still have a marginal advantage in probably being the only woman and therefore not so forgettable as her male counterparts, she has still to face a selection committee that may be more or less hostile to her simply on grounds of her femininity. Clearly, as the Equal Opportunities Commission has shown, discrimination is a most difficult thing to prove. How does a woman know that she was rejected because she was a woman and not because of some other quite relevant aspect of her personality or abilities, and what is more important, how could she prove this? The assumption of an anti-feminine conspiracy on the part of selection committees is one of the unproved, and probably unprovable dogmas of feminists. Although it is perhaps statistically or indeed empirically, an imponderable, it is possible to get an impression of how far this may be the case by reference both to the composition and probable attitudes of selection committees and the experience of candidates themselves. Neither seem to lead to any necessary assumption of anti-female bias. Yet just such bias is assumed by, for example, Patterson who asserts that 'the paucity of women M.P.s is not attributable to the hostility of the electorate, whose deeply ingrained habit of voting for the party and not the person would probably not be radically altered by an increase in the number of women standing as candidates, but to the suspicion and reservations and prejudice of the selectorate'.[4] In the same vein in 1964, *The Times* (12 September) reported Conservative Central Office and Conservative candidates themselves regretting the fact of so few women being selected and put it down to the bias of selection committees. Few of the women members I talked to however claimed to be aware of discrimination at the selection stage. This may, of course, be because they are the successful products of the system and, having themselves been selected, they are the living proof that women do get chosen. Yet it is not as simple as this. Most of these women had tried, unsuccessfully, more than once before they got a winnable parliamentary seat to contest. Many of them have therefore had the experience of rejection, yet few wanted to put this rejection down to discrimination. Indeed, they adamantly dismissed the idea saying that discrimination is in the eye of the beholder, or claiming that if she is good enough, a candidate need not fear her sex counting against her. This was particularly the response of the Conservatives who almost to a woman have a very strong sense of personal efficacy and a belief that their fate rested (in tune with their general political philosophy) largely in their own hands. They seemed to regard the idea of anti-feminine bias as largely an excuse put forward by the unsuccessful. As one of them said to me, summing up this attitude, 'Sex discrimination is like race discrimination. It's not that it doesn't ever exist, but if you start to think like that, you can see it everywhere and put everything down to it.' The Labour women on the whole, on the other hand, although equally insistent on the insignificance of discrimination in their own cases, were more likely to be aware of it as a possibility. Many of them stressed the existence of sexist, rather than discriminatory attitudes on the part of selectors and gave examples of this in the kinds of questions they had been asked at selection conferences. For example, almost all of the married women recounted experiences of being asked about their family situation and often in terms which suggested that they might not be able to give sufficient time and care to their husbands and children. As this is clearly a condition of the job which affects men with families quite as much as women with families, it is an indication of a pretty widespread belief among selectors about the incompatibility of at least motherhood and parliamentary involvement. On the other hand, one aspiring candidate I talked to had been put on the short-list when she was clearly several months pregnant, and of the present crop of younger married women in the House at least three or four were possible candidates for motherhood, if not already mothers, when they were chosen.

In general the attitudes of selectors to women candidates which Conservative Central Office and others assumed and deprecated in the 1960s seem to have, at least to some extent, changed. It is not the general rejection of women as women which the M.P.s themselves refer to, but a rather more secular questioning of their suitability given their female characteristics. For example, will they be strong enough to take the obvious physical demands of electioneering or even the necessary constant appearances at meetings and rallies and conferences? In the case of one M.P., she was even asked whether she could drive a car. Some of these questions may be irritating, but mostly they are intelligible as an attempt to see whether this particular candidate with her particular attributes, characteristics and commitments could in fact successfully fulfil this particular role.

On a rather different point, it seems not to be the case that women selectors are necessarily in favour of women candidates. Several of the women M.P.s said they had been asked particularly hostile questions, often about their domestic arrangements, by other women. Some of them felt that this might reflect the belief of these women that being an M.P. was not a woman's (particularly a mother's) job and that she ought not to be abandoning her family commitments in favour of a political role. Again, this could be related to an assessment of the particular individual for the job in question. A woman who has herself stayed at home to bring up her children may well feel that it is indicative of a certain lack of responsibility (hardly a characteristic to be ignored in a putative M.P.) on the part of another woman not to do the same. Or she may subconsciously feel some jealousy for another woman's greater political involvement, all the more likely since, if she is serving on a selection committee, she must have a high level of political interest herself. Once again, it is impossible to generalise on this point as women can be and often are very predisposed to support other women and even if hostile in a particular case, this may simply be due to a greater understanding, through personal experience, of the difficulties which face a woman, if elected, say, in maintaining any adequate home life.

The inbuilt prejudice of selection conferences is not then a well-attested fact, and probably a greater general problem for women candidates is the ambivalence of their position as both woman and politician As discussed in Chapter I, the criteria of acceptability of the two roles are rather different and in some cases antipathetic. A woman candidate therefore has to show that she is sufficiently forceful and committed, opinionated and articulate to be a good M.P. while still retaining her femininity. Many people, not just men, still have a 'seamless web' theory of women so that women who act in particular ways are seen as that 'kind of woman'. Such ascriptions are almost always uncomplimentary, as when for example it is assumed that a woman who is self-confident and forceful enough to launch herself into public life must also be ruthless, unsympathetic and probably sexually promiscuous! At any rate, women are in something of a double-bind situation here in that to be 'one of the boys' clearly won't do, yet to be obviously feminine is to be questionable (at least in principle) in terms of fitness, robustness (both physical and intellectual) and general ability to cope. Again the impression gained from the women themselves is one of an often unconscious sexism rather than any full-blown discrimination. And this of course is a general social consciousness rather than a specifically political reaction. Sally Oppenheim, for example, is aware of always being 'blonde Mrs Oppenheim' which is hardly how male M.P.s with fair hair are typically described. And yet in the peculiar circumstances of politics and politicking, there can be an element of manipulation in all this. As Jo Richardson pointed out, if a colleague asks why you are shaking 'your pretty head' in the midst of a heated debate, it rather precludes a relationship of total equality.

In the atmosphere of a selection conference however, the mechanics of such attitudes are altogether more diffuse and it is probably the influence of political myths and half-truths surrounding women in general and women candidates in particular that militates against their chances of selection. The woman candidate for example has often been thought to be a vote-loser. This however, is extremely contentious. Most people vote for a party and not an individual, the personal vote of a candidate being reckoned at most at about 500 votes. Yet such uncertainties are regularly trotted out as absolute truths. *The Times*, for example, in analysing Mrs Thatcher's chances of victory in a general election, takes as read the likelihood of anti-feminine prejudice and states as a well-attested fact that 'the barriers to women set on a political career are mainly erected by other women'.[5] Yet none of this is certain. It is however a potent disincentive to constituency parties to select a woman when such ideas have gained the status of uncontested fact.

Again, the more general political image of women as less well-informed, more politically passive, more interested in personalities than in issues, all in an indirect way contrive to make women seem less likely political candidates. Yet recent research on all these points is leading at least to a questioning of the received opinion on women's political attitudes and political understanding. McKenzie and Silver,[6] for example, have compared men and women in this context and find very little sex difference. Recent studies also suggest that women are anything but passive when it comes to political opinions. More women than men, for example, have been found to be opposed to conscription, to the Vietnam War, to nuclear weapons and racial discrimination.[7] This also seems to give the lie to the idea that women are necessarily less radical, more right-wing than men.

Certainly, if these characterisations ever were true of women, they seem to be less and less so of today's women.[8] Indeed it now seems likely that younger women at least are not significantly different from men in terms of their political interests and affiliations. Yet the image remains, with the result that a woman candidate still has the appearance of an oddity—in attitudes as much as numerically. And oddities are not what selection committees are after. All constituencies may not want a youngish, middle-class, professional man, married with a couple of children, but many of them, both Labour and Conservative, do. Successful women candidates are in fact largely middle-class, professional and often married too. But even the marital state is, in the case of women, an added uncertainty. Whereas bachelors have tended to be looked on with some dubiety, both married and single women are suspect. The married ones have domestic involvements while the single ones are like their male equivalents, 'unusual', perhaps even rather 'odd'. And it is quite irrelevant for party conferences to present resolutions to the effect that more women must be encouraged into political life.[9] When it comes down to it, a constituency is choosing a single individual and is less than likely to opt for an outsider. A woman, given both the general and specifically political image of women, is an outsider and is disadvantaged accordingly.

Interestingly enough, democracy may well be disadvantageous to women in the context of selection, particularly in a single-member system. The Conservative Party's method of selection of candidates was fairly drastically overhauled by the Maxwell-Fyfe Reforms of 1948. There was thereafter to be more openness and consultation in the selection of candidates and the process by which short lists were drawn up. When this was done, selection by committee meant a far greater likelihood of the unusual candidate being rejected. It is pretty well impossible to imagine now for example, a situation parallel to that of Lady Davidson in Hemel Hempstead, in 1937, where she 'evolved' as M.P., following her husband. Other candidates were not considered. She was known and respected in the constituency and that was enough for the small number of people who made the effective choice at the time to appoint her. In a context of much greater discussion, wider deliberation, the involvement of different interests and groups, the candidate chosen is probably going to be if not the compromise choice, at least the individual without glaring peculiarities, all the extremes of class or sex or whatever tending to be excluded. This is not to say that a woman (or a working-class or coloured candidate) would necessarily be the best in the circumstances, just that they might be given their chance more often under a rather different system of selection. Equally, one is certainly not suggesting that the people (particularly the women) who were selected under the pre-Maxwell-Fyfe system were simply incompetent appointees. In the case of Lady Davidson, circumstances may indeed have conspired to give her a parliamentary chance which, had they been different, she might not have had. Yet she was clearly well-qualified even before she took her seat and proved herself a most able M.P. whose quite outstanding career included her being the first woman elected to the 1922 Committee, and has culminated in her own elevation to the peerage.

Having crossed the hurdles of selection, a woman is still not anything like home and dry. Roughly two-thirds of all constituencies are regarded as safe seats and these are clearly choosing not just a prospective parliamentary candidate, but to all intents and purposes, an M.P. Yet women do not seem proportionately to share this virtual certainty of election, for they are rarely selected for safe seats. In the October 1974 election, for example, 161 women stood as candidates of whom twenty-seven were elected. For men in the same election the figures were 2252 candidates yielding 608 M.P.s. This means that where a man's chances of election worked out at 3.7:1, a woman's were 6:1. In the light of this, it is hard not to agree with Bernard Shaw who wrote to Margaret Bondfield after her selection for Northampton (which then had a Conservative majority against her of more than 5000), '. . . why Northampton? You are the best man of the lot and they shove you off to a place where the water is too cold for their dainty feet . . . and keep the safe seats for their now quite numerous imbeciles'.[10] Even without tendentious references to mental calibre, the point is well made.

It is interesting to consider whether certain types of constituency are more liable than others to return a woman member, or conversely whether there are constituencies which are unlikely to see a woman as an appropriate representative. This might seem to be partly a matter of party attitudes. It is probably most unlikely that a woman would get far in a Conservative safe seat like Bournemouth. Yet Finchley was hardly a Conservative marginal when Margaret Thatcher was returned there in 1959. Equally the Liberals did not appear to be imposing any ban on women when Nancy Seear was selected to follow

Ludovic Kennedy in the Liberal plum of Rochdale (perhaps all the more significant in that there are so very few Liberal plums). Nor is it the case that rural constituencies are necessarily more conservative in their attitudes to women. (Although, for example, Helene Hayman says she was once told at a selection conference that 'the farmers' wives won't vote for you', a sly suggestion of the compounding of rural by female conservatism.) Several women have in fact sat for rural constituencies. Joan Quennell was returned for the safe Conservative constituency of Petersfield without previously ever having contested a seat. On the other hand, a woman standing in an urban area has often been thought to be disadvantaged by the industrial component of such a constituency, prompting questions about how she will deal with male factory-workers, dockers and so on. But again women like Bessie Braddock (Liverpool Exchange) and Alice Cullen (Glasgow, Gorbals) have been returned in such constituencies and the triumvirate of Josephine Richardson (Barking), Millie Miller (Redbridge, Ilford North) and Oonagh McDonald (Thurrock) sat by 1976 for London constituencies where it was confidently claimed no woman would ever be returned.

There seems then to be no 'kind' of constituency where women appear to be necessarily excluded. But neither are there any which would seem predisposed to accept a woman. Even in constituencies where women members have given long and distinguished service, there is little evidence of a woman being followed by a woman. One exception is Lucy Middleton who won Plymouth, Sutton when Lady Astor stood down in 1945, although Mrs Middleton took the seat for Labour when it had been Conservative since well before 1919. In general, however, women do not necessarily break down barriers and open the way for other women.[11] As is the case inside the House, a few outstanding individuals may make their own way and achieve great personal success, but this does not accrue to women in general. Each time, it appears, the ground has to be ploughed anew.

If there are indeed any 'kinds' of seats which are more open to women, they are the marginals or newly created divisions. This is not the case because the electors in such seats have any sort of feminist bias so much as because these are the seats for which women are most likely to be selected, and landslide victories for one party or another have often brought women to Parliament in much higher numbers than expected. The Conservative victory in 1931, for example, brought ten new Conservative women into the House, most of them representing seats which were either very marginal or which had been previously held by Labour. The 1945 Labour victory brought twenty-one Labour women to Parliament many of whom again could not have expected to be there but for an exceedingly large swing to the Socialists. The Conservative women, with the single exception of Lady Davidson, all lost their seats.

The women who are finally elected to Parliament are a minority of a minority. They have somehow managed to break out of the social framework which casts them as politically uninterested if not naive, and more, they have managed to convince a selection conference and an electorate that they have done so. In this context, it is interesting to see how they have made this break and what are their pre-parliamentary political experiences and involvements.

There are two or three main routes by which an individual, male or female, can get involved in national politics. One of these is local government; another is the national party at the local level, or (and perhaps as well as) the various organisations such as youth sections, women's sections etc. which are connected with and affiliated to the party itself; yet another, mainly the preserve of the Labour Party, is the trade union movement. None of these is of course a necessary pathway to Parliament, but most M.P.s have trodden one or all at some stage.

Local government is clearly an important training ground for national political aspirants, and many local councillors do use it as such. Many if not most of the women M.P.s past and present have been involved at some stage in their lives in local government. Clearly it is a training which most women particularly would get nowhere else. It gives them experience in public speaking, in committee work and in political cut and thrust. It is in this context that many women get their first taste for politics, having originally become involved in a quite practical way in matters which they saw as directly concerning themselves and their families. Most of the women who go into local government—as indeed most of the men—never get personally involved in national politics. Others however, get the political, as opposed to simply the decision-taking, bug and want to pursue their interest in the development of strategy at Westminster, rather than confine their focus to the local scene. Only some of those who do come up in this way however seem to be consciously seeking national political office. Many are simply there at the time and are asked to stand—probably locally—for a parliamentary seat. Those who have come up like this—almost *faute de mieux*—are often, when they get there, the least interested in Parliamentary life and the most uncertain about its values. They probably liked local government for itself and did not consciously see it as any kind of a take-off into the national stratosphere.

The national party at the local level is also an important nursery for politicians. Again, the chairman and members of a general management committee of a local party may have no aspirations beyond service to the party at this level—the arranging of educational programmes, canvassing during elections, raising of funds and so on. Yet all the while these people are becoming known within the local and perhaps even the national party itself, and should their aspirations become wider, it will stand them in good stead in being considered for a constituency. Some of the same experience in organisation and committee work as accrues to those involved in local government is available there too. Again, both men and women can get their political apprenticeship in this way, but women with perhaps less original self-confidence, and especially less political self-assurance seem to benefit particularly. It is difficult to over-estimate the importance for most women of being seen to be efficient and competent in a public job. It may give them the confidence they need, even at the highest levels, to try within a wider context. Karen Soder, Foreign Minister of Sweden and the first woman ever to hold that position in any democratic government, says she had to be persuaded to take the job and in the end 'accepted because my colleagues . . . made it clear that they thought I was capable. That is important. One must have the feeling that other people think you can do a job and do it well'.

About a third of Labour M.P.s are sponsored by a trade union, with union subventions playing an important role in their constituency party finances. In the 1970 election, 39% of all Labour M.P.s, but only a very small number of women were sponsored in this way. There has in the past ten to fifteen years been a substantial increase in the number of women joining unions. In 1958 for example there were 1,850,000 women trade unionists. By 1973, this figure had grown to 3,046,000. Yet there is little evidence that women are involved to any great extent in trade unions as office-holders and it is largely from this base that they might be expected to go on to involvement in national politics. Even the unions with relatively large female member-ships do not have many women among their leadership. The likely reasons for women's lack of participation have already been discussed, but Margaret McCarthy suggests that, although the actual number of women shop stewards is hard to come by, it is probably on the increase.[12] Yet old attitudes die slowly and women themselves are often not as active, even given domestic and other involvements, as they might be. The 1972 T.U.C. Women's Conference might put forward resolutions 'to secure the extension of T.U. organisation among all women workers', but this was little more than an acknowl-edgement of the low representation which exists and the reality is much more accurately expressed in the numbers of female delegates at the 1974 T.U.C. Conference, where only sixty-one out of 1027 were women. Even a union like the N.U.T. with three times as many women members as men, sent only five women among its delegation of twenty-seven.

In the light of women's lack of major participation in the trade union movement as a whole it is largely in the specifically female sections of the movement that women get their political education. It may be argued that unionisation is itself a potent politicising experience and that in being more aware of the issues of their own employment terms and conditions, women become more generally politically aware. Yet this still does not of itself encourage women to acquire the tech-nical skills—of public speaking and organisation—which are so valu-able a by-product of both local government and constituency party involvement. And so it is largely in the Women's Conference organ-ised by the Women's Advisory Committee of the T.U.C. that women begin to get this sort of training. The Co-operative Women's Guild (the women's section of the Co-operative Movement) also plays a part in disseminating political information among women and giving them the chance to learn fundamental techniques of speaking and of committee work. Again only a small number of women have ever been sponsored by the Co-op but it is the more diffuse educative function which such sections perform that is their main contribution.

Recently however, there has been widespread disagreement par-ticularly within the Labour movement about the value of women's sections and women's conferences. The argument goes that they are out of time and place in these days of equality of opportunity. They underline differences, set women apart and so on. Yet realistically, it would seem wrong to suggest that women can or will immediately take their proper place with men in the general meetings and conferences. And if they do not, there is a very good chance that their particular interests and problems will not be given anything other than a statutory airing. It is in this context that Angela Phillips, writing in *The Guardian* (20 June 1977) claims that 'Separate organisation is vital if women are going to fight for their rights,' and Lady Young, Vice-Chairman of the Conservative Party, expresses the fear that women may shut off avenues for themselves in the name of equality, before they have established new openings. Moreover, the confidence to put their point of view forcibly in front of a large audience is going to be less easy to find for women denied the chance to build up this assurance in the perhaps more sympathetic framework of the women's sections.

Each of these training-grounds however—local government, the constituency party and the trade union—has its limitations. They are none of them, of course, any kind of direct route to Westminster, for either men or women. Yet the great majority of M.P.s will have experience of one or all of them. In the 1974 Parliament for example, Millie Miller was an obvious example of a woman gaining her political experience largely in a long and distinguished local government career. Sally Oppenheim was chairman of a constituency party before her election and Joan Maynard has experience of all three areas, having served on the West Yorkshire County Council and been a magistrate there. She has been a member of the Labour Party since 1941, was a Party agent for 21 years, and she has been on the Labour Party National Executive since 1970. She has also been National Vice-President of the National Union of Agricultural Workers. So, although it is true that each of these involvements has its own particular hierarchy and there is no reason why someone involved in local government or T.U. activity should necessarily want to get out into national politics, it just is the case that some do, and most of those who make the national scene have had just such experience.

The small number of women involved in trade unionism is not entirely carried over into local government or local party work. But in the latter, women are very much less represented in an office-holding capacity than their numbers in party membership might suggest. They appear to be content to do the general work of canvassing and fund-raising, rather than seeking official status with the local party

leadership. In the case of local government too, the idea that women
virtually run the show is not carried out by the figures of around 12%
of council members being women. More importantly, the number
seems not to have risen substantially since before the War. Indeed, in
1934, *Labour Woman* reported that almost a quarter of the Labour
councillors in London were women. By 1974, the Greater London
Boroughs elected only just over 18% women Labour councillors.
And London, as the Maud Report would suggest, is here well ahead
of the national average. Local government too may increasingly be
seen by women with national political aspirations as limited and
parochial, not to say time-consuming. Some of those I talked to were
clearly of this opinion and the pre-election political experience of
several of the younger women now in the House, who rather chose
to involve themselves in their party organisation at both the local and
the national level, would seem to confirm this. It may be that there is
in this respect a kind of 'cultural lag' effect for women. Local government has probably become less important as a political background for
men since 1945 and party research work in Transport House or
Central Office or the unions, much more so. Men like Clement Attlee
and Herbert Morrison, with their local government experience have
given way to those like Denis Healey and Peter Shore with research
backgrounds. The younger women elected in 1974 seem to be more
in the latter mould, and indeed of those under thirty-five, only Ann
Taylor had a local government background.

In view of all this, the prospects for increasing the numbers of
women in national politics through their participation in party and
trade union organisation look fairly bleak. It is often said that the
Conservatives have both nationally and locally wooed women while
the Labour Party has lost out by the assumption that they were, after
all, the main party of women's political representation and social
equalisation and could therefore count on female support. Yet neither
of the major parties has a particularly sparkling record in its encouragement of women into its organisation, although in terms both of
numbers of candidates at general elections and numbers of elected
M.P.s, the Labour Party is consistently ahead of the Conservatives.

Since the choice of an M.P. is often effectively made at selection
conferences, one obvious remedy might be to increase the number of
women there, both as involved in the selection process, and as candidates. The precedent for this kind of positive discrimination, may well

exist in Part V, para. 49 of the Sex Discrimination Act of 1975 which allows seats to be set aside for women on elective bodies, if this is thought necessary to 'secure a reasonable lower limit to the number of members of that sex serving on the body'.

More women selectors however, even if this could be arranged, would seem to be something of a double-edged sword. As has already been pointed out, women can be the harshest critics of other women and there is certainly no reason to expect that were there more women on selection committees, more women would be selected.

The point at which more women are needed if more are to come through to the electoral stage is among candidates at the selection conference itself. Barbara Castle, often a severe critic of women's differentiating themselves as a group, says she would be in favour of having women represented at this point in proportion to their numbers on the electoral register. And this view may be more than just a hope that more women standing will produce more women selected. There is also the argument that if women cease to be an oddity in this context, if more of them are seen to enter politics, the attitude of other women to this particular involvement will change and they may begin to consider it as a possibility for themselves.

Another idea which it is worth considering briefly at this point is that the single member electoral constituency is not the most advantageous that could be envisaged for women at this stage. It is historically true that multi-member constituencies when they existed in this country, were more likely to return minority candidates since their share of the vote was not voided by the first-past-the-post system. Eleanor Rathbone, for example, was Member of Parliament for the Combined English Universities from 1929–46. She stood as an Independent and therefore without the formal support of any major party. The Universities' seats, however, were elected by proportional representation by which method it might be said her status both as woman and Independent was not the disadvantage it might have been in a single-member seat. It may seem strange to consider women as a minority when numerically they are clearly not such. Yet their characterisation as a social minority has a well-documented history in sociological writings. Many of the criteria used to characterise minorities—from cultural differentiation and social and economic insecurity, to restricted legal and property rights—have until very recently applied to women. If single-member constituencies (both selectorate and electorate) are less likely, for all the reasons mentioned, to choose a minority candidate, then women, on this criterion, are disadvantaged and the only really effective remedy may be to change the electoral system. Mrs Castle, although dubious about the more general political outcomes of proportional representation, says that she probably got her political chance in 1945 because at that time Blackburn returned two members. The selection of a woman, she thinks, was more likely where there was already in the area a safe male candidate.

Again the suggestion here is not simply that changing the electoral system would increase the chances of women already coming forward to contest seats, but that if more were visibly successfully involved, women's general attitudes to the feasibility of this kind of involvement would be changed. Nothing succeeds like success. Whatever reasons can be adduced for the very low involvement of women in national politics, the fundamental one still has to be that very few women come forward. Most of the M.P.s I interviewed made the point one way or another that women do not think in terms of doing this kind of job yet, they said, it is quite possible for a woman with enough incentive to do it. The incentive however may never be conceived, or may easily be stillborn if the possibilities for women making good in national politics are seen to be as limited as they are today. At this level, it may be a chicken and egg problem: for more women to come in, more women must be seen to be already there. But this question will be looked at in more detail later.[13]

CHAPTER IV

Sisyphus and the Ancient Mariner

'If you want anything said, ask a man. If you want anything done, ask a woman.' Margaret Thatcher, M.P.

'We don't call Churchill a *man* M.P.' Susan Lawrence, M.P.

It was Eleanor Rathbone who once said that for a woman to be politically successful, she must combine the virtues of 'the Giant Sisyphus, King Bruce's spider, the Ancient Mariner and the Importunate Widow'.[1] Having got through the hurdles of selection and election then, what kinds of women finally arrive at Westminster? The short answer is, all kinds. There is certainly no stereotype 'woman M.P.' any more than there is a standard male equivalent. They differ quite radically from each other in backgrounds and attitudes, education and experience. And yet there are common threads in such backgrounds and education which make it possible to develop, if not a typology, at least a framework of common experience and characteristics.

'Background' probably initially and fundamentally means home and family, and it is common for political commentators to point out that the origins of M.P.s are frequently political. There are the obvious cases of the political families, well-known for generations in public service. Winston Churchill M.P. is the latest representative of his family who, Churchills and Marlboroughs, have been in politics for hundreds of years. Likewise the Devonshire family have had contemporary representatives in Harold Macmillan and Robert Boothby (now Lord Boothby), both related to the family by marriage. Maurice Macmillan M.P. of course followed his father into politics. Among women, Lady Davidson's family involvement has already been mentioned and Lady Megan Lloyd George at one time sat in the Commons with both her father and her brother. Today, Gwyneth Dunwoody M.P. is the daughter of Morgan Phillips, sometime General Secretary of the Labour Party, and Shirley Summerskill follows in the tradition of her mother Dr Edith (now Baroness) Summerskill.

Even where the connection with politics is not so long-standing, the women I interviewed had in almost every case come from a family where politics was not just important, but where some degree of political activism was taken for granted. One or both parents were usually involved in constituency party work, some also in local government. At the least, there was a strong sense within the family of the importance of political discussion if not participation. The politicising background of Shirley Williams is obvious. Her parents were well-known Fabians, her mother a writer and feminist and her father a university teacher of politics. Similarly, the young Barbara Castle was bred to political concern by a father who was a leading light in Socialist circles in their home town and who inspired such younger men as Victor Feather, later General Secretary of the T.U.C. The fathers of Betty Harvie Anderson, Lynda Chalker, Margaret Thatcher, Joan Lestor, Joan Maynard, and Ann Taylor were all actively involved in politics in one capacity or another. Audrey Wise and Maureen Colquhoun trace a family commitment to Socialism back several generations. And even where such specific involvement is not there, most of the women could mention a family concern with social and political arrangements which was extraordinary. Judith Hart, for example, tells of the formative importance of her mother, a teacher, who was 'full of 'isms', pacifism, liberalism, femininism and vegetarianism and who inspired political interest with a strong moral and religious tone. In a rather similar vein, Joyce Butler's parents were members of the Society of Friends and, although officially uninvolved in politics, they had a deep interest in community and social work.

The importance of the original family background is perhaps obvious in the development of political consciousness, as much for men as for women. But it is not always the case, of course, that political beliefs of the parents are taken over intact by the child. It is the value of political activism itself which may be directly conveyed and there are many examples of children, who, although equally politically committed as their parents, are yet committed to different values. Susan Lawrence, for example, was brought up in a strongly Conservative family and started her own political life as a Conservative councillor. Joan Lestor on the other hand says she owes her original political education to a father whose views were well to the left of the Labour Party, while Oonagh McDonald's family were, she says, Liberals.

In general, the political involvement of parents may give their children not only a sense of the significance, acceptability and importance of politics, but also a direct help on the way to active involvement. This need not take the form of any kind of nepotism, but simply means the advantage of, say, having a name that is known, and having perhaps met socially the people who are important in the party at the time. Over and above this, it may be particularly important for women who on the whole are much more reticent than men about political participation, to have the area of politics as it were 'legitimised' by parental approval and concern. The general belief that politics is 'not a woman's business' is counteracted by the family's political interest. And the daughters themselves will be encouraged, implicitly as much as explicitly, either not to develop, or to overcome, the belief which seems to overtake most adolescent girls, that it is only men's judgements that are respected and listened to in the political sphere, and which seems to result in many girls failing to maintain even their early political interest.

Perhaps most important of all, girls with political backgrounds are helped to overcome a major hurdle to political success and that is the development of a sense of personal efficacy—a belief that the individual can personally affect the course of social development and the way society operates, and that individual problems and injustice should be acknowledged and can be resolved. What is more, they can be resolved by people themselves and some of the 'resolvers' are women. Many women seem not to have a very high level of self-confidence in this respect. They simply do not believe in their own competence. And indeed the very limited number of examples of women in our society publicly exercising such qualities must confirm most girls in the belief that politics is a male occupation and probably best left to men. Again, the effects of socialisation and education, the almost unconscious sexism of the media, conspire to give girls the impression that they are less competent, less dynamic, less informed, less politically and socially aware than men, and consequently they become less opinionated, less articulate, less self-confident and, to complete the vicious circle, less politically competent. People, in other words, tend to fulfil the expectations that others have of them and it is generally only in politically involved families that girls encounter such expectations. As one would expect, almost all the women I interviewed had a very strong sense of their effectiveness as witnessed by their belief in their ability to do things and to change things, and particularly their satisfaction in the part of the job which allowed them to 'do things for people'.

Political education and socialisation are clearly important. So too is the more general educational background of the woman M.P. As has been mentioned elsewhere girls do not fare too well compared with boys when it comes to formal educational achievement past the age of sixteen. In spite of their early educational superiority to boys, they progressively fall back until by the stage of post-graduate studies, there are little more than half the number of women compared with men. Yet it is clear that M.P.s male and female are better educated than the population as a whole. This is the case across party lines, although the Conservative Party has always tended to have a greater percentage of graduates than the Labour Party. The early Labour women M.P.s on the other hand were very highly educated, women like Susan Lawrence, Dorothy Jewson, Jennie Lee, and Ellen Wilkinson all had university degrees (the latter two financed on scholarships), while the Conservatives were for many years much stronger on titles than on scholarship. As is to be expected, the increase in the number of women in higher education has meant an increase in the educational level of women M.P.s. In 1945 42% of them had degrees. By 1959 that figure had risen to 52% and by 1974, it was 63%.

If this increase was to be expected, it might also be assumed that women would generally be more highly educated than their male counterparts. On the assumption that women need the confidence of formal educational achievement to launch into national politics, it would seem reasonable to expect more of them, proportionately, to have university degrees. And this assumption would seem to be given greater probability by the fact that the figure for men is bound to be lowered by the proportion of working class, manual working representatives returned by the Trade Union sponsored seats. However this assumption is not borne out by the figures. For as the proportion of women graduates in Parliament has increased, so too has the proportion of men with degrees. In 1945 it was, as for the women, 42%. By 1959, it was 53% and by 1974, it rose again to 67%. Thus, the proportion of male graduates is at all times since 1950 slightly higher than that of female graduates. The explanation for this is partly to be found in the smaller numbers of women (both in absolute terms and as a percentage of their age groups) who go to university compared with men. Indeed, many able girls still do not go to university at all, but are directed into training colleges or commercial colleges where they do not receive degrees. Even when these colleges are taken into account and the numbers of college diplomas as well as degrees are considered it is still the case that women get only rather less than 30% of the total.[2] And so the 63% graduate women in the present House of Commons are indeed the female educational cream while their male counterparts are less exceptional, if not much more representative of the population as a whole.

In the present House, the younger women are, almost without exception, graduates. Many of the longer-standing M.P.s, too, were similarly educated. Mrs Williams, Mrs Castle, Mrs Thatcher and Mrs Kellet-Bowman were all at Oxford and Mrs Short, Dr Summerskill, Mrs Ewing, Mrs Hart, Mrs Jeger and Ms Colquhoun are also graduates. There are also those with teachers' training certificates and diplomas of one sort or another (Janet Fookes, Joan Lestor), or a secretarial and commercial background (Betty Boothroyd, Jo Richardson). Two of the present female membership were trained in drama (Sally Oppenheim and Gwyneth Dunwoody), which, given the irreducible histrionic component in any successful political career, is perhaps the most appropriate background of all.

It has often been claimed that the professional backgrounds of M.P.s follow a clear pattern in that a high proportion of them have always been members of the so-called 'articulate' professions—particularly the law, teaching and lecturing. Part of the reason for this is the professional convergence already referred to. There are aspects of a legal training which are clearly quite directly useful in the pursuance of a political career. The most direct convergence is probably between the role of the barrister and that of the politician and it is not surprising that barristers have almost always made up the greatest single professional bloc in the House and there are, for example, between three and four times as many barristers in the Commons as there are women. Although in the 1970 Parliament there were proportionately as many lawyers among the women M.P.s as among the men, in 1974, both the February and the October elections produced proportionately fewer legally trained women, while the numbers of those with secretarial training has risen in that period from one to three.

Women have always been very well represented too among the teachers and lecturers in the House. Again, the utility of the pedagogic training is perhaps not hard to find and there have often been a higher percentage of women teachers than men in the House. Since 1970 this has always been the case, with 18% of the women returned in October 1974 having this kind of background, compared with the men's 14%.

The number of company directors among M.P.s has always been high while the number of women in the population as a whole in this role has always been small.[3] The percentage of women M.P.s who register their interest in companies as directors is thus relatively high, with 11% of them so recorded in October 1974. It is probably the case that, although the figure looks high, particularly when compared with that of the men for the same time (i.e. 13%), the women are mainly non-executive directors. Many of the male M.P.s do in fact have executive interests, in some cases in more than one company, while the women are almost without exception full-time M.P.s. This is, therefore, the case too among the women barristers and solicitors who, unlike many of their male counterparts, do not maintain a practice while in the House.

It is perhaps significant that since the October election of 1974 none of the women in the House have designated themselves 'Housewife'. In 1970, two (8%) did so, as did the same number (making 9%) in February 1974. In 1955, the figure was nearly 20%. It is unlikely that over the interval the type of woman coming into Parliament has changed so very much. Indeed other indices would suggest that this is not the case. Rather it seems that the women are seeing themselves in terms of their occupation outside rather than predominantly inside the home. Also, the increase in the number of younger women, either unmarried or without children, probably means that these women have never adopted that particular designation for themselves.

In her book, *Political Woman*, Melville Currell cites a decline in the number of married women among parliamentary candidates between 1966 and 1970. She sees this as a trend which she thinks will continue as politics is seen by more women as a career possibility. In the candidates' lists as of June 1977 to which I had access, this did not seem to be the case. Among the women M.P.s, however, there has since 1945 been a progressive fall in the number of married women. From 75% in 1945, the figure declines to a low of 56% in February 1974, with only a slight rise to 59% in the October of that year. The shortfall however is not taken up by single women who in 1945 made up the remaining 25 % of women M.P.s but largely by those who are divorced. Until the early 1960s, the social stigma attached to divorce meant that women, and men, in public life either avoided legal dissolutions of marriage altogether or in the last resort, if this became necessary, kept it out of the public eye. This was probably even more of a constraint on women than on men as is evidenced by the total lack of divorce statistics for women in Parliament before 1964. Since then, the figures have progressively increased—from 7 % in 1964 to 26 % in February 1974. This reflects, of course, the much greater social acceptability and legal facility of divorce over the past ten or fifteen years. It also perhaps reflects, in the specific context of political involvement, the enormous pressures to which the personal and family life of an M.P. is subjected. And these pressures are almost always increased if the M.P. is a woman. Whereas a man can, and mostly does, take for granted a certain level of domestic order for which he is not responsible, this is not the case with a woman. Many, particularly of the younger male M.P.s are now themselves becoming aware that their wives are not any longer prepared simply to arrange a household around their needs and hours of work. Increasing numbers of wives, for example, themselves work and cannot fulfil a role as social secretary, hostess and unofficial constituency M.P., as well as housekeeper, cook and nanny. Such pressures on all M.P.s and on their families are the main reasons for the recent suggestions from Lisanne Radice[4] among others that the hours of parliamentary attendance at least ought to be rationalised.

Yet the pressures of the job would remain, whether with more standardised hours or not. And they are pressures which fall very heavily on the families of the members. And where that member is a mother and wife, the importance of family support is extremely relevant. Many of the women M.P.s I talked to stressed the importance of co-operative families—particularly supportive husbands. Society is currently so organised after all that whereas men may expect to get the support and encouragement of their wives, women need not necessarily expect this of their husbands, particularly where their jobs are to any extent in conflict or competition. And almost any job a husband may have would be seriously rivalled by the political career of his wife. In terms of time alone politics takes up not only the long and erratic working hours, but as much 'free time'—weekends, holidays etc.—as the individual is prepared to give to it. Many men would find this an intolerable situation and would be unprepared to support a wife's political aspirations. Just as important is the potential for serious loss of *amour propre* involved in having a well-known and successful wife. Whereas most women might be proud and pleased to have a successful husband, most men, if they are honest, would probably admit to some misgivings about walking forever in the shadow of a famous wife. One man who had the sense of humour to cope with this situation was Lord Astor, no doubt at least partly because of his own successful if less well-known political career mainly pursued in the Lords. He was fond of telling the story against himself of an American journalist who approached him during a trip the couple made to the United States, saying, 'Lord Astor, I've seen you called upon several times to speak and I want to tell you I think that you ought to think seriously about going into public life also'. Yet support, one way or another, a woman must have, even it be what Baroness Young, Tory Party Vice-Chairman, calls 'negative' support—that is the acceptance of a household run in a less than conventional way with a great deal of freedom for the partners. In fact most of the most successful political marriages have been based on a very positive support, indeed on a strong shared political commitment. One immediately thinks of Bessie Braddock some of whose fire undoubtedly went out when her consort and political confident, her husband Jack, died. Barbara Castle, Renee Short, Judith Hart and Audrey Wise, for example, all have husbands who are politically interested or active. On the other hand common political engagement did not maintain the marriages of Gwyneth Dunwoody (who once sat in the House with her ex-husband, Dr John Dunwoody) or Lynda Chalker (whose ex-husband was a fellow Young Conservative). Like the strains of political marriage, the gains of shared involvement can perhaps be overplayed. The greatest gain from a stable marriage is probably not that wished for by Ellen Wilkinson bemoaning the fact that she had to type and post her own letters and cook her own dinner, but the psychological comfort of coming home, when in disgrace with fortune and men's eyes (a not uncommon situation in politics), to a loyal and supportive spouse.

To have a supportive husband then, seems to many of the women to be essential to their success. It is in any case probably not without significance that the woman who has gone further than any other in British politics, Margaret Thatcher, has a husband several years older than herself, who had come to the end of his own successful career just at the point where Mrs Thatcher's star was in the ascendent and who has since been able to relieve her of any guilt that she might have had about competing with her husband or coping with the potential role conflict of being both a wife and a political leader.

If the percentage of married women M.P.s is falling, the percentage of those with children seems to be increasing. In 1950, seven of the women M.P.s, or 33 %, had children. In October 1974 fifteen of them, or 55 %, had children. Most of these children are now grown-up, or at least teen-agers, but it is not the case that women only come into national politics when their children are grown. This used not to be a problem for middle class women who, as mentioned before, employed nannies or sent their children away to school from an early age. For the women now in the House, however, there have been problems here too. Mrs Short, for example, talked of how she had deferred her national political ambitions until her children were old enough to be left. Mrs Butler on the other hand speaks of a series of au pairs while her children were young; Mrs Hart had her mother-in-law living in the house providing a necessary continuity for her young family; Mrs Thatcher had a nanny for her twins, as has Mrs Hayman for her son, and Mrs Williams shared a house and baby-sitting with another couple when her daughter was little.

The arrangements these women have made to have their children looked after while they are at Westminster are varied and more or less ad hoc. It is hard to bring up a young family and also be involved in anything as exacting as politics. Yet the figures, and the personal evidence of the women themselves, show that women have increasingly been managing to do just that. Indeed the fifteen women who have children have between them thirty-three children which works out at an average of 2.2, rather higher than the national average. It does not seem then that being married, or having children, even more than the average number of children, is any kind of necessary limitation on a political career.

Children and domestic commitments may however affect the career patterns of women in politics in the age at which women feel able to get involved in this kind of life. It is clear that they tend to miss out in any career structure in that the very years, from twenty-five to thirty-five, when they would be establishing themselves in a job and getting into the zone of promotion, are the years when most women are most heavily committed on the domestic front. As we have seen, many of the most successful political women in the past have given up the family role, either by remaining unmarried, or at least by having no children. Margaret Bondfield, Susan Lawrence, Ellen Wilkinson, Eleanor Rathbone, Florence Horsbrugh were all unmarried and have their counterparts in Parliament today in Betty Boothroyd, Janet Fookes, Margaret Jackson, Joan Maynard and Jo Richardson. Bessie Braddock and Jennie Lee had no children and neither do Betty Harvie Anderson or Barbara Castle or any of the six married women M.P.s under forty with the single exception of Helene Hayman.

Whether or not there is a growing trend among younger women considering politics as a career to choose to remain single or childless (and both of these are becoming much more viable options given changing social attitudes to marriage and the role of women) is at best uncertain, but what is clear from the figures is that women do not appear to have suffered particularly from their domestic involvements, at least in considering the ages at which they get into Parliament. The average age of women in the 1950 Parliament was 47 years 4 months, and of the October 1974 Parliament 45 years 8 months. That average age did rise into the 50s from 1955 to 1966 but has been falling steadily since. It is, as might be expected, slightly higher than that for men, but the difference is not vast. What is perhaps more interesting is the difference in age distribution between men and women. Whereas men figure at the top end of the age distribution, women do not at all. Rather they more than hold their own with the men at the lower end of the scale—whereas just over 11% of the women elected in 1974 were thirty or under, only 1.8% of the men were. In the perhaps critical age group thirty-one to forty, however, where careers are being made and office often won for the first time, there were only 7% women compared with over 21% men.

Having sketched their social, educational, personal and political backgrounds then, how do these women see themselves and what are their attitudes to their role as M.P.? Firstly, in spite of Lady Astor's aspirations, they all see themselves primarily as M.P.s and only after that as women. They are not 'women M.P.s', but M.P.s who happen to be female. This is not at all to say that they are unsympathetic to women's issues or problems, in fact in many cases the reverse is true, but simply that they are primarily in politics to pursue certain wider social ends for men and women, people, regardless of gender. Also they are all full-time M.P.s. This has always tended to be the case, perhaps initially because so few women had careers to pursue which would have been compatible with membership of the House of Commons and latterly because most women have other, mainly domestic commitments over and above their political ones which make it unlikely that they will have time for much besides this. All of the women M.P.s I interviewed in any case stressed the importance they attached to being full-time, the advantages this gave them in terms of dealing with their constituency as well as parliamentary work, the greater freedom to serve on committees and so on. The women M.P.s undoubtedly do a great deal of work for their constituents, they almost all have very regular surgeries and most of them think that they get more enquiries and problems at this time than a man would. It may or may not be the case that people feel happier to confide in a woman or that women are better listeners than men, but the women M.P.s themselves tend to believe that they are approached more often than men by constituents with personal problems. There may be something in this belief, over and above the image of the sympathetic mother-figure which women M.P.s may create, and that is that constituency work may appear to some men as of limited importance. It is not of great personal political value to them, particularly if they have a safe seat, and it rather smacks of the do-goody, social working ethos which most men probably feel sits more easily with women. At any rate, several of the women I talked to claimed that constituents officially of neighbouring male M.P.s came to them with their problems and that organisations in the area, hospitals, schools and the like would ask help of a woman, whether officially in her area or not, presumably on the basis that women are interested in such 'domestic' or welfare issues. In her book, Jean Mann recounts some of the constituency problems which came her way, including one of touching faith in her ability to find 'a wife for our Willie'. Yet women cannot claim any monopoly of this kind of interest, and although most of them are known as good constituency members, so are many men.

The demands of constituency involvements were not lost on the family of one M.P., David Penhaligon, who told me that his young son, on being informed that they were going to another fête that day, responded, 'Oh, it must be Saturday'.

Like most professional women the women M.P.s generally give the impression of great diligence and involvement in their work. They are, to begin with, almost always available during the session within the Palace of Westminster, in their offices or in committees or in the Chamber. An article analysing the work of backbench M.P.s in terms of the committee attendance, questioning of Ministers, and voting record in the 1974–75 session, found only one woman to be in the low attendance category.[5] Indeed women sit on committees more than in proportion to their numbers. They are conscientious to a degree and, as the report says, are not among those 'habitually inactive M.P.s whose outside interests . . . severely limit the time they have for the more mundane chores of the House'. As one of the women said, women are in the House in the morning when many men are not and they get the work to do then—the rooms to book for meetings for example, which means being there to claim them and therefore being involved.

The conscientiousness of women M.P.s is perhaps largely the conscientiousness of insecurity. Not that they are in most cases personally insecure, but that they are aware of being women and as such to some extent on trial, aware that if they do make a mistake, or fail to do their homework, they will be maligned as 'just a woman'. Nor is men's attitude here necessarily self-consciously discriminatory. A successful woman will be given her due just as a successful man will. But an unsuccessful woman will not be simply ignored or patronised like an unsuccessful man. Rather she will immediately revert in male eyes to the paradigmatic female, incompetent, illogical, not very capable. Most professional women will work very hard in order to avoid this happening. They can stand the impugning of their femininity, until recently the traditional male shibboleth for keeping women in their place, but the impugning of their competence, their professionalism, is another matter. Also it is for this reason that so many of the political women for so long sought the chance to develop their professionalism in direct competition with men, not just by being in their club, Westminster, but by involving themselves in 'hard', 'male' issues—like foreign and economic policy—rather than the 'soft' areas—health, welfare and consumerism—they had so often been allocated.

When the women M.P.s themselves were asked what they thought were the most important and valuable characteristics for a woman in this branch of public life, two or three almost invariably came up. As well as the requirement of application and diligence already referred to, toughness and resilience, persistence and 'not too thin a skin' were constantly mentioned. Women have to overcome a socialising experience which leads them to fear making a fool of themselves, which is somehow archetypally 'unfeminine'. And yet politics demands the ability to fall on your face, and get up again as if nothing, or nothing too much, has happened. Even to get into the race for Parliament may mean attendance at several selection conferences, several rejections before final success and women seem particularly prone to opt out whenever they sense rejection or defeat. And if this is difficult, Barbara Castle's account of what it was like to be sacked from the Cabinet makes it clear just how much courage, toughness and resilience it takes to survive, even when you appear to have reached the top in politics. She says: 'The first day after you've been sacked, you go into the Chamber and find yourself walking to the Front Bench . . . then you slink to a seat three benches back. Everybody's eyes are on you. You feel naked. It took me four days before I could force myself on to my feet to ask my first supplementary question as a back-bencher.'[6]

Allied to the requirement of toughness and resilience is the basic self-confidence that is needed to get involved in a sphere as opinionated as politics. Women in our society are often not encouraged to develop a sense of the value of their own opinions, and more, such self-opinionated women as do emerge, are frequently dubbed 'brash' or 'arrogant'. To acquire such self-confidence is however an essential of political participation, far less of electoral success. When Mrs Thatcher was asked about this in a newspaper interview, she was quick to point out that although confidence was so necessary for a politician, especially a leading one, 'It does take longer for a woman to get it than a man. I've often noticed the difference'.[7] Several of the younger M.P.s had much the same impression. Ann Taylor, for example, talked about the 'confidence barrier' that women, more than men, had to break through. She cited the case of very competent women in local party organisations who had not the confidence, although clearly the ability, to go any further in politics. Again Margaret Bain talked about this failure of confidence among women outside, as well as inside Parliament, and spoke of her own surprise, that, when she was teaching before entering Parliament, so few women even tried for promotion. She always applied and so ended up as a head of department at only twenty-six.

Self-confidence is clearly largely dependent on a strong sense of personal value and particularly perhaps in politics a strong sense of one's own efficacy. As already mentioned, girls are not generally given the impression (unless in the exceptional circumstances of a 'political' family) that politics is a 'female' activity. Rather they acquire a picture of the world which shows men in almost all positions of power and influence and in almost all the jobs involving decision-taking. The world in other words, is very largely run by men and there are few female models for girls in terms of whom they can acquire a strong sense of their own value.

Yet political women do acquire just such a sense of themselves, many of them probably largely as an outcome of their family's political connections. Others of them may be motivated by what Joyce Butler calls insecurity, an inferiority complex for which they over-compensate by an external confidence which is really no more than bravado. But in the end, of course, bravado on its own would not do because confidence can only be maintained if it is underpinned by competence. And competence involves not only having the belief in one's self to attempt a course, but actually carrying it through. It was Mrs Thatcher's competence on which Jean Mann remarked when she said that having acquired a couple of degrees and a couple of children with seemingly so little effort, 'Margaret should be capable of the Foreign Office and quads'. The quads were quite clearly not on Mrs Thatcher's agenda, but the self-confidence which she claimed to be slow in acquiring has taken her well beyond the Foreign Office.

Although the women are adamant about their femininity being only a contingent factor in their political lives, many of them feel a sense of unity, almost an *esprit de corps*, with the other women. Perhaps it is truer to say that all of them feel it to some extent at some times. The Labour women in the 1974 Parliament are most strongly aware of it, partly no doubt because they are far and away the largest group and their party is of course in government and this may give them a greater sense of their own strength. Even the Conservative women, who generally claimed no strong corporate sense, emphasising rather that 'we are all individuals', agreed that at times this feeling was there. There is almost a tradition, for example, that all the women regardless of party, will go to hear the maiden speech of another woman, and it is recounted that Margaret Thatcher finding herself one day the only woman in the Chamber felt constrained to stay there at least until another woman appeared.

In general however, it is the Labour women, and specifically the Labour women of the 1974 Parliament, who have developed a strong group sense. This was probably largely the result of the threats to the 1967 Abortion Act (the proposed amendment by James White, and later that of William Benyon) which drew them together in support of the already existing liberal legislation. The almost ad hoc organisation which grew up among the women to deal with this, in the Chamber and in committees, has been there to be mobilised again in other contexts. The Lady Members' sitting room is much used, by the Labour women in particular, for informal discussions and ideas have emerged from such discussions which allowed the women to present a virtually united front, or at least to know where each of them stood, when it came to public debate. Women members who have won a place in the ballot for Private Members' time have apparently discussed this with their female colleagues and taken account of the general view about priorities for a Private Member's Bill. It is also said that when the women members of the Committee on the Abortion Amendment Bill resigned en masse in 1976, this tactic had been discussed by many of the Labour women, including those not on the committee, well beforehand.

There is no suggestion that there is anything formal here. Simply that this particular group of women have organised themselves, galvanised perhaps by a series of issues, so that Mrs Hart could say that since 1976 at least she was aware that such issues were constantly being monitored and that if her colleagues needed her support, it would be sought. She was at this stage a minister once again and therefore to some extent out of the immediate circle of backbench discussion, but believed that the extent of organisation and cohesion among the women was unprecedented.

It is sometimes suggested, particularly by political women themselves, that a woman has to be more radical in politics than a man, if only in that she cannot afford to be thought uncertain or uncommitted. Men can perhaps appear more moderate and commonsensible without giving the impression of having only a milk and water political philosophy. Most of the women I interviewed thought that, certainly at the selection stage, a woman had very clearly to show her passionate commitment in order to be taken seriously. Once in the Commons, however, their opinions differed greatly, some being convinced, clearly from their own case and experience, that the women were more radical and extreme, while others thought there was no sex difference here at all, and at least one thought that women were 'more sensible' rather than more radical. (This was Judith Hart whom many might have put in the 'radical' camp.)

However, it can at least be said that in the 1974 Parliament women played a large part in the formal and informal opposition to the Government, not only in their almost united stand on abortion and anti-discrimination, but on wider issues of economic policy. In March 1976, for example, when the Government was defeated by abstentions on the part of their own supporters on Public Expenditure cuts, six women were among those who abstained. This figure is high when it is remembered that six of the other women were in governmental office at the time and therefore supported the Government, which left only a further six who were not and who might have opposed their party line.

Again, during the Grunwick dispute, out of eight M.P.s who joined the picket line in June 1977, three were women, and in the backbench revolt which almost toppled the Government in July 1977, of the two M.P.s who finally voted against their Whips on the Finance Bill, one was a woman. It is always possible that these are simply cases of particular non-conforming individuals but the fact is that there have always been such individuals among women members (outstanding examples are Ellen Wilkinson, Bessie Braddock and Dame Irene Ward) and as a proportion of the numbers of women, they are significant. And it is not only on opposition to particular issues arising during the Parliamentary session that women have, at least in the past few years, taken independent lines. Fourteen of the eighteen Labour women elected in October 1974, for example, were avowedly anti-Common Market and indeed spoke in favour during their campaigns, of withdrawal from Europe.

Although the women M.P.s acknowledge that they are accepted in the Commons as equal partners with men and that there is no intentional discrimination against them, they are yet aware of the problems of being a woman in an environment heavily dominated by men. It is not only the ritual and the club atmosphere of the place with which a woman has to come to terms, but also the finding of a satisfactory image which will, as Mackie and Pattullo say in *Women at Work*, 'be both socially acceptable and will avoid misunderstanding with her male colleagues'. As one of their interviewees has it 'If you're successful, you're accused of . . . chatting people up and so on—and if you're not successful they'll say it's because you're a woman. You have a double bind to get over' (p. 85). Women who are successful have to establish working relationships with men which are conducive to co-operation without giving the impression that they are in any way trading on their sex. Tears and tantrums would hardly seem to be the scene of a Margaret Thatcher or a Shirley Williams, yet if all is fair in love, war and politics, the temptation to use every weapon must sometimes be very strong. David Wood of *The Times* recalls how Barbara Castle could sometimes cheat on the strict rules of sex equality. She wept at a meeting with newsmen at the time of the collapse of 'In Place of Strife', and he says, 'as she intended, my heart went out to her. I thought and probably wrote, what rotters that male Cabinet were'. Willie Hamilton too recalls a disagreement with Judith Hart which ended in her 'dabbing her eyes with a hankie', with the desired effect: he did not persist in the course to which she so objected.

When asked about their personal motivations in politics, almost all the women replied initially in terms of the satisfaction of being able to 'do things for people'. Most of them denied any real sense of personal ambition beyond that of being an M.P. and many of them said they would not even be happy to accept office. Now clearly politicians of either sex are probably not going to publicise any strong personal urges to power they may nurture. By the self-selective process of actually pursuing a political career they have shown that they care about being in a position of command and taking decisions. Yet for most of them a fundamentally important part of the job was the contact they had with constituents and other people for whom they could be a mouthpiece and whose problems they could help to solve. Jo Richardson, for example, made this point in mentioning the importance she attached to her Bill for the protection of battered wives.[8] Here was something that she tried to achieve for people in a situation of pressing need. And this pragmatic attitude is there to a greater or lesser extent in all the women. Their values are largely in contact with people and in, as they see it, 'helping others'.

This attitude spills over to some extent into the way women conduct themselves in the Chamber and in committees where they tend to be utilitarian in their speeches and pragmatic in their proposals. Baroness Summerskill puts this down to biology. 'A woman speaker', she says, 'rarely burns much midnight oil on inventing aphorisms or flights of oratory; her biological structure may have something to do with this approach to speech-making. Nature has planned her primarily on strictly utilitarian lines and her functional sense rejects the superfluous.'[9] But it is perhaps more a matter of socialisation. Women may feel less constrained than men to compete in every situation and they may not therefore be so prone to the desire to score personal points in argument. There are, of course, the exceptions, and they may be on the increase. There are women who have always looked on politics as a career and have gone for office, have been aware of their exceptional ability and intent on using it to the full. Without in any way necessarily dismissing the everyday problems of the people they represent, they also have a wider vision, a social and political strategy which they want to see implemented and which they seek the power to develop. And there are among the younger women M.P.s of both major parties, such women. They are coming into politics in their late twenties and thirties with the intention, the electorate willing, of making politics their life. Usually, they have had interesting and responsible careers before their election which they could have chosen to pursue to the top. It is unlikely that they are going to be content with anything less in their newer role.

For all this however, almost all the women agreed with one of their number who said that politics was 'a drug'. They love the life of politics, the electioneering, the challenge of public meetings, the debate, the power, the personal acclamation. Significantly almost all of them said that if they were not returned at the next election they would try again (in spite of the fact that M.P.s once defeated, do not often come back). They could think of no other life that they would prefer. Perhaps significantly too the few who were uncertain about whether they would, if asked, stand again, were those who like Millie Miller, had reservations about national politics, and like her believed they might do as much or more good in some other more specific capacity.

From this brief analysis of the backgrounds and attitudes of the women in the Commons, it is clear that no 'ideal type' woman M.P. can be adduced, which would sum up and incorporate their widely varying qualities. Yet there are common threads in backgrounds and early training and experience, the predominance of politically active parents, a high educational level, membership of the 'articulate' professions and so on. Perhaps one can go further than this and say that although there is no one type of woman who is likely to become an M.P., there are, among the women who do, a number of 'types', which might for convenience be designated, 'the pragmatist', 'the moral reformer', 'the committee woman' and 'the imperator'. These categories are not necessarily exclusive, in that most women have elements of some or all of them, but all the women seem to be able to be categorised more or less successfully using these heads.

The pragmatist is primarily interested in solving problems here and now and sees politics as the most practical arena within which this is possible. She has a commonsense attitude to life and sees her own problems as soluble. She probably believes that most people are less capable of dealing with their problems than she is and she has a great desire to sort out the disorganisation of individuals, and of society at large, the latter being mainly seen by the pragmatist as a massive collection of much smaller confusions which can be cleared up individually. The pragmatist is therefore a rationalist, believing that grand strategies are not very helpful and indeed frequently obfuscate the more basic issues which, taken one by one, are soluble. She is therefore likely to be less than strongly partisan, the immediate problem and its solution being relatively more important for her than the party line. Many of the women in the past have been pragmatic in this sort of way. Eleanor Rathbone did not have a party to support and she pursued her independent line precisely because she did see politics as being about problems of a specific and soluble nature. Her long and finally successful campaign for family allowances, for example, while certainly informed by a strong moral tone, was her attempt to deal with a number of social problems which she thought her policies would relieve. Edith Summerskill had a similar approach. Her speeches and her books are almost dauntingly practical and full of commonsense. She could cope very expertly with her own life and its complexities and she has given her very considerable talent in this sphere to helping other people cope with theirs. Among the present women at Westminster, Sally Oppenheim and Lynda Chalker appear to me to have something of the same attitude and talent.

The moral reformer is also a type of which there are many examples in the history of women's participation in politics. The early Labour women were almost all, to a greater or lesser extent, motivated by a strong sense of social injustice. They wanted not just to make a few ad hoc, piecemeal alleviations to the widespread misery they saw among poor families, they wanted to change the system which they believed created that misery. Their passion was all for the underdog, the victims of an iniquitous society. In the sense that their motivation is based on a violent reaction against what exists at present and its replacement by a whole new way of life developed in the party programme, these women have tended, unlike the pragmatists, to be strongly partisan. Even when they oppose their own party it is frequently because they believe it to be selling out on the real values and aims that it ought to stand for. Ellen Wilkinson, 'the fiery particle', was of this ilk. She experienced the desperation of the unemployed in Jarrow and walked at their head for much of the way on their famous march to Westminster. Jennie Lee, from a working class background which she describes so vividly and wittily in her books, never forgot her origins or the difficulties with which 'her people' had to contend. Similarly, Bessie Braddock may have shocked the House by the brutality of her language in describing conditions which she felt were scandalous, but her sincerity and commitment were evident and her political life was dedicated to the righting of what she saw as moral wrongs. Today, Audrey Wise carries on this tradition of strong moral commitment (wedded in this case to a fairly comprehensive social and industrial strategy), and on the other side, Jill Knight has a tenacious grasp of what she considers to be the moral inadequacy of contemporary society.

The committee women are an important part of the solid backbone of parliamentary life. Whether literally sitting on committees or not they are the organisers and managers of the schemes which are largely dreamed up and hotly debated by others. They are the ones who deal in the details, who arrange the practicalities of policies. They are able and conscientious, unlikely to be flamboyant or to kick over the traces, but highly respected and necessary members of the parliamentary community. They are generally good party women, not in any sense simply mindlessly following the party line, but taking their ideological commitment as a background to their real work. Mrs Wintringham was probably the first of this breed. She had wide experience of committee work, being vice-president of the Lincolnshire Total Abstinence Association (an interest which was immediately to put her on good terms with Lady Astor), a magistrate, a member of the County Agricultural Committee for Lincolnshire and on the Grimsby Education Committee. Lady Davidson too was a respected committee woman who, although she did not speak much in the House, became well-known for her industry behind the scenes. Among the women now in the Commons, Betty Harvie-Anderson has the same hard-working reputation, as has Joyce Butler on the Labour side.

Finally, there are the imperators, probably the rarest sub-species of the parliamentary species. They are the women committed to leadership, convinced that they have a strategic as well as a simply tactical contribution to offer. They too are good party women—except when they think the party is wrong and this generally means wrongly led. They are probably the most ambitious, opinionated and determined of a group whose ambition and determination would seem self-evident. They are aware not just of their own competence and ability, but also of their influence with others. The charisma of the politician is often referred to in the context of his or her appeal to the electorate but it is of course of equal importance in its influence on colleagues. The leaders command the respect and attention even of their parliamentary opponents as is evidenced by, for example, Lady Astor's irritation when Margaret Bondfield was given in 1923 a government post, but not a Cabinet one. With characteristic asperity, Lady Astor told a meeting of the women members 'Some people say she was not admitted because she had no parliamentary experience . . . I know the Cabinet pretty well and there are some men in it whose parliamentary experience is not to their credit'. Margaret Bondfield, even from the other side of the House, was clearly a leader. Similarly, Barbara Castle recalls how, even as a youngster before the beginning of her parliamentary career, she was speaking at a meeting at which the chief guest was Susan Lawrence. In her own speech, Miss Lawrence referred to the then Barbara Betts and told her audience that they had just been listening to 'one of the future leaders of our party'. Party loyalty and encouragement of youthful ambition aside, she was right.

Right from the beginning too, Margaret Thatcher was clearly unusually well-endowed with the requisite qualities for political success. She gave what is acknowledged to have been one of the best maiden speeches on record, in 1960, on the second reading of the Private Member's Bill for which she had had the great good fortune to be drawn at the beginning of the session.[10] The speech, delivered in all its complexity without even a note, made a very great impression on the House and this ability to marshal facts and shred the arguments of opponents with devastating logic has been one of her great strengths ever since. In 1975, she took the opportunity offered her by the events of the leadership battle in the Conservative Party and went for the top. As she herself said at the time, 'You cannot go so far up the ladder and then not go to the limit, just because you are a woman'.

Obviously such typologies are not exclusive. Leaders can also be at times moral reformers or indeed pragmatists. Barbara Castle for example has often gone out on a limb for what she thought was politically and ethically right. Elaine Burton had the reputation of being a diligent worker and committee woman, yet hearing her talk about her experiences in South Wales in the 30s, it is clear that her socialism is very much based on moral beliefs. Again, Lady Astor, not unexpectedly, does not fit easily into any category, or rather at times she fits into them all. She was a pragmatist by instinct. She dealt with problems as they arose and she was a typically uncertain party woman in consequence. She was also strongly morally committed to certain ideals—her long involvement with the Temperance League is a clear example—and had qualities of leadership none would dispute, yet a quite cavalier attitude to the niceties of political convention which allowed her (probably rightly) to be passed over for office again and again. This said, the typologies can be seen not as vain attempts spuriously to categorise the quite distinct and vastly divergent personalities and characteristics of the women but to suggest that there may be some underlying coherence in their attitudes and political behaviour.

CHAPTER V

Women for Women

'I am too old for Women's Lib.' Judith Hart, M.P.

'Women no longer want to be surrogate men.' Helene Hayman, M.P.

Whatever Marx or Lady Astor might have to say about it, women are in politics as people and not mainly as women. For this reason they have never seriously contemplated forming themselves into a group or using their combined strength except in a rather ad hoc sort of way. As Eleanor Rathbone said, 'A woman's party is never possible because of politics', because of the fundamental questions of party policy which divide political women much more conclusively than any common femininity can unite them. To this day they are politicians who happen to be women and most of them dislike the suggestion that their femininity has any important bearing on their professional life. And yet, as they are also aware, it does. Not just in the sense that their experience is different from that of their male colleagues, but in that their constituency is not only the parliamentary one which they officially represent but the women, singly and in groups, who see them as their particular champions. They are aware of this special responsibility and it is this central ambivalence, their wider interests as politicians, and their awareness of their special competence in putting the woman's case, with which it has always been difficult for them to cope. A few of them are not very sympathetic to 'women's issues', mainly on the basis that they are in Parliament to help 'people' and this brief does not involve them in particular sympathy with their own sex. Many more are frustrated with the amount of time they feel constrained to spend on putting the woman's case, while yet others take the line that nobody is compelled to get involved in this kind of issue if they do not choose to do so.

Initially, of course, the women are aware of advantages as well as disadvantages in being a woman. They mention the value of being 'outstanding' at a selection conference, and even before that it is

comparatively easy for a woman to get on to the party lists of candidates, just because so few women come forward and national candidate
selectors are always on the look-out to bring up their numbers. Even
in an election campaign itself, there may be advantages. Again, simply
being more unusual than men can be a help and increasingly it seems
women are predisposed to support other women. Many of the M.P.s
were convinced that women were their greatest advocates and defend-
ers; for example Barbara Castle, told of how the women's section of a
local party threatened to go 'on strike' if her name were not put
forward for selection. Several women recounted electioneering experiences where women, not necessarily of their own party, came up to
congratulate them on a speech or to wish them luck. There can also
be a specific advantage in a particular case. Margaret Jackson recalls
her campaign at Lincoln, standing against the Labour rebel and sitting
member Dick Taverne. She did of course have the advantage of being
the official party candidate but she thinks she also gained from the
uncertainty in the Taverne camp on how to deal with her as a woman.
They couldn't be too rude because, she says, Lincoln is a rather old-
fashioned town. Largely because of these advantages, some of the
women said they would rather fight an election against male candidates
than against other women.

There is some American evidence to suggest that women, the higher
they go in electoral politics, get less supportive of other women.[1]

Yet the case seems more complicated than this. There are few women
who want to keep other women out of politics on the grounds that
their own prestige and extraordinariness would be limited if their
presence were diluted by an influx of their sisters. Such 'pulling up the
ladder' women do exist in any profession, but I did not come across
any such, at least overt, opinion among the women M.P.s. Rather
the reason for their sometimes rather equivocal attitude is to be sought
in the historical development of the role of women at Westminster.
During almost that entire history, women have themselves been
aware that women's problems and concerns were relegated to a kind
of ghetto area. This has not just been the case in politics: there are
acceptable female specialisms in all the professions—women in
business and the Civil Service tend to go into personnel management,
lady lawyers often specialise in family law, matrimonial cases etc.,
and women in Parliament will usually be expected to have special
interest in health and welfare, consumerism, education and the like.

Now these areas are clearly important in themselves, but more than this, they were the areas defined by men for women's participation. They were the areas in which women were supposed to have special competence, and conversely in economic strategy or foreign affairs they were not encouraged to participate. 'Stick to women's issues', Herbert Morrison advised Lena Jeger when she gave her maiden speech. He was not impressed when she chose to speak on the Berlin Conference and charged her with not heeding his advice. 'Isn't peace a woman's issue?' she retorted.

For a long time, however, women seemed typically to be pre-occupied with 'women's issues', the so-called 'Housewife M.P.s', Jean Mann and Agnes Hardie, personifying this image with their voluble attacks on the price of meat or the shortage of potatoes. There was bound to be a reaction and this came among women who saw themselves categorised as the purveyors of the woman's point of view, bound to be interested in house-keeping and child welfare to the virtual exclusion of all else. They saw the only way forward in rejecting specifically women's concerns (not necessarily at this point suggesting that they were everybody's concerns, but simply refusing to be completely involved in and dedicated to them).

Barbara Castle, for example, as far back as her participation in local government, in London before the war, recalls her own fierce resentment of a move to co-opt her onto a committee on maternity and child welfare on the basis that she was a woman. And all through her political life she has shown the same desire to be accepted as a competent *person* with political interests which were not in the least dictated by her feminine experience. She says that she always made it clear that she did not want to be given a post in education or consumerism, but stuck out for her real interests in transport and industry. Judith Hart thought, in much the same way, that it was only by tackling the areas beyond those traditionally assigned to women that she could establish herself as a credible politician and she felt that it was a most important breakthrough when Barbara Castle got the Ministry of Transport and she herself soon afterwards was made Paymaster General.

With these women, had begun the serious and systematic questioning of the framework within which women had mainly operated since their entry into the House. There they had exemplified very clearly and experienced in particularly acute form the roles and responses of women outside the House, in a society which was predominantly masculine in its values and standards. As Viola Klein points out, in this situation, the minority will tend to take over the values of the dominant group rather than develop their own.[2] At first this con- sisted in women taking their cue from the men and involving them- selves in the appropriate areas accordingly. The first rejection of this, as evidenced by Mrs Hart and Mrs Castle, is still within that same framework. It simply rejects the exclusion of women from certain spheres and demands entry to them. The values however, the defi- nitions, are still those of Klein's 'in-group', and are taken over, rather than rejected by those of the 'out-group' who want to be recognised. The rejection of women's issues in these terms is not a rejection but a reinforcement of the male values, an acknowledgement that men were indeed right to relegate these issues, and to try to keep the ones they defined as important, to themselves. The reactions and comments of women at this stage confirm this thesis. They claimed to find women's issues trivial or uninteresting and pressed (many still do) for and end to women's sections in the parties and unions on the basis that this simply underlined differences and perpetuated the discrimi- nation of separate spheres.[3] In other words, they took over the largely male definition of what was weighty and what was domestic or trivial and in view of their educational and professional experience, refused to indulge in the trivial which they saw as a distinct, if not conscious, limitation of their potentials. They wanted to be the equals of their male counterparts and that involved playing the men's game by the rules which were already in existence.

This reaction is sometimes stigmatised as arrogant, particularly by other women (the men more often call it disloyal). Yet at the time it was probably the only possible response for a woman who did not see her destiny in the assigned areas. Since the advent of the women's movement, however, women have acquired a great deal more self- confidence and the reaction now is more likely to involve a questioning of the male definitions and priorities themselves, rather than an attempt to assimilate them. But in the early sixties, this possibility was scarcely there. For the questioning of a whole framework to be successful, most people involved in its operation must at least begin to be uncertain about its validity, and at that time the questioning of the largely male-inspired system of priorities was hardly seriously attempted. This could not seem the method, to these women brought up in the belief that the way to equality was through direct competition, by which women would be taken seriously.

In the seventies, however, the argument is on a rather different level and informed by rather different beliefs and attitudes. The younger women M.P.s are to a woman ambitious and able. Yet most of them do reject the denial of the importance of women's concerns. They, like Mrs Castle and Mrs Hart, are the products of their experience and times. It is not that they are different kinds of women. Their educational and social backgrounds are almost identical. They are mainly equally ambitious and probably as competent, but they have lived their formative years at a time when the whole position of women in society has been very much discussed and is very much in flux. As Mrs Hart said, 'I am too old for women's Lib.' She did not mean by this that she rejected the questions which the women's movement has prompted, but simply that her attitudes and aspirations were largely established before that movement got under way. She had chosen her political involvements and specialisms at least partly because of their secular, non-feminist orientation and although she would gladly support such women's issues as she believed in, she could not be expected entirely to reject a scale of priorities in terms of which she had largely lived out her political life.

Butler and Stokes, in *Political Change in Britain*, develop the idea of generational cohorts which would seem to be enlightening in this case. They argue that (in their case) the electorate's view of politics can be divided by the social perceptions of different 'generations' and not just by class or party attitudes *per se*. The relative affluence of the post-war period, for example, has created attitudes and expectations in the generation growing up at this time and knowing nothing else, which divide them sharply from those whose experience is rooted, say, in the depression of the thirties. Perhaps it is not to extend this framework too dangerously to suggest that at the centre of the differing attitudes of the political women to women, is the difference resulting from such varying experiences. A woman young enough to be significantly influenced by the women's movement of the late 60s and 70s need not by this token be rabidly feministic. Indeed she may well be less militant in her views than many women of earlier generations. But she will take for granted certain priorities and assume as rights things which an earlier generation would have seen as outré.

Such diffuse social changes in attitudes to women, their finding their voice in many areas, and their demand to be taken seriously on their own terms, would seem to have been crystallised in the parliamentary sphere in the key issue of abortion. Again, it is not the case that these women are all militant feminists. Indeed they are a part of the institutional fabric of a society which most of the politically inspired section of the women's movement, with its strong Marxist orientation, would reject. They are also, as has been repeatedly pointed out, mainly concerned with much wider political strategies than the merely feministic. Yet they are influenced, to a greater or lesser extent, by the claims of women for social justice and equality. And they are constantly reminded by the lobbying of women's groups and sections, of the practical importance of these issues for women.

The re-emergence of the abortion issue after 1974 was visited on the women by the decision of male colleagues. First James White M.P. and then William Benyon M.P. in 1975–6 and 1977 introduced Bills which would, one way or another, have limited the working of the 1967 Abortion Act. It is very unlikely that, unless these Bills had been introduced, the women would have concerned themselves with this issue. While they are mainly in favour of a liberal abortion policy, only a few favour abortion on demand and probably none of them would have felt the need to rush into amendment of the 1967 Act as high on their list of priorities. Once the limiting Bills were introduced however, they did feel constrained to act and there did develop an unprecedented unity among most of them on this issue.

This unity was, according to many of the women involved, at least in part the product of male apathy. Even the men who were willing to support them saw the issue as not important enough to devote a great deal of time to. And it did take a great deal of time simply not to allow the stages of these Bills to go through almost by default. The men were willing to oppose, but not to organise the opposition. It was left to the women therefore to arrange the marches and compose the petitions and collect the signatures, to say nothing of the time taken up in committee. This left some of the women at least with a feeling of resentment that the men could be so blasé, as they saw it, about such a critical issue. It also seemed to surprise the men that such a large section of the women members took it so seriously. And perhaps it went deeper than this. For here were women in significant numbers, taking a stand on an issue which men had not dignified by their particular concern. Here were women sufficiently self-confident to suggest that an issue was important because they defined it as such. The comparison with the House's attitudes to some issues which women had tried to characterise in this sort of way in the past is very direct. In 1961, for example, Barbara Castle tried to bring in a measure, under the ten minute rule, to abolish turnstiles in women's public lavatories.[4] Her argument was that these caused unnecessary difficulties for the old, handicapped and pregnant, and in any case, no such toll was levied on men. The request was greeted with many a joke and ribald comment, and Mrs Castle may well have wished she had never got involved in the matter. (Patricia McLauchlin's 1963 Private Member's Bill abolished the offending turnstiles.)

The comparison between the turnstile and the abortion issues may seem an unlikely one, but the point remains that the House was able to demolish Mrs Castle's case by smiling at the wrong, or the right, time. No such expedient was open to it, although many of its members would like to have side-stepped involvement, in the case of abortion.

Many of the women are now far more willing, and able, than in the past to put up for discussion ideas and issues which they think are important, because women so define them, and the men are, on these issues, increasingly unable to call the tune. This has perhaps made some of them rather defensive. When the abortion debate was in full swing again in 1976, there was one occasion when procedure required the women to intervene in the Chamber when the motion was called.[5] The time for such an intervention is uncertain, depending as it does on previous business, and the women started to gather in the Chamber some time before the motion was due. At one stage, there were twelve of them sitting, as they do not typically do, together, on the back-benches awaiting the Speaker's sign. This apparently was too much for some of the men who came into the Chamber (it was in the evening) from elsewhere in the Palace to view this unholy alliance, laughing and making suggestive remarks, perhaps more than anything to cover their own trepidation.

Yet this emphasis on the galvanising effects of the abortion debate on women in the House is not intended to give the impression that they are all converts to the women's cause in a way that would have delighted Lady Astor. Indeed she would probably have been pleased with their sense of unity, however sporadic; but they are not a unit, nor are they primarily devoted to women's affairs. They quite self-consciously share around the committee membership and so on, on sex discrimination and abortion for example, partly so that the very real burden of such involvement is not borne by a few individuals, but also so that no individual acquires a purely feminist reputation or image. This is probably no longer, in the majority of cases, because they see women's issues (in the wider sense, including education, welfare, consumerism etc.) as secondary, but because they do, many of them, have other specialisms which they are keen to pursue.

Part of the same pressure which has encouraged women to 'stick to women's issues' has also been at work in the past in making them less willing than they might have been to champion women's causes. Again the male image of women, as illogical and irrational, particularly when it comes to emotive issues like rape, abortion and childbirth, has probably made many of the ablest women wary of getting too involved in these areas. Those who see themselves as serious professional women want above all to be taken seriously and if this means avoiding feminist contention, they will generally concur, when to do otherwise is to risk being stigmatised as emotional and tendentious. And although the older women now in Parliament are many of them in favour of women's rights, they will not seek out this risk. What some of the younger women are now asking, however, is what the accusation of being tendentious here really amounts to. Isn't political debate always tendentious, they ask, doesn't it always involve talking about what you know, and isn't it often extremely emotional? No one castigates a union sponsored M.P. for putting his members' case. No one suggests he is not being objective or only talking about what he knows. This response seems largely to be reserved for women, talking about women. This reaction is not confined to the Commons itself. Ronald Butt writing in *The Times* (30 June 1977) castigates the women for their tactics in sabotaging the Abortion Bill by procedural tactics—'spying strangers', filibuster and the like—thereby 'making a mockery of the free vote' on the issue. Yet most of the male members of the House did not support the Bill, they wished that it would just go away. The women, more realistically, simply ensured that it did.

There are of course women in the House who have no special sympathy for women's problems. They are often very good constituency M.P.s and firmly believe that their responsibility is to this wider representation. A few believe that the claims of the women's movement have had too much attention already and they do not want to be associated with what they consider to be the excesses and unjusti-

fiable demands of that movement. Miss Harvie Anderson and Mrs Jill
Knight are of this opinion with which Miss Betty Boothroyd clearly
has some sympathy. Mrs Oppenheim too, regretting perhaps her early
involvement with the women's lobby, when she sponsored Willie
Hamilton's Anti-discrimination Bill in 1971, thinks that things have
gone 'too far'. Mrs Thatcher, who is of the same political generation
as Mrs Hart, is on record as a qualified supporter of women's rights.
'In politics, if you want anything said ask a man, if you want anything
done, ask a woman', she said in 1964, and at the 1969 Conservative
Party Conference, she quoted Sophocles to the effect that once a
woman is made man's equal, she becomes his superior. And she has,
it might be said, personally proved her point. She believes that a successful woman is the best advertisement for women's equality, without
perhaps acknowledging that women have had personal success, even
in politics, for a very long time without its meaning any more than the
acceptance of an exceptional individual.

Over time women have acquired a much healthier sense of their own
worth and consequently their own competence. Jean Mann, writing in
1962 about her parliamentary experience from 1945 to 1959, more or
less dismisses the efforts of women in the higher reaches of Government. Margaret Bondfield, she says, suffered always from the assumption that 'being a woman, she was almost bound to make a mess of it'.
Florence Horsbrugh gets equally short shrift—'she was removed to
the backbenches and her job given to a man of inferior ability'—and
she remembers Edith Summerskill as being more thrilled by her son's
affection than by any of her political successes. Nobody who has seen
Mrs Castle or Mrs Thatcher or Mrs Williams perform in the Commons
could now doubt their standing with their colleagues, and their
competence is taken for granted. Women have been Cabinet Ministers
and done well at it. And yet the ambivalence sets in again when the
uncharted seas of the premiership are mentioned. Women once more
become tentative, afraid of failure, and many of them in considering
Mrs Thatcher as a future Prime Minister are uncertain of her ability
(and they take this to be fundamental) to continue to convince the
men, inside and outside Parliament, of her undoubted powers. Others,
on the other hand, see even her elevation to the leadership as an
enormous boost for women in that, as a number of them said, she was
acknowledged 'as the best person, never mind the best woman'. The
reservations and the support which were expressed went across party

and even the reservations were seldom intended as any disparagement of Mrs Thatcher's acknowledged parliamentary mastery and impressive grasp of the intricacies of policy formation. They were rather indicative of the residual fears which women have that one of their number will fail and bring derision on all of them, for unlike success, failure does seem to accrue to the breed. Lady Astor made a similar point in a debate on the war effort in 1941 when she mentioned Margaret Bond-field and the Duchess of Atholl as examples of women who had been dropped by their parties, while, she said 'men fail time after time and back they come to the front bench'.

There have, of course, been occasions in the past when women have acted together to pursue policies in their common interest. During the war, for example, Mavis Tate and Lady Astor were instrumental in persuading the government to debate what they thought was the under-utilisation of woman-power in the war effort. Again, in the post-war period, Jean Mann and the other 'housewives' put forward the claims and grievances of the women of the country in the shortages and rationing of the late 40s and 50s. 'What this country needs', declared Mrs Mann then, 'is a Housewive's Union',[6] and she did not mean it simply to oversee bread prices or protect the consumer. She believed that the women of the nation did think alike on many important social issues and by uniting behind the women M.P.s they could hope to influence the seat of power. The areas of particular female concern which she mentions however have little to do with modern preoccupations. Equal pay is never mentioned, nor anti-discrimination or abortion; rather the concern is all for law and order, anti-pornography legislation and tighter laws against homosexuals.

Yet neither of these had the impact of the Abortion Debate; they were episodic and related to a particular historical situation. Abortion focussed attention on a particular issue and has, inside and outside the House, concentrated women's aspirations and self-awareness on one issue—rather as the suffragettes did in earlier days. Both gave women a focus, something precise and specifiable and central to their developing self-consciousness. The claim to control their own bodies, to choose maternity or otherwise, was both more politically impressive and more psychologically satisfying than diffuse and vague claims for 'liberation'. And yet in the abortion issue was also symbolised the wider demand by women that their ideas and priorities should be taken as they were presented and neither defined by men, nor distorted by being presented as seen through the lenses of male opinion. In this sense it was more important to the women in the Commons than for example the anti-discrimination legislation. This was diffuse; it was necessarily unspecific, and as the Equal Opportunities Commission's problems have shown, its value was uncertain. Indeed the 1975 Sex Discrimination Act was not given unqualified support by the women M.P.s, precisely because many of them saw it mainly as publicity concocted for International Women's Year. Again, it was largely dreamt up by men who once more had taken the initiative in producing legislation for women which incorporated their priorities and their attitudes and values to a great extent, as even the least sceptical women believed, so that the Bill and particularly the E.O.C. itself could be pointed to as the proof of our advanced social equality.

But the Abortion Debate has highlighted these diffuse changes in attitude. Women, as Mrs Hayman put it, no longer want to be surrogate men. The younger women are aware of this groundswell of opinion and are therefore prepared to back it politically. And more than this, they are, many of them, keen to encourage other women in their stand for their rights. The whole perhaps rather tired verbiage of 'consciousness-raising' does yet express a fundamental reality of which many of the M.P.s are aware: if women are to take their stand they must be given a greater sense of their own value—as women. What the successful political women of the past have tended to do is to cut themselves off from this by appearing to show that women could only succeed if they pursued the male goals in the same way as men. They underlined, for most women, the difference between themselves and most women and the futility, in the context of achievement, of feminine mores and values.

What many of the younger women are aware of now is their responsibility, as opinion-formers, to encourage women's self-confidence, not just by succeeding themselves, but by their willingness to discuss their own problems, as women, and to seek solutions which will benefit all women. Helene Hayman's stand about feeding her baby was a case in point. Her motive was not self-publicity but rather publicity for the impossible situation of a woman in the—quite natural—position of a mother who is constrained by an institutional framework largely geared to men. Thousands of women are in a similar position and if they are constantly given to believe that this is simply the way of the world, they are in a psychological impasse. If however, a well-known woman has the courage to let other women see her struggles, they may be inspired to seek changes in their own position.

It is only, of course, since the women's movement that such public pronouncements have been valuable, for only since then has there been a background within which such claims have any impact. In the past they would have been inappropriate, as the majority of women would themselves have seen them as such, they too believing that that was how the world was. Audrey Wise tells women's sections of the Labour Party about her 'secret vice', reading women's magazines, not primarily so that women can be given a comfortable feeling that women M.P.s are after all 'just like us', but rather so that they may begin to be confident enough to define the framework, in this case of relaxation, which appeals to them, without feeling that they have to apologise for it. After all, she adds, men have their football.

In similar vein, Mrs Hart suggests that many men have in the past perhaps tended to devalue constituency work because they were not all that good at it. Women have always been acknowledged to be strong in this area and it was consequently lowered in status for the men who felt it to be less incumbent on them to make an impact there.

There are indications too apart from the specific ones mentioned, that significant changes in attitude are taking place. There is the beginning of a much wider acceptance that many issues, hitherto regarded as of interest only or primarily to women, are important general areas of social concern. Policies governing abortion, child-care, education and welfare are often indices of social advance and although this acknowledgement has perhaps not penetrated here as deeply as in Scandinavia, for example, it is becoming much more widely accepted that women's concerns are everybody's concerns. A case in point was the resolution at the T.U.C. Conference in September 1977, which recommended that special provision should be made at work-places for mothers who wanted to breast-feed their babies. This was accepted on the basis that women at work should be looked on as what they are, an integral and essential element of the work-force, and not as a dilettante minority expected to conform to the male industrial ethos.

The differences in attitudes to women among the women M.P.s are partly generational, the outcome of their differing perspectives and self-images. They are also partly the result of different political positions. The older women are more conscious of their status as

M.P.s. They are the products of a more hierarchical and deferential social climate than that of the present and one in which the professional classes expected and were accorded a certain standing, which is no longer seen as theirs as of right. Society increasingly challenges its doctors, its teachers and its politicians to substantiate their opinions and decisions and with this questioning their assured status has largely been eroded. The younger women, of whatever party, are the products of this changing view and consequently are themselves unlikely to feel the need to maintain distance as a prerequisite of gaining respect.

Party attitudes too are apparent in that the Conservative women, as would be expected, place great significance on the personal qualities of the individual. They espouse, after all, a political creed which suggests that individual effort is to be rewarded by individual success and they are therefore perhaps sceptical of social arguments about exploitation or deprivation when applied generally to women or any other section. They are, of course, aware of the problems which a woman may have to encounter in professional, and particularly political, life but they see these as superable. After all, they are the living proof that success is possible. As Miss Harvie Anderson says a first-class woman will compete with first-class men. A second-class woman will lose to a second-class man. A woman, to succeed, has to be better than her male counterpart. The Labour women, on the whole, do not take this line. While they place more emphasis on the difficulties facing women, they do not see discrimination as a reality in their own cases and they do not subscribe to the idea that women must be superior to compete. They are, like the Conservatives, aware of their own struggle to succeed, but they are much more likely also to introduce the element of luck, of being in the right place at the right time, of contingencies like health and strength and physical and psychological toughness. This is again relatable to a political creed which sees individuals as much less personally efficacious, much more at the mercy of circumstances—whether physical, psychological, economic or social—than the Conservative. It is not that the Conservative women are not aware of these circumstances, but rather that they do not acknowledge them as barriers. Mrs Kellet-Bowman, for example, admitted that she had been asked discriminatory questions at selection conferences, mainly relating to her children—and she did after all have three under three when she first started on the parliamentary path—but she says she brushed these aside. She did not herself perceive a problem here; personal difficulties of organisation involving vast supplies of energy and commitment on her part, yes, but no insuperable hurdle in her way. Mrs Renee Short, on the other hand, hardly a slacker herself and quite unaware of personal discrimination, catalogues the problems which women face if they contemplate the move into politics. Although she as an individual may have made it, she cannot generalise, as things stand, that position.

Taking the individualist line makes the Conservative women appear more ambitious too. They have a very overt sense of their own efficacy and a clear belief in their own competence. But for all their genuine concern for the circumstances in which women struggle and which may defeat their enterprise, the Labour women are really no less self-confident. It is a pre-requisite of the job. Indeed their concern for others is if anything an indication of their recognition of their own extraordinary qualities, a recognition of their ability to cope and to succeed where the odds are against them.

In conclusion, then, the women have no very clear and certainly no enduring sense of themselves as a group. They certainly have no desire to form any kind of a female mafia. What has emerged since 1975, largely as a result of the Abortion debates, is the articulation of a new self-confidence which will survive. Whether the more or less ad hoc organisation which grew up then will continue to exist in some form, to be used perhaps in other circumstances, remains to be seen. Yet even if it does, Eleanor Rathbone's comment quoted at the beginning of this chapter is still most apt. The women are too interested in and too divided by politics to contemplate any kind of corporate unity. Even within the Labour Party itself, there is no question of support for women colleagues simply on the basis of sex. In the 1976 Labour Party leadership election, Shirley Williams, generally acknowledged as a most able and popular candidate, collected the vote of only one other woman. Questions of policy are, and probably always will be, more important than any feminist loyalty.

CHAPTER VI

Women in the House

'English party politics are essentially masculine in style, combative, assertive . . .' Ronald Butt in *The Sunday Times*

'A few women are regarded as exceptional and carted round like magnolias.' Pat Derian, U.S. Assistant Secretary of State for Human Rights

Women came on to the political scene rather late. As electors, they did not have a say until 1918, and then only if they were over thirty, while men had been, to all intents and purposes, enfranchised since 1884. It was not until the early twenties that women started to join the political governing elite in any numbers and since that time they have participated in many of the important areas of government and of the administration of the House. Yet there are equally areas which they have never penetrated and roles which they have never been asked to fill. No woman has, in 1978, been Prime Minister or Foreign Secretary, Defence Secretary, Chancellor or Home Secretary. No woman has been Speaker of the House or Chief Whip. And yet many of their number have been accepted as having outstanding ability, which seems in many cases not to have been fully exploited.

On the basis of women's late entry into national politics, Melville Currell suggests a comparison between their assimilation and that of working-class men, another group of late-comers, into national politics and political leadership.[1] As she points out, neither women, nor working-class men came into the formal political structure without any previous political experience. The men had had trade union and Co-operative involvement, although until 1906 they had no political party of their own. Similarly, women had participated as workers, if not voters, in party organisation and in women's sections and suffrage organisations. The great advantage which working-class men seemed to develop over women was in the progress of the Labour Party which espoused their cause and gave them a specific hierarchy which has never been available exclusively to women, in the absence of a women's party. And yet the Parliamentary Labour Party has never been to any great extent the party of the working man. Its composition has always been strongly and, as time went on, increasingly middle-class. Even its backbenches have only a minority of working-class members, while its frontbenches have always been predominantly middle class. The MacDonald Cabinet in the 20s, for example, had only about half its members of working-class origin and the Cabinets of Harold Wilson were largely middle class. The representation of women at Cabinet level is, of course, very tiny.

Where working-class men and women in general seem often to have fulfilled a similar function is in being sometimes accorded a statutory position. Both groups have at times been the victims and perhaps the beneficiaries of tokenism (i.e. sitting on committees or other representative bodies as a 'token' member of one's class, sex, race or whatever).

Such symbolic representation of working-class men has declined since the war. With women the situation is rather more complicated. For a long time, the statutory representation of women was seen as at least a way of getting women on to committees and boards where they would otherwise not have sat. In the past few years however, there has been widespread resentment among women themselves that they are perhaps being patronised. This suggestion will be dealt with in more detail later.

In general, the comparison of women with working-class men is perhaps interesting, provided that the dissimilarities of the two groups are borne in mind. It emphasises again that women's political development can well be seen as the experience of an 'out-group', in Viola Klein's term, and that the problems they have faced in assimilation and acceptance, are largely the problems of such groups. It seems to be stretching the evidence, however, to suggest that these groups have been given posts—particularly Cabinet jobs—which were likely to bring unpopularity to their holders. Arguing thus, Currell quotes Jean Mann's description of Margaret Bondfield's problems as Minister of Labour, Ellen Wilkinson facing the 'onslaught of opposition from her own Party' and Edith Summerskill's difficulties as 'Food Minister when there was no food'. And she adds, Barbara Castle walked 'the tightrope as Secretary of State for Employment and Productivity', while Margaret Thatcher's problems were not hard to seek as Secretary of State for Education 'when that sector was a subject of heated controversy'.

But the scarcely veiled conspiracy theory suggested here is not really convincing. To begin with, it is one thing to say that women and working-class men may at times have been given jobs partly because it was politically expedient that their group be seen to be represented. It is quite another thing to suggest that they were thereby handed the hot potatoes, or the jobs that nobody else wanted. On the one hand, politics, and Government formation in particular, irreducibly involves this kind of group representation, not only of women, but perhaps of Trade Unionists, regional members, and all shades of backbench opinion which are significant at the time. On the other, it seems unlikely that any government post, and particularly one in the Cabinet, can be seen as an easy job. All such jobs are ones in which reputations are made and broken and it would be hard to predict which were liable to be most pressured in a particular administration. There is no reason why easy glory should be any more forthcoming at the Foreign Office than at the Ministry of Education, and if one were looking for a scapegoat office, surely that of Chancellor, never held by a woman, would come high in such stakes in almost every administration since the war.

What then have women achieved in the House since their entry in 1919? In the first few years, their progress was slow. They had to acclimatise themselves and to become accepted members of the parliamentary community and it was not until 1924 that they began to be given office. In January of that year, after Baldwin's resignation and the formation of Ramsay MacDonald's government, Margaret Bondfield was asked by the Minister of Labour, Tom Shaw, to become his Under-Secretary of State. The first woman Minister had been appointed and although, as already mentioned, Lady Astor thought Miss Bondfield had been sold short by not being immediately included in the Cabinet, it was a remarkable achievement for anyone, far less a woman, to be given ministerial office without having been either Whip of Parliamentary Private Secretary, and with scarcely a year's parliamentary experience. Later the same year, Susan Lawrence was made a Parliamentary Private Secretary and at the end of February, on a vote on women's suffrage, Dorothy Jewson and the Duchess of Atholl acted as tellers. Women had thus penetrated both the ministerial and the organisational hierarchies of the House and seemed well on their way to being fully assimilated and utilised to the same degree as their male counterparts. This assumption was no doubt partly posited on the belief that women must come into the House after their slow start, in ever increasing numbers. Having already achieved ministerial office when their numbers were so few, they must have felt confident that more of them would mean more governmental representation. And to some extent, they have been proved right, for as more of them have come in, more of them have held office. In proportion to their numbers in the House, the last two Labour administrations, for example, have employed women in office to almost the same extent as men. However, where they were perhaps optimistic in their calculations was in assuming that women's representation in the House would go on growing, and that reasonably quickly. But, as has been pointed out, women are always particularly vulnerable to the vagaries of political fortune. Women have always tended to be given the marginal seats and to come into Parliament on landslides. Landslides for one major party however, mean destruction for the other, and where relatively large numbers of women have been returned for the victors of such an election, their marginal seats having been won in the general swing to their party, the women on the other side again with the less stable seats, are most vulnerable to swings against their party and are the first to go. Women have only occasionally, and relatively recently, built up anything like a solid base of safe seats where women would, almost regardless of 'swings', be returned to Parliament at any general elections.

This is probably most obvious in the case of Margaret Bondfield who having achieved her ministerial appointment early in 1924 was not returned in the general election of that year. The text of the Zinoviev letter was published a few days before the election and partly at least because of the 'red scare' which this occasioned, the Conservatives were returned with a large majority. Of the four women who came into Parliament only one, Ellen Wilkinson, was a Labour representative. Thus Margaret Bondfield was unable to consolidate her ministerial position, or even to gain experience and party prominence as a member of the Opposition. It is an indication of her first-rate ability, clear even on her short parliamentary and ministerial showing, that when she came back into the House, she was soon again called to office, this time to the Cabinet, as Minister of Labour in the ill-fated MacDonald administration.

In the same year (1929), Susan Lawrence became the first woman Chairman of the Labour Party. Women's achievements in the organisation of the parties are much more strongly and widely based than in government itself. This is partly because their involvement in extra-parliamentary party organisation is greater and of much earlier origin than their venture into national electoral politics, and partly because of the special voting arrangements whereby women standing, for example, for the National Executive Committee of the Labour Party, compete only against other women. In the Tory hierarchy, there is always, for example, a woman Vice-Chairman of the party. Dame Caroline Bridgeman who was Chairman of the women's organisation of the Conservative Party was never herself involved in electoral politics, but became, in 1926, the first woman Chairman of the National Union of Conservative and Unionist Association, and so the first woman chairman of any political party. Lady Iveagh, a Conservative M.P. since 1927, became Chairman of the Party Organisation in 1930. In the Labour Party too following Susan Lawrence, many of the well-known Labour women have been Chairmen of the Party.[2] The National Executive of the Labour Party too has always had a fair proportion of women members, both parliamentary and otherwise. By common consent, that is where a good deal of policy-making power in the party lies and women have never been excluded. And in the Conservative Party, both within the national party organisation and in the powerful 1922 Committee of backbench M.P.s, women have made their way. Lady Davidson was the first woman to be elected there and Miss Harvie Anderson is a current member. Compared with their experience and influence in governmental posts, the women of both parties have done rather better in their respective party organisations than in the battle for ministerial office. The Labour Party has perhaps a slightly better record of ministerial appointment than the Conservatives—if only in that they did appoint women, albeit very few, early on and so set a trend which had at least to be maintained if not extended by the Conservatives. In spite of having appointed a woman to office in 1924, and having had women Party Chairmen in 1926, 1930, 1936 and 1937, it was not until 1953 that the Conservatives brought their first woman, Florence Horsburgh, into the Cabinet.

In 1936, just before the constitutional crisis which was to develop over the abdication of Edward VIII, Florence Horsbrugh moved the

Address in reply to the Speech from the Throne. In her speech, although she did not, she said, want to suggest that the occasion heralded 'the crumbling of some fortress wall which has defended this citadel of male prerogative', she did see it as 'an opening of a gate into a new field of opportunity'.[3] Yet the fortress wall was perhaps stronger than she imagined. It was to be another seventeen years before even a woman of her ability was to be made a Cabinet Minister and in the meantime, only one Labour woman, Ellen Wilkinson, was to be accorded that position.

Outside the realms of ministerial office, women have always made a contribution, well in proportion to their numbers, in parliamentary committees. This is partly as has been mentioned, a result of the women's full-time involvement in parliamentary duties, few of them ever having any outside occupation, and therefore being, as Lady Burton put it recently, ready 'committee-fodder'. It is also perhaps partly too the result of the general preoccupations and experience of many parliamentary women. There are, and always have been, a large number of them to whom committee membership has been almost a way of life. In view of this, it is perhaps surprising that it was not until 1946 that the first woman joined the Speaker's panel of Chairmen of Committees, and in this capacity, Florence Paton presided in 1948 over the whole House, in Committee, in a debate on the Scottish Aviation Estimates.

Although Mrs Paton was the first woman to preside over the whole House, she did not take the Speaker's chair. It was thus not until 1970 that this was to be occupied by a woman for the first time in the history of the office, when as Deputy Chairman of the Committee of Ways and Means, the Rt. Hon. Betty Harvie Anderson took the chair. She recalls that she told the Prime Minister that she would take the job on a three months' trial basis because she was uncertain if it could be done by a woman, and if she were not accepted simply as the Speaker, the job itself ('persuasion by reference to precedent', as she sees it, 'not dictation') would have been impossible. She was asked by the Speaker when she wanted to take the chair and when the press release should be made. She said she wanted no release and she would take over immediately. She did so, wearing the blue sleeveless dress she happened to have on (and next morning, she says, nobody could recall what she had worn). After this, she occupied the Chair many times, coping with the stormy Industrial Relations Act in the 1970–1 Parliament, and the equally impassioned Common Market debates. Another first had been quietly and capably recorded by women, in an area where their involvement had always occasioned uncertainty about their capacity to maintain order, a debate which like so many similar ones was shown, when put to the test, to be simply irrelevant.

Again perhaps surprisingly, since women have always taken their fair share of arrangement and organisation within the parliamentary parties, it was not until 1964 that the first woman, Harriet Slater, became a Whip. Since that time, a number of women have held this office (both in the Commons, and as baroness-in-waiting, in the Lords), which can often be an important step on the way to higher office.

By 1975, then, women had been Whips and Parliamentary Private Secretaries, and Ministers, both inside and outside the Cabinet. They had chaired committees, including committees of the whole House, and sat in the Speaker's Chair. In the Cabinet, however, there had been few of them—only seven in forty-five years, and four of these had been Ministers of Education, an approved 'women's area'. No woman, as has been said, had ever been Chancellor or Home or Foreign Secretary, although one, Barbara Castle, had been First Secretary of State. It was, in view of this, surprising to many people when the Conservative Party elected as Leader a woman, Margaret Thatcher, in February 1975. Yet, the internal politics of that election aside, she perhaps confirms the trend among women politicians for exceptional individuals to carve out their own place regardless of precedent. If Mrs Thatcher becomes Prime Minister it is most unlikely to pave the way for women any more directly than Margaret Bondfield's achievement did over forty-eight years ago. In 1930, there was one woman in the Cabinet, and in 1978 there was also one. In 1968, there were briefly two women in the Cabinet and that high was repeated in 1974 when both Barbara Castle and Shirley Williams were there. Outside the Cabinet, the record of ministerial appointment is equally episodic (two in 1964, two in 1977). Yet if these numbers seem in absolute terms to be unimpressive, in relative terms in recent years, they have been nearly as high as for men. In the Labour administrations from 1974, two women (Barbara Castle and Shirley Williams) have been in the Cabinet, Judith Hart has resigned and then been re-instated at Overseas Development, Shirley Summerskill, Joan Lestor and Margaret Jackson have been Parliamentary Under-Secretaries, while Ann

Taylor has been a Parliamentary Private Secretary. (Also Betty
Boothroyd and Gwyneth Dunwoody are members of the European
Parliament.) In other words, nine women out of nineteen have at
some time held some office between 1974 and 1977, at least six (that is,
about a third) of them at any one time, a similar proportion to that
of Labour men in office over the same period. The problem for women
then is not that, once there, they do not make anything of their parliamentary chances, but that the number who are actually elected is so
small that their achievement is constantly numerically dwarfed by
that of the men.

It is sometimes assumed that women have been excluded from
certain offices—the Home and Foreign Offices, and the Treasury—
because their interests and talents lie elsewhere, in welfare and education, for example. Perhaps the original justification for this hiving-
off process was that women have often historically been interested in
matters relating to the family, to children and social welfare questions.
This has given rise to the impression that women are more tender-
hearted, socially concerned, and above all, interested in people than
men. In general they have perhaps seemed stronger on individual
grievances and problems than on policies and this has made their
political concerns appear episodic rather than informed by any all-
embracing political strategy. This is only partly true. It is certainly
the case that women have often been primarily interested in individual
people and their problems and concerns, but there have always been
those who had a strong commitment to a much wider political vision,
a strategic understanding of the kind of society they were in politics to
bring about. This was certainly the case with many of the early Labour
women. Susan Lawrence and Margaret Bondfield were indeed personally committed to individuals and their problems, (they were both,
for example, good and popular constituency M.P.s). Many of Barbara
Castle's most impassioned speeches have been on issues of social
justice for individuals about whom she clearly cares deeply and Margaret Thatcher can wax eloquent in defence of the little man and the
unfairness of his treatment. Yet they cannot see themselves as simply
social workers manqué. Beyond this personal level, lies another wider
and deeper perspective, an understanding of the kind of society where
these individual injustices and prejudices would not exist. And such
an understanding inevitably takes the M.P. beyond the purely ad hoc
or episodic interest in people, to a concern with the organisation of

society in its wider economic, industrial, commercial and international framework. They are inevitably drawn, that is, beyond the personal and domestic, beyond 'women's issues', into economic and foreign policy. It was perhaps this realisation that led one writer recently to suggest that a woman M.P. to whom he was talking was 'better with causes than with people'. It apparently struck him as odd that a woman was clearly involved in politics for reasons other than simply 'liking people' and wanting to help them. As Lady Young has said, M.P.s must 'like people', and women have no monopoly here, but to be successful they must increasingly have a strategic appreciation of their political aims, and it is this more than anything, which has taken the women beyond 'women's issues'.

It would appear then that women are not significantly disadvantaged solely on grounds of their femininity. Indeed femininity may be, as some of the younger M.P.s both male and female assured me, an advantage, all else being equal. It is not of course the case that women can get by on femininity, but in the first place that any ability they have will be noticed, there being so few of them, and also that they are particularly useful to both Government and Opposition in the contemporary political scene, where account has to appear to be taken of the idea of female equality. In this context the appointment of a capable woman may strengthen the administration, not only in making available to it her abilities, but also in making it clear that its attitude is modern, liberal-minded and non-discriminatory.

Because of their small number however women's representation in whatever political capacity must often appear symbolic. The statutory woman on committees, panels and tribunals of all sorts was a fact of political life long before the women's movement started to take issue with the idea. And in a way, such symbolic representation is very much a part of the formation of governments. It is unlikely nowadays that any Prime Minister in choosing his administration would fail to include some women, just as he would be politically unwise to fail to represent the main bases of his political support or not to give a post to a Scottish or Welsh representative. In this sense women ministers are no more examples of tokenism than is the Secretary of State for Scotland (who would normally come from a Scottish constituency). But in the same way they are symbolic; their appointment is assumed to indicate not only their personal ability, but the fairness and liberality of that government. Still, there are few of them in governments

and fewer in Cabinets. An eloquent testimony to the lonely splendour
of the statutory Cabinet woman is to be found in Harold Wilson's
account, in *The Governance of Britain* (p. 45), of the case of the chairs
at the Cabinet table which were so rough as to cause Barbara Castle's
stockings to be laddered. He arranged for the chair's legs to be covered
in cretonne, and recounts that it was then allocated to Mrs Thatcher
during the Heath Administration!

If women get a sense of their purely token representation in government appointments when, as has been shown, they have recently
relatively speaking been as well represented as men, they have far
more reason to see this as a reality when it comes to Government
Enquiries, Royal Commissions and public bodies. There, they really
are under-represented by any standards. Very occasionally, such a
group may be composed of almost equal numbers of men and women
(the Latey Committee on the Age of Majority had five women and
six men), or even more rarely, a woman may chair such an enquiry
(e.g. the Lane Committee on Abortion), but in general, women are
not well represented. The Whitehall lists of well-known and experienced people who are generally called upon to staff government
committees, councils and governing bodies (the lists of the so-called
'great and good'), are sparse on female representation. On public
bodies too, women's representation is often not only limited but non-
existent. Neither the Electricity Council, the National Bus Company,
nor the Civil Aviation Authority had in 1977 a single woman on its
governing body. Similarly the Research Councils for Science and
Medicine, Agriculture and Natural Environment have no women
representatives at all. Even the Design Council and the Arts Council
which one might have supposed would have been deemed highly
suitable for female participation can only muster three women each, in
the former case out of a membership of twenty-eight, and in the
latter out of twenty. In May 1975, Maureen Colquhoun attempted to
introduce a Private Member's Bill entitled 'Balance of the Sexes',
which aimed to ensure equal representation for women on public
bodies. It failed to get a second reading. And the arguments made
against it are strong enough. It would be quite illogical, it is rightly
said, to bring in women in large numbers, simply on the qualification
of sex, who have no experience or expertise to offer in the particular
fields. This is unanswerable. If it really is the case that there are no
suitably qualified women in these areas, then it is clearly self-defeating

to dilute the quality of the advice given or the decisions taken purely on a quite unrelated point of principle. And yet it does seem strange that in the 1970s, when women have been established in the professions for more than half a century, when their educational and professional backgrounds are similar to those of men, many more of them are not thought to be suitable and sought out for such public work. Here as elsewhere, the problem becomes one of the chicken and egg variety. In order to get more women, more women must come forward and more women will only come forward if these are seen to be areas in which women succeed. The positive discrimination of the sort Ms Colquhoun suggests is one attempt, however blunt and unsubtle, to break into this circle of self reinforcing under-representation, and crude as it may seem in this case, it may initially be necessary in one form or another if a better balance is to be achieved.

The twenty-five Private Members' Bills which have been successfully introduced by women do seem to show a preference for women's concerns. No less than three relate to alcohol or drunkenness, three to protection of animals, nine to women and children directly and four to consumer interests. With almost the single exception of Mrs Thatcher's Public Bodies Act (1959), they encapsulate feminine ideology. It is clearly not the case that women have the monopoly of concern about social and animal welfare or consumer protection, yet these are the areas in which women are encouraged to specialise and in which they may feel competent to introduce legislation when given the chance. These Bills are of course hardly a perfect indication of the preoccupations of women in the House during the period. After all, Private Members' Bills are essentially arbitrary in selection in that the member has first to gain a high place in the original ballot and then to secure enough time to see the Bill through the House. Most of them therefore depend on government supporting such Bills, and many measures originating in this way are either taken over by the government, or are dropped by the initiator when the government takes some other relevant action.

Women in the House have had difficulties, and to some extent still do, in operating in a working environment which was developed without their involvement or influence. Not only are the facilities of the House itself rather limited—this is the case for both men and women—but the ritual of the House with its formal methods of debate, its intricate procedures and its general club atmosphere can seem alien to women. Getting the respect of the House often involves being able to hold its attention in the Chamber, and having such respect and attention is a prerequisite of getting a serious hearing. Women on the whole have less experience, whether through schooling or later professional life, of dealing with such ritual and form and many of the women M.P.s said that, at least initially, they felt this as a barrier to their expressing themselves successfully in the Commons

Again women do face special difficulties in trying to keep their domestic life going. Some of these difficulties they share with all working women, but some are particularly acute for women living so much of their life in the public eye. Like all professional women, at least, they have felt the need not to appear to be too involved with the demands of their children. Mrs Butler mentioned that at the time when her children were small she felt other people took domestic involvement as an indication of unprofessionalism. Domestic ties were, until quite recently, seen as a largely female responsibility and a woman who was always rushing off to see to the children could soon get a reputation for being unreliable. The roles of mother and professional woman are still felt by many people to be incompatible. The kind of conflict which can develop in this situation was brought home very clearly to a Swedish male M.P. who told me of taking his baby daughter to his room in the Riksdag, where in the middle of a nappy-change, a division was sounded. The conflict of loyalties, he said, was profound. While the mother who is also a lawyer or doctor or academic has to deal with social uncertainty about her involvements in this respect, she does not have to do so in the full glare of publicity which surrounds a member of Parliament. When Helene Hayman's son was born, she had an enormous mail on this subject, some supportive, but some clearly antipathetic. The press too exacerbated her problem and she tells of journalists besieging her house, and when she finally emerged, blocking her way to her car while they took pictures of the baby. She was then accused in some quarters of subjecting her child to unnecessary publicity.

The attitude of the women M.P.s themselves to this question is rather mixed. Some of them feel that it is a good thing for women M.P.s to be clearly and publicly involved with their children. Joan Lestor, for example, often takes her children with her on her weekend visits to her constituency, but she admits to being aware that although she thinks it right that they came along, they should not be in any way exploited in the process. Again Barbara Castle said she thought it would be beneficial for the House as a whole if women did bring their children. Most of the men there are 'the products of institutions', the public schools, the trade unions and professional associations, and she would think it a good idea for them to be taken beyond this institution-alised framework by the introduction of a more domestic note, for the good of everybody.

On the other hand, several of the women clearly felt that such domesticity was inappropriate, that women were in the House to do a particular job and this could only be impeded by their importing other, necessarily conflicting, priorities. Baroness Phillips took this line, and Mrs Oppenheim underlined the separation of home and job when she asserted that women 'can't have their cake and eat it'. What is clear from all these attitudes, however, is the general acceptance that children and home still are primarily a woman's responsibility, and a woman working outside the home is expected to make arrangements as far as possible to the detriment of neither of her duties. There is a contrast in social attitudes here in comparison with, for example, Sweden, where the whole notion of women being solely or even mainly responsible for children is being challenged. It is this challenge which informs Sweden's day-care policy for pre-school children, where centres are being developed not at the mother's place of work which, it is argued, would underline her responsibility here, but on a neigh-bourhood basis, emphasising the family orientation and the involve-ment of both parents in child care. This double load which most political women carry of family and professional responsibilities is perhaps not helped by the fact that they are on the whole enormously diligent and hard-working. They take both their parliamentary and their pastoral constituency duties very seriously. Some of them think that this can be a disadvantage, for although almost all have secretaries, they seem to be bad at delegating and admit to doing much of the routine work themselves. Often of course, they cannot afford to hire staff to take some of this load from them, but when they do (Mrs Oppenheim, for example, has a personal assistant and a full-time secretary) there are obvious advantages.

If women claim on the whole to be aware of little discrimination against them in the selective process, they are equally adamant, most of them, about the equality of treatment they receive once in the House. Apart from the fact that they claim that the men assume a conspiracy if two or three women sit together in the tea-room, on the whole they accept this as banter rather than anything more serious. There is, however, still the inevitable sexism of the male response, even if it amounts to nothing more than an assumption that women will organise the domestic arrangements of the House itself. Maureen Colquhoun recalls a male acquaintance coming up to her soon after she entered Parliament and saying how glad he was to see her, because 'now you can do something about the food in this place'. Ms Colquhoun responded that he'd better see to the food himself as she intended to be Chancellor of the Exchequer.

It can of course go deeper than this. Male attempts to keep women in their place, to render them harmless and manageable, by overt reference to their dress, or by sexual innuendo, have already been referred to. And women have often been in something of a double bind here with regard to their feminine attraction. The more physically attractive, the more orthodoxly feminine they are, the easier it is for men to categorise them within the confines of the eternal feminine and to demand the appropriate response from them. Several of the early women M.P.s were intuitively aware of this and affected a mannish appearance in clothes and hair-styles to counteract it. They, on the other hand, were frequently looked on as odd women just because they did not conform to the accepted standards of femininity in these respects. The inspiration of such reactions can be both an advantage and a disadvantage for women. Jean Mann for example, claims that when Lady Tweedsmuir, the House 'glamour girl', spoke for the Conservatives, 'our men hesitated to attack her and were only too pleased when Mr Speaker called on me to follow'.[4] Yet several of the women complained that it was very much easier for them to catch the Speaker's eye when the debate was one on social questions or education, than when it was on, for example, the economy.

Inside the House, the women do not see themselves as having any strong *esprit de corps*. At the most, the Labour women are, as previously mentioned, aware of a certain camaraderie and unity of purpose about some basic issues. But beyond this, the use of the Lady Members' Sitting Rooms is almost the only outward manifestation of any feminine clique. Even there, some of the women profess to disapprove of the use of separate rooms by Conservative and Labour women which has, quite informally, developed in the last few years, and some of the older members make a point of not frequenting only one of these in the belief that such divisions by party are harmful. Still others expressed a dislike of the whole idea of even separate sitting-rooms for women members, pointing out that all the other reception rooms of the House are used by both sexes and suggesting that it would be better for women's full integration if they did their socialising and held their discussions, like the men, in the bars and Smoking Room.

It is difficult in reviewing women's achievements in the House not to feel a certain sense of anti-climax. It is even more difficult to say exactly why this is so. After all, they have reached almost the top office, and they are represented in office in almost the same proportions as men. Perhaps their total commitment to their job gives them less variety and colour than the men. There are among the women, for example, not only no practising barristers or doctors or academics, but no novelists or actors, or even television personalities! There have of course, been 'characters' among the women as among the men. Lady Astor, Eleanor Rathbone, Ellen Wilkinson and Bessie Braddock were all, in different ways, quite as outstanding personalities as any of their male colleagues. Again, small numbers play their part here. The great rump of worthy but unremarkable male backbenchers is of course there, but there seem proportionately more men who are outstanding in one way or another partly because there are simply numerically many more men altogether. Still, the fact that the women are professional M.P.s without apparent involvements or interests outside politics does contribute to the impression that their efforts are very much concentrated, and that the men appear able to achieve at least as much politically and still have time to write or act or sail or play the piano or violin.

Perhaps all this shows is that the women are not so good at self-publicity as many of the men and that the qualities asked of an M.P. are here being stretched to cover those required in show business. Yet part of the job of an M.P. is selling ideas, of which the ability to sell oneself is an integral part. And women are often reticent about this. They are hard-working and competent, but they do not want to be challenged in other areas. To this end they refuse to make themselves vulnerable by revealing anything of themselves other than the professional persona which they feel able to defend in public. Almost without exception, the women I interviewed stressed the importance of keeping their 'private lives' to themselves and registered horror at the idea of having to 'perform', as one of them called it, in any other than the political arena.

In these days of the women's movement with the strong political appeal of women's issues, it is tempting to see women M.P.s as having here a ready-made constituency with particular current appeal. As has been said, many of them are very uncertain about the advisability of becoming associated primarily with women's concerns. Yet it might be argued that this is precisely what they should do: they should cease to accept male definitions which designate such issues as 'soft' or 'easy' politics and use their influence unashamedly for the Women's Lobby. But this is not either as simple or as productive as it might seem.

To begin with, the last ten years or so have seen an enormous increase in the number of pressure groups of all kinds and of women's pressure groups in particular. These range all the way from the well-established ones like the Fawcett Society and Josephine Butler Society, through the more recent like the National Council for One-Parent Families, to the radical and political, such as Woman's Place Collective and Women's Charter. Some of these groups work happily within the conventional political system, but others are, for one reason or another, less satisfactorily accommodated within it. Most of the pressure groups use conventional lobbying tactics, in the process of which they often get in touch with women M.P.s; but the women are neither their exclusive allies nor are they always necessarily even the most useful. As Lady Seear points out, in her experience both as President of the Fawcett Society and as Chairman and Spokesman in the Lords for the Council for the Single Woman and her Dependents, it is always worthwhile lobbying men in a woman's cause. It is very important strategy, she suggests, to have male support, just as it is generally important as far as possible to have all-party support. In this context, Lady Seear mentions the work done for the Council by Sir Keith Joseph and other male M.P.s which she thinks has given the single woman's claims greater impact and credibility than if they had been canvassed exclusively by women.

A woman M.P., then, desirous of establishing a reputation as a woman's champion could find that, welcomed as she might be by the Women's Lobby, she could not expect to establish any kind of female hegemony, the right sexual mix being as important to successful lobbying in many cases as the right party-political mix. There is also the problem of sheer volume. There are vast numbers of women's groups, and even to keep up with the particular interests and views of some of them is time-consuming, without trying to keep pace with them all.

It has been argued too, within the last few years, that conventional party politics itself is giving way to pressure group politics. If this thesis is correct, and politics must now be conducted on what Anthony Wedgwood Benn calls the 'stiletto heel principle: that if you put all your weight on one place you can go through almost anything',[5] then all M.P.s, men and women, are in a difficulty. They, after all, are supposed to be the generalists par excellence, able to form an opinion on anything and decide between priorities and differing demands in society. But 'the new politics', as Wedgwood Benn dubs it, does not call for this kind of ability as much as for specialism and commitment to a particular cause. Leaving aside the problems which this approach may bequeath to politics, when politics becomes what Trevor Smith characterises as 'a bewildering myriad of "one off" approaches and "one best way" solutions',[6] it also makes life difficult for M.P.s by removing, or appearing to remove, the locus of power from Westminster to the Lobby itself. Indeed there is among some lobbyists a general suspicion of conventional parliamentary processes. May Hobbs, militant leader of the office cleaners says, 'If I was in Parliament, that would put me out of reach of the people I am trying to help while it would suit a lot of . . . the other side to see me muzzled by all their parliamentary procedure and compromises'.

Even if this is not always the case, it would seem to be the presupposition of at least some of the women's groups which are intensely suspicious of conventional political frameworks which they regard as male-dominated. They do not seek to operate through M.P.s because they see them—both male and female—as instruments of a system which is exclusively male-oriented. For example, when the Working Women's Charter held a fund-raising meeting at Alexandra Palace in February 1977, there was disagreement in exactly these terms among the organisers about whether a woman M.P. should be asked to open it. One faction claimed that women in Parliament were part of the male establishment while the other saw benefits in the support a well-known woman would attract. On the other hand, groups which can hardly be seen as fitting within the conventional framework do not all take this feminist line. Erin Pizzey, for example, of Chiswick

Women's Aid Group, has her reservations about being 'linked with the feminist ideology—it's too political, too anti-men', and records her debt to men like Lord Goodman and David Astor for their involvement and support.

One way or another then, it would seem facile to suppose that political women have simply missed their opportunity with women's pressure groups, that they have failed to capitalise on an area where they could, for the asking, have been much more dominant than they are. It is not just the reticence of women M.P.s, not predisposed to become too involved with women's concerns, which is relevant here, but also these attitudes and policies of the groups themselves which affect and often limit their relations with the women at Westminster.

The extent to which women have progressively won recognition in the House has been at least partly a reflection of the wider social integration of women and indeed of their developing sense of their own significance. In the past women have attempted in all sorts of ways to establish their individuality and credibility as people in their own right and perhaps one example, that of names, makes clear the change in attitudes which has taken place in the past few years. Edith Summerskill recounts amusingly the problems she encountered when she decided to take her seat in her maiden name, the name by which she was known professionally. She felt strongly, and her husband agreed, that she had a right to her own name, and indeed both her son and daughter adopted this and not their father's name. Her insistence in this matter (in the face of questioning by the Chief Whip and the former Attorney General) was for her an assertion of her individuality and an important personal stand. Thirty-six years later, when Helene Hayman was returned to Parliament, in spite of having become known in her maiden name and indeed fought the 1974 elections as Helene Middleweek, she decided to be known by her married name. Although believing that in a more rational society, the convention of taking a husband's name would not continue, Mrs Hayman does not think this particular self-assertion is necessary. It is not the case that Edith Summerskill was wrong in her stand. She was at the time making the point as a specific example of a general problem—that women were not appendages, were not to be subsumed even under a husband's name. But nobody would now seriously even suggest that they were and this social consciousness, largely developed by women like Lady Summerskill herself, had made it possible for them to be more self-assured and less prickly about details like dress or nomenclature.

Another Summerskill, Shirley, in seconding the Address to the Queen's Speech in 1966, reminded the 'Right Honourable Gentlemen in the Government that the railings around the Palace of Westminster can be used again'. It is unlikely however that today's political women would feel the need for any such symbolic gestures. If they feel maligned or unfairly treated, they have other practical political methods of asserting themselves. Women in politics have to this extent come of age. Symbols and tokens of whatever type are no longer adequate or appropriate. Yet *The Times* can still commiserate with what it saw as women's political handicap—having to 'prove something about their femininity'.[7] The force of this argument rests on a female stereotype which is rapidly losing credibility: only if it is believed that there is something inherently unfeminine about politics, and something inherently unpolitical about women, does it have force. And the more women are politically active the less would it even seem plausible to suggest that in this role their femininity might stand in any need of proving.

CHAPTER VII

The Men's Response

'Personally I care little for giving women the vote, except
as a means of getting them on public bodies. If you have
served, as I have, for years on Health Committees trying
to persuade a parcel of men who regard women as angels
and subjects for loose jest ... that women require sanitary
accommodation as well as men, ... you would not press me
for my reasons.' George Bernard Shaw

'First and foremost today, the Welfare State means the
state controlling the way in which the woman does her job
in the home servicing the worker and bringing up their
children.' Beveridge Report

Any account of Women Members of Parliament which leans as heavily
as this one does on the responses and views of the women, both past
and present, is initially open to the charge of female tendentiousness.
Although I consulted many male M.P.s in the process of my research,
I felt that the attitudes of the men to their female colleagues, and to
women in general, could best be discovered by a review of party
literature, manifestoes and debates on women and their concerns. This
also reveals changing—and indeed some unchanging—views of
women, and often too the self-perceptions of the women themselves.

By the time women's suffrage came to be discussed in the Parliaments of the 1920s, women were already represented there, and the
legislation which was debated in 1924 and 1928 might be thought to
have been simply a tidying-up operation. Women over thirty already
had the vote (and indeed those over twenty-one were eligible to stand
for Parliament). The demand for votes for women on a par with
men—at twenty-one—would seem to have been a clear demand of
logic and justice. And yet old habits of mind die hard. 'The woman
question' had been so long on the Parliamentary calendar that it
almost seemed as if some members were unwilling to let it go, and
consequently at least some of the arguments made in 1924 and even
1928 were exactly similar to those advanced since 1870 when the

whole question had originally been raised in Parliament. In all these years, all parties had been involved in the Debate. Conservatives like William Forsythe and Sir Albert Rollit, Liberals like Jacob Bright and William Woodall and finally, after 1906, Labour members like W. Crooks and Keir Hardie himself were instrumental in introducing bills which would in one form or another have extended the suffrage to at least some women. This is not however, to suggest that there was a majority in the major parties in favour of women's suffrage. Even in the Labour Party, generally assumed to be supportive of the idea, there was, as will be seen, considerable dissent.

The arguments used throughout the period from 1870 to 1914 scarcely changed, although sometimes one or two were stressed more than others. It was suggested for example that since Queen Victoria herself occupied the supreme position of Head of State it was ridiculous to exclude women from participation in Government. Yet the Queen rather quashed this argument by revealing a profound distaste for 'this mad, wicked folly of "women's rights", with all its attendant horrors on which her poor, feeble sex is bent, forgetting every sense of womanly feeling and propriety'. Just as the anti-suffragists could use the royal will as an argument against women, so they turned the granting of the vote to women in Australia (between 1893 and 1909) and New Zealand (1893) against women in the mother country by stressing that the former did not have an Empire to supervise. This was an argument which did not fail to turn up as late as 1928. Again, it was argued that women were politically uneducated and that they would not be able to make reasoned political judgements. And if deprecating their general ability and intelligence was insufficient, women could always be depicted as too pure and too frail for the debasement and hurly-burly of politics. If all else failed, the appeal was made to masculine fear of female unity and hegemony. After 1918 this was seen as a matter of numbers, women being a majority of the adult population, and hence of the projected electorate, after the war. The fear appeared to be given some ground by the activities of the militant suffragettes, especially in the period from 1911 to the beginning of the war. When, for example, members of the Women's Social and Political Union ran amok in Oxford Street and Bond Street smashing windows (and Mrs Pankhurst herself put four stones through the window of No 10 Downing Street before being arrested), this was taken by some as an indication of the irresponsibility of the women, and of their clear unfitness for political participation. It was also suggested that such behaviour was quite obviously atypical of women and that the suffragettes therefore represented nobody but themselves. In a letter to *The Times* in 1912, Sir Almroth Wright launched a violent attack on them in exactly those terms suggesting that the participation of women in politics was, as every decent woman knew, unnatural, and those who pressed for it were simply psychological misfits. The strong implication was that 'normal' women, 'decent' women, were above the grossness of politics and were happy to allow their men to represent their interests in this sphere of national life. And many women did feel just this. Yet in spite of the arguments made on grounds of female sensibility and purity, clear also throughout is the male desire to maintain political control and social domination, which Lord Pethwick Lawrence, an ardent suffragist himself, exemplifies in the reaction of his appalled parliamentary colleagues: 'Votes for women, indeed: we shall be asked next to give votes to our horses and dogs'.

Although the Conservative Party passed a resolution in favour of women's suffrage as early as 1887, the party leadership was extremely uncertain about such a measure. The Liberals, in spite of having many prominent suffragists in their ranks, were equally split on the issue. The rank and file of the party were probably broadly in favour, but successive leaders, Gladstone and Asquith in particular, were against. The latter continued to maintain that there was no evidence that women wanted or needed the vote. Democracy, he said, had no quarrel with the distinctions created by nature. Roy Jenkins suggests that, although he appointed women as Factory Inspectors during his term as Home Secretary (in 1892), Asquith's failure to support votes for women was probably the result of his natural conservatism in social affairs.[1] Constance Rover however, suggests that his distrust of women was more fundamental and quotes him as writing in the most contemptuous terms, as late as 1920, of women as 'hopelessly ignorant of politics, credulous to the last degree, and flickering with gusts of sentiment like a candle in the wind'.[2]

Lloyd George's record too is somewhat ambivalent, for although he was ostensibly a supporter of women's suffrage, he opposed the Conciliation Bill of 1912 on the grounds that it was too limited, giving the vote only to propertied women. Although he may genuinely have favoured a wider suffrage than this, as Rover points out, 'no real friend of woman's suffrage would have opposed a measure which broke the sex barrier on the grounds that it was not generous enough. One might as well refuse a starving man half a loaf because he needed a whole one'. His case is perhaps made even more dubious by the fact that Winston Churchill opposed the Bill on the same grounds and Churchill, originally an avowed anti-suffragist was, according to Sylvia Pankhurst, even by 1912, 'an opponent at heart'.

Even in the Labour Party, the extension of the suffrage to women was not supported by all, on any grounds whatever. The Socialist claim was adult suffrage and it was often argued that the extension to women on a property qualification would simply extend the middle-class (i.e. Tory and Liberal) vote and leave large numbers of the working class, the Labour supporters, still unenfranchised. In spite of this, Keir Hardie, as Leader of the Independent Labour Party and Chairman of the parliamentary party from 1906 to 1908 accepted the limited enfranchisement of women as a step on the road to total adult suffrage. He was followed in this by subsequent chairmen like Arthur Henderson and George Barnes. Ramsay MacDonald supported the women's claim generally, but he also accepted the Cat and Mouse Act[3] of 1913, believing that the militants had only themselves to blame for this measure. Philip Snowden too although a suffragist from the early days, opposed the militant tactics after 1912, saying that the women had 'forgotten the cause in the intoxication of the methods they were using'. George Lansbury's support on the other hand was quite unequivocal. He felt so strongly about the issue that he applied for the Chiltern Hundreds and fought a by-election on it in his constituency. He lost, but continued to fight for the women's cause, going to prison in 1913 and finally being released on licence, under the Cat and Mouse Act.

Although the I.L.P. were broadly in favour of women's suffrage, other areas of the Left were hardly as enthusiastic. The Fabians had what Margaret Cole describes as a 'lukewarm attitude' to the whole question.[4] Beatrice Webb, for example, while still Beatrice Potter, in 1889 had signed a protest, arranged by Mrs Humphrey Ward, objecting to the demand for the extension of the suffrage, although she changed her mind on this after 1906, and the Society did from that time take a more active part in the women's campaign.

The extreme left-wing of the Labour movement too was somewhat uncertain of the value of votes for women. The Marxist Social

Democratic Federation, although having among its leadership some who were committed suffragists, also had Henry Hyndman, who told Sylvia Pankhurst 'women should learn to have influence as they have in France, instead of trying to get votes'. Another S.D.F. leader Belfort Bax who suggests in his *Essays in Socialism* that to enfranchise women would put men in the political minority and that in any case women were, rather than oppressed, shielded from the reality of the crass, cold world, where men had to make their way and support their families. For this, men deserved the vote; women did not. These were arguments which, with minor variations, were used again and again, as late as 1928, by the anti-suffragists.

There were of course men, of all parties, who were consistently favourable and actively supportive of the women's cause, who saw the denial of votes to women as grossly unjust and clearly illogical. They too made themselves heard in the debates up to and beyond the end of the First World War but their fundamental message is put by Arthur Balfour as early as 1892, when he castigated his Parliamentary colleagues for their willingness to 'give a vote to a man who contributes nothing to taxation but what he pays on his beer, while you refuse enfranchisement to a woman because she is a woman whatever her contribution to the state may be. She has sufficient ability to look after lighting and paving[5] but is not so fitted to look after the interest of the Empire as a man who cannot point out on a map the parts of the world of which the Empire is composed'.

By the time women came into the House of Commons, these activities and priorities had perhaps become somewhat less extreme, but the drama of debate still brought them out from time to time. When the House finally passed the Bill to give votes to women over thirty—in December 1917—although it was clear from the vote (364 in favour, to 23 against) how the great majority of the men now viewed the issue, it was still necessary to oppose again the aruments that had been made at least since the 1870s. At the end of October 1918, the House considered the case for women's eligibility to stand as parliamentary candidates. Although this was passed by 274 votes to 25 with Mrs Humphrey Ward's son, Arnold, accepting the Bill without opposition, the old guard were still represented by Sir Hedworth Meux, Admiral of the Fleet and Conservative Member for Portsmouth, who claimed that the House was not 'a fit and proper place for any respectable woman to sit in'.[6]

After the election of 1918, although no woman was actually in the House (Countess Markiewicz having refused to take the oath of allegiance, thus forfeiting her seat), Ray Strachey[7] claims that 'their absence in person was much less important than it had ever been before, for every member there knew that he owed his election to the votes of women as well as men, so that the whole atmosphere of Parliament was changed'.[8] Be that as it may, the continuing debate on the franchise in 1924 and 1928, when women had finally made their way into Parliament, still shows the at least residual hostility of some members to their wider political participation.

In February 1924, the House debated the second reading of the Representation of the People Act (1918) Amendment Bill which set out, among other things, to extend the franchise to women over twenty-one. What became clear in this debate was that not only men but some women too were still opposed to the measure, and on grounds which had been used to fight the granting of the female franchise in the first place. The Duchess of Atholl challenged the notion that women really wanted this change. 'I agree that there are women's societies that are very anxious to see [it], but I would like to ask what evidence . . . there is . . . for this among women in general'.[9] She went on to reiterate the argument that women were not politically educated and indeed had neither the time nor the inclination to become so. 'My experience', she said, 'is that the men go to meetings and leave the wives at home to manage the children.'[10]

The Labour women adamantly opposed her (Dorothy Jewson had seconded the introduction of the Bill), as did Mrs Wintringham who sought to refute another of the time-worn arguments about women in politics and Parliament by referring to the present case. It had often been feared, she said, that women 'will work together and there will be essentially a woman's party against a man's party. This Debate shows that women are not at all in agreement'.[11] Lady Astor, too, joined in the rejection of her colleague's argument and claimed that the Duchess was 'like Canute, trying to keep the waves back'.[12]

Although the women were, with the one exception, in favour of the measure, some of the men were still uncertain, and mainly expressed this uncertainty by initially claiming not to oppose votes for women, but some quite practical and undesirable outcome of the franchise extension. Lord Hugh Cecil, for example, claimed that 'It is neither a sex question nor a class question', but explained his opposition to the

Bill by his unwillingness to 'increase suddenly by 3,000,000 or 4,000,000 the least experienced and least trustworthy part of the electorate'.[13] Some of these practical concerns were clearly not simply excuses either. Sir Sydney Russell-Wells, for example, agreed that women were under 'grievous disabilities',[14] and that it was 'a ridiculous thing that a woman who takes a degree . . . should have to wait until she is thirty to get the vote, while her brother can get it when he reaches the age of twenty-one'.[15] But he went on to register disapproval of the general content of the Bill which aimed not just at the further enfranchisement of women but at universal suffrage with its attendant virtual ending of the property qualification. This the promoters of the Bill ought openly to acknowledge, he said, and not shelter 'behind the skirts of women voters'.[16] The argument, in other words (and this is true of the tone of the opposition in the debate generally) is less concerned with the inappropriateness of women having a wider political voice, than with the positive evil of the uneducated and propertyless being given the vote.[17]

There is still, however, beyond this practical concern, sometimes a certain yearning for pre-war standards of femininity which were so clearly losing ground to the 'flappers' of the twenties. 'The older I get', confessed Sir Martin Conway, 'the more wonderful, the more beautiful and the more admirable to me is that glorious flourishing time of the young woman between the ages of 21 and 25.' She should then 'be paying attention to other matters than voting . . . she ought to have her eye upon the glory of life at the threshold of which she stands and upon the prospects of family and of man's development and all that area of activity and command which is open to a woman'.[18]

Since this Bill failed to get through, the House was again debating the topic in March 1928, in the Representation of the People (Equal Franchise) Bill. Sir William Joynson-Hicks, the Home Secretary, opened the debate by asking if anybody would be willing to 'get up in this House in the year 1928 and say that we dare not give votes to these women',[19] and Philip Snowden, a long-time friend of the women's cause, went on to assert that 'No change in the attitudes of the political parties . . . has been more remarkable or more rapid than the change of attitude [on the issue] . . . during the last 15 years'.[20]

Yet for all this, the opposition was still there. Sir George Cockerill, moving an amendment opposing the Bill, reminded the House that such a measure would put women in the political majority and went on to ask 'in all seriousness whether women ought to be the determining factor in our political life'.[21] His appalled suggestion that the 'Vox populi, vox dei' would then be 'no longer the voice of the gods—but of the godesses'[22] was greeted with 'Hear, hear' by Lady Astor.[23] The noble Lady was again to interrupt his rhetorical questioning when he demanded to know what natural right women had to be in a position of permanent majority over men adding, 'I ask, has man less spirit, less vision?', to which Lady Astor promptly replied in the affirmative.[24]

Nor was Sir George a lone voice, for Colonel Applin supported him by arguing that women made little economic contribution to the nation. His economic analysis was however somewhat jejune, depending as it did on simply looking up the wills for the last year and finding, unsurprisingly, that women had left only £6 million compared with men's £58 million. When he went on to draw the conclusion that 'if we are to have a majority rule by women in this country, we are handing over to them the taxable wealth of the country, to which they have contributed only one-tenth',[25] the official report of the proceedings records 'Laughter'.[26]

The old Imperial connection was once again stressed and it was Colonel Applin who warned the House that 'If we let this Bill become law, what a weapon we will put into the hands of the agitators (for Indian Home Rule) if we tell the Hindus of India that we are to be ruled by a majority of women'.[27] Nor was the Colonel to be put off by the interruptions of Ellen Wilkinson, who volubly objected to some of his more extreme comments, and it was she who provoked him into his final outburst where he referred to the—clearly abominable—possibility of a woman Chancellor of the Exchequer. To Miss Wilkinson's 'Why not?' he riposted with relentless logic, 'Imagine in the middle of her [Budget] speech a message coming in, "Your child is dangerously ill. Come at once".—I should like to know how much of that Budget the House would get, and what the figures would be like'.[28] Most of the House however, agreed with the Countess of Iveagh that 'This measure is the outcome of logic and of justice',[29] and the Bill went through with only ten noes to 387 ayes.

Social changes in the position of women in the 20s and 30s, and in the way they were regarded, were reflected in the attitudes of the House. The First World War had meant not only that women were for the first time employed in traditionally male jobs, but also that the massive loss of men in battle and the huge numbers of war wounded left greatly increased numbers of women unsupported by men. Ray Strachey says that a third of the female population had to be self-supporting and quotes the census figures for 1921 which gave 9,316,753 'unoccupied' women and 4,209,408 working. In spite of this, the image of women reflected in legislation in the 30s and beyond is still largely that of wife and mother, and that meant of dependent female. Inevitably perhaps, after the loss of such a large proportion of the population, there was a great emphasis on the restoration of numbers and women were encouraged to do their duty by producing the next generation and increasing the birth-rate. There was also the economic impact of the slump which encouraged the idea that women in the work force took jobs from men. Yet women were frequently employed in unskilled and part-time jobs which men either would not take, or in which employers favoured women mainly because their wage rates were considerably lower. Thus women, particularly married women, found themselves in a double bind, being encouraged on the one hand to remain dependent on their husbands and succour their families, yet often forced by economic circumstances to seek employment. Eleanor Rathbone was quick to point this out to the House when it debated the Unemployment Insurance (No. 3) Act in 1931. She objected to the fact that women, when they married, would by the terms of the Bill cease to make contributions and would thus become ineligible for benefits,[30] In 1932 the House again debated Health Insurance,[31] and Miss Rathbone was quick to defend the section of the population whom she thought were most discriminated against. She said:

> The married woman of the working class always gets the worst of it every way. If she decides to give up her job and look after her home and children, she is entering on one of the most dangerous occupations in the world. She does not get a penny of wages and is expected to live on what her husband can spare her out of an income which is no larger than that of a bachelor, but out of which she has to keep her husband and children. If she retains her job, everyone looks at her askance. Her employer looks at her as one who may be irregular in her work, the Trade Union looks at her as a potential blackleg, and the spinster often asks why there should be two incomes coming into the same house. The Govern-

ment watching these things with one eye on their finances and the other on the electorate, thinks that married women are fair game.[32]

Nobody contested this. Still the attempts to raise the birthrate continued, while women were treated as a bad health insurance risk mainly, as Miss Rathbone herself pointed out, as a result of motherhood.

As the construction of a welfare system continued, and particularly into the 40s and 50s, this notion of women, inside and outside the House, was enshrined in successive stages of legislation and it was only in the late 60s and 70s that the very existence of the Equal Pay and Sex Discrimination Acts acknowledged the inequalities and injustices of many of these attitudes. The Beveridge Report, for example, talks about women in exactly those terms. 'First and foremost today, the Welfare State means the state controlling the way in which the woman does her job in the home servicing the worker and bringing up their children.'[33] This was stating the priorities to be adopted in the post-war world. As it was, by 1943, there were $7\frac{1}{2}$ million women in the work force, as compared with the official projection of $6\frac{3}{4}$ million had there been no war. The extra $\frac{3}{4}$ million were all the more noticeable too because they were once again in 'men's jobs'. Between 1939 and 1943 women in engineering and allied industries rose from 411,000 to 1,500,000 and from 18% to 30% of the total labour force. In this context, it is not surprising that the women in Parliament should have been very keen to discuss the role of women in the war effort and this they did in both 1941 and 1942. The debates are interesting indications of the attitudes to women, both changed and unchanged since the 20s which predominated in the midst of a war of which they were very much a part.

On 20 March 1941, the first ever debate on woman-power was opened by the Joint Parliamentary Secretary to the Ministry of Labour, Mr Assheton, who bravely asserted, 'I am no feminist myself',[34] only to be assured by Dr Edith Summerskill, 'You will be, by the end of the War'.[35] While maintaining that women clearly had an important part to play in the war-effort, Mr Assheton was dubious about this being of the same nature as men's contribution, because, as he saw it they were 'more individualistic and perhaps less easily used to discipline than men . . . [and] are certainly very much attached to their homes'.[36] Whatever the role of younger and unattached women in the war, mothers of young children must be exempted from active war-work, for 'nothing is more important than the future of the race, and clearly there is no form of national service for any woman more important than the guidance of a home and the upbringing of young children'.[37]

Irene Ward was not, however, to be fobbed off with protestations about the importance of motherhood, and charged the Government with the reality of what actually took place in the sphere of women's employment—particularly noting the 'wide differentiation between the wages paid to women and those paid to men'[38] in government training centres. She went on to raise a point made again and again by the parliamentary women in the course of the war, that 'we feel very strongly that right through the range of the war effort we have had no executive or administrative job of real responsibility'.[39] Thelma Cazalet-Keir echoed this when she complained about the lack of women in top jobs not only in the war-time Regional Commissions, but in the B.B.C. and the Civil Service.[40] Sir John Anderson picked up this point later in the debate, and said that more women in such jobs would make for 'a very admirable arrangement, but there are not nearly enough qualified women to go around'.[41] Such arguments and counter arguments are still frequently made.[42] Plus ça change . . .

In spite of these criticisms, most of the women displayed an enormous sense of patriotism;[43] indeed this often appears to be the fount from which their feminism flowed. Edith Summerskill, for example, castigated the Government for making inadequate use of propaganda, which if it had been properly utilised would, she thought, have made conscription (registration) of women unnecessary. The radio, she suggested, could have been used 'in such a way that every family in the country with an idle woman sitting in their midst would look at her and experience the same shame that they might feel if they had a deserter from the army in their midst'.[44] And she went on, 'we even find young men with childless wives feeling that it is a reflection on their manhood for their wives to work. Where is our propaganda? It is not a reflection on their manhood if their wives should work, but a reflection on their patriotism that their wives should not work'.[45]

There was, however, a clear realisation among those who spoke in the debate that, as Dr Summerskill put it, 'the modern woman is an entirely different person from the 1914 woman'.[46] And part of this realisation was the acknowledgement that the modern woman was aware of her economic and industrial strength in a way in which the women of the earlier war had not been. The constant demand for nurseries in the speeches in the debate, the denial that women would be content to be a source of cheap labour, and the many allusions to the position of women in industry beyond simply the exigencies of wartime, made this clear. Thelma Cazalet-Keir, for example, raised, not for the first time, the question of compensation for women, and the inequality of a situation which repaid its women wounded at a lower level than its men. 'I cannot think of a single good reason', she said, 'for giving different rates to women and men ... they are running equal risks'.[47] And looking ahead in what turned out to be a most prophetic way, Mrs Jenny Adamson warned of the dangers of women believing

> that the politicians are going to give them equal pay for equal work. The men workers in this country have learned by painful experience the necessity for Trade Union organisation, and the best advice that we can give women ... is that they should get inside their Trade Unions, build up a powerful organisation and have collective action and collective agreements ... it is through the power of our organisations that we can compel the employers to give justice and fair play to our women as well as to our men.[48]

And many a present-day trade union organiser might echo her words and say that women have never paid them sufficient heed.

By 1942, when the second woman-power debate took place, women's registration for war-work had become mandatory. Both sexes were liable for national service, either in the forces or in civil defence, or industry, and girls born in 1920 and 1921 were already being called up. Enormous stress was again laid, in this debate, on the importance of developing adequate nursery facilities for the children of working mothers. On the other hand, reservations were apparent about the advisability of encouraging women to forsake their domestic duties for outside work. And here were highlighted the two, seemingly incompatible demands being made of women—that they produce and nurture the next generation and on the other hand that they fulfil their other patriotic duty in the war effort. There were, of course, exemptions from call-up for women with children, yet if all of these women left the factories, it was clear that the gap could not easily be filled. The answer seemed to be the day nurseries the provision of which Jenny Adamson said, ranked in importance 'with the building of factories and the machines which will ultimately be operated by women'.[49]

There was again some criticism by the women members of the preponderance of men on all the committees and commissions on warwork and Dr Summerskill asserted that she was 'beginning to feel that the war is being prosecuted by both sexes but directed only by one'.[50] In general, the assumption of the men was that the women's role was, and had to be, a subordinate one. 'Women are not mechanically-minded like men', said Sir George Broadbridge, but went on to agree that they could 'certainly replace men in the Pay Board . . . in order that the men be applied more to the war effort'.[51] Nobody reminded him that the Pay Board might have something to do with the war effort, and indeed even Dr Summerskill, for all her fiery feminism, assumed the same stance when she suggested that women might be suitably employed 'to replace men in the Home Guard, who could be released for more competent duties'.[52]

It was left to Megan Lloyd George this time to refer pointedly to the future for women. Lamenting the 'prejudice, indifference and contempt with which very often [working] women were regarded',[53] she wanted to know if employers took a longer view of women in industry. How much, she wondered, did they recognise the potential value of their women workers and was their employment 'due to material considerations which have absolutely nothing to do with the war-effort? How much is it due to the disinclination to pay a woman a man's wage and again, how much is it due to the consideration of post-war conditions?'[54]

It was only Eleanor Rathbone who consistently argued for real equality. In expressing her lack of sympathy for girls who were unwilling to go and work wherever they were needed in the country, even if this meant leaving the security of home for the first time, she claimed that she had fought for many years for women's rights, by which she meant 'the rights of women to be regarded as equal citizens with men, but I have always insisted that equal citizenship should bring with it equal responsibilities as citizens'.[55]

Men did not speak in great numbers in either of the debates, but when they did, there generally emerges a quite clear acceptance of women's part in the war-effort, although that part is seen as largely subordinate to men's. In general, too, it is apparent that the men were being brought face to face with the 'modern woman' as Edith Summerskill called her, and they are rather uncertain of how to treat her. Outside Parliament, the special circumstances of the war meant that she was necessary to national survival and as such must be given much more freedom and economic independence than had hitherto been the case. Even inside the House, there is a perceptible change of attitude. The women members were, many of them, the clear representatives of the new woman. Women had been in the House for over twenty years and had fitted in, on the whole graciously, to the surroundings and conventions which were largely man-made. There had, it is true, been the odd individualist who had always been feministic and even at times aggressive, but this new phenomenon of a combined attack was virtually unknown and certainly unknown in any sustained kind of way. The men may well have felt that the debate was, at a rather deeper level, indeed about 'woman-power'.

Perhaps because of this, the coy references to the fair sex with which most of the male participants prefaced their remarks, strike an oddly jarring note. The women were not playing. They were discussing as colleagues, the very real problems which faced half the population. The little gallantries, and often they are no more, thus come across as gratuitous, if not insulting. They add nothing to the substantive content of the debate, and they sometimes appear, no doubt unconsciously, like an attempt by the men to regain control by reminding the women of their proper place. Sir George Broadbridge, for example, felt that he might be 'rushing in where angels fear to tread',[56] while Sir John Anderson rushed in 'where angels have ceased to tread'.[57] Their uncertainty is clear, especially when Sir George went on to make a particularly foolish pun, with no significance beyond its male/female reference and which he felt obliged immediately to disown as one 'to which I do not necessarily subscribe'.[58] Sir Walter Womersley too prefaced his remarks in 1941 with a rather long-winded and clearly fabricated account of what purported to be the essay of a schoolgirl, which had the final devastating punch-line, 'Both men and women sprang from monkeys, but women sprang the furthest'.[59]

On one level, this is nothing but a little innocuous flattery, quite in line with the usual tradition of parliamentary speechifying. Yet it sometimes reads like patronage, largely because the women were not maintaining the tradition; rather they were hitting where it hurt. Perhaps the men took the point, yet feared the consequences of Mrs Cazalet-Keir's opening remark in 1941, 'If we had 40 or 50 women members of Parliament instead of the present small number, I doubt whether this debate would have been necessary because many of the things which we are discussing today would either never have occurred, or would have been automatically rectified at a much earlier date'.[60]

When the war was over, the real construction of the Welfare State could get under way. Retrospectively, it is possible to draw out some of the basic attitudes and assumptions which were fundamental to this particular social welfare edifice. Contained in the Beveridge Report of 1942, for example, and in the legislation which sought to implement many of its major recommendations, is a view of women, of their role and capacities, their economic and social status, their priorities and values, which was to dominate not only social attitudes, but the consciousness of individual men and women, for at least a generation.

Part of the return to normality after the war meant the return of women to the home from the Forces or the factories where they had been involved during the crisis. Women had, since at least 1941, left their homes and their children, on the express encouragement of the politicians, and twelve-hour nurseries had been provided to facilitate this. During the war, this was legitimised; in peacetime, it was not to be sanctioned. Thus Beveridge: 'The attitude of the housewife to gainful employment outside the house is not and should not be the same as that of the single woman. She has other duties . . .'[61] Again, whereas women could contribute most by being members of the work-force in war-time, when their menfolk were in most cases not at home to need ministering to, in peacetime the priorities were different. Women were there fundamentally to service the returning male workforce, and without this servicing, industry would not run efficiently: 'the great majority of married women must be regarded as occupied in work which is vital, though unpaid, without which their husbands could not do their paid work and without which the nation could not continue'.[62] The logical development of this position was that women must be seen as themselves financially dependent, since their employment however 'vital' was 'unpaid'. Thus the benefits which a woman might be entitled to were derived from her husband's—the worker's—contributions in National Insurance etc. Beveridge makes the point quite explicitly: 'Since paid work will in many cases [for women] be intermittent, it should be open to any married woman to undertake it as an exempt person, paying no contributions of her own, acquiring no claim to benefit in unemployment or sickness.'[63] The woman is thus classified as a dependent, with her husband supporting her.

It is not that the Welfare State was conceived as some kind of vast conspiracy to get women back to the home and keep them there, financially dependent and socially conditioned to their subordinate and supportive role. Rather it embodied the attitudes to family life and women's place within this, which the disruption of war had encouraged in those who afterwards sought to implement what they saw as a fairer, juster and more prosperous Britain. The emphasis on the integrating qualities of the family was very great. Relatives had been split up after all, by military service, evacuation and the general disruptions of war and now was the time to restore the even keel of family life. The role of women as the static centre of this life was crucial and not one which could be adequately fulfilled, it was believed, by a woman who was spending large parts of her day outside the home. Again, the importance of producing children was emphasised. Not only was this a personal fulfilment for a woman, but it was a responsibility to society. Again and again, the danger of working mothers being unable to bring up their children adequately was stressed. In the woman-power debates in the Commons, for example, the demand for nurseries was counterbalanced by concern about the advisability of young children being away from their mothers for any extended time, and the importance of ensuring the proper development of the next generation. Beveridge makes no bones about this. Women might have been doing their duty in one way during the war, but he and others of his colleagues were dismayed by the falling birth-rate and therefore keen to emphasise that 'In the next thirty years, housewives as Mothers have vital work to do in ensuring the adequate continuance of the British Race and of British Ideals in the world.'[64]

Through the period of reconstruction and into the 50s, too, politicians continued to advance this view of woman as fundamentally— and rightly—wife and mother, and as generally employed full-time in the maintenance of her family's welfare. This image is clearly accepted, indeed promoted, in the various Government inspired education reports of the 50s and 60s. The Crowther Report of 1959, for example, recommended that the education of girls should take account of 'the prospect of courtship and marriage' and that girls' 'direct interest in dress, personal appearance [and] in problems of human relationships should be given a central place in their education' (p. 136). Again, the Newsom Report suggested that if girls don't like domestic science and homemaking subjects because they have already had 'their fill of scrubbing and washing-up and getting meals for the family at home', all the more reason for them to have 'the education a good school course can give in the wider aspects of home-making, and the skills which will reduce the element of domestic drudgery' (p. 135). By the time the Plowden Report was published, the numbers of women working outside the home was increasing by leaps and bounds and the Report's response to this is to advocate part-time work for married women and the provision of part-time nursery facilities. The suggestion is that full-time nurseries are for the 'deprived child' with a mother who is unable or unwilling to look after her child herself. The ideal is still the woman looking after her own children in her own home.

Thus well into the 1960s, the attitudes to women legitimised and promoted by politicians were not very different from those of the pre-war period. The modern woman, as Edith Summerskill had said, no doubt was a different creature, by 1942, from the 1918 woman. Yet those with political and social influence did not acknowledge this in any very fundamental changes in the status of women, at law, in education or welfare during that period. Whether the late 60s and the 70s, the post-permissive society, with its much-vaunted social and sexual equality, has in fact brought such changes in attitudes, is what the next chapter will attempt to establish.

CHAPTER VIII

Present Discontents

'Nothing infuriates me more than the current fashion, amounting to a world-wide conspiracy, to pretend that women are the peer of men and equally human.' Letter in the London *Evening News*, 1972

'The chief weakness of the Movement's concentration on suffrage, the factor which helped it to fade, disappear and even lose ground when the vote was gained, lay in its failure to challenge patriarchal ideology at a sufficiently deep and radical level to break the conditioning processes of status, temperament and role.' Kate Millet

On 20 March 1962, Judith Hart's Bill to change the basis of jury service was debated by the House of Commons. In the course of the discussion, Mr Charles Doughty opposed the measure on the basis that if it went through, 'it is likely that the majority of juries would consist more of women than of men. Some people might think that a good thing . . . One reason which, I think, militates against them—and I say this with no disrespect to any Honourable Lady in the House—is that women are undoubtedly rather more emotional than men'.[1] The argument is almost exactly parallel to that used so frequently by the anti-suffragists almost forty years before when the appalling prospect of more women than men on the electoral roll was one major factor in their argument, and women's emotional instability, another.

It is not the case that Mr Doughty's claim in 1962 would be unheard of in today's House of Commons (as I shall want to show, some of the most sexist, if not discriminatory remarks made about women in the modern period have been uttered in the period often thought to be the most enlightened, that is since the early 70s). Yet changes in the extent of concern about women's position in society have clearly taken place since the 1960s, as becomes clear when the party literature and the manifestoes over this period are examined.

The party manifestoes produced before the 1964 election have very little to say specifically about women. And even the Conservative manifesto for that year, 'Prosperity with a purpose', contains no specific reference to women, except a passing comment in the section on 'Competition and the Consumer' about restrictions on shop hours 'which are particularly inconvenient to the growing number of women at work'. The Labour manifesto for the same year is similarly lacking in any policy specifically aimed at women, although it did refer to widows for whom Labour intended to abolish the Earnings Rule. The Liberals too in their offering 'Think for yourself', show no plans to change the status of women.

By 1966, the emphasis in the manifestoes, as in the election campaign itself, was on the financial crisis. A deficit of £750 million may have encouraged the Labour Party to entitle their programme for that year 'Time for Decision' and to concentrate on the economy. There is at any rate no section of the document which refers specifically to women, and the Conservative's 'Action not words' has a similar blank in that area. The Liberals did promise improvements in family allowances with, for example, allowances payable to the eldest child, but there was nothing more specific on the situation of women.

In the run-up to the election of 1970 the Labour Party did make it clear that they would undertake the introduction of legislation to ensure equal pay, but in their manifesto for that year the emphasis was still very much on the economy and it was largely on this issue that the election was fought. Because of the emphasis on inflation and on prices, women were courted as housewives, and it was in this capacity that the two major parties largely appealed to them in their platforms.

The change in emphasis which had taken place by the time of the October 1974 election is enormous. International Women's Year was coming up (in 1975) and the import of the women's movement, reborn with a vengeance in the late 60s, had begun to be acknowledged even by those who strongly opposed its aims and ideas. The proportion of the manifestoes devoted to winning the support of women and to displaying a proper concern with women's issues is very large compared with anything that has gone before. Labour's 'Britain will win with Labour' for example, includes a whole charter for women covering such issues as equal pay, family planning, equality of treatment in social security, maternity leave, child allowances and rapid extension of nursery education and day-care facilities. The programme also promises changes in Family Law and new Family Courts, reform of Housing Law to strengthen the rights of mothers on the break-up of marriage, and increased educational opportunities for girls. Legislation was also promised directly on the Government's White Paper on sex discrimination[2] with machinery to enforce such measures.

And the Conservatives were not to be outdone. They too devoted a section of their manifesto, entitled 'Women—at home and at work', to the female half of the electorate. They promised, among other things, child credits for mothers, equal pay, improvement of pension schemes for married women, and improved widows' benefits (in the light of the Finer Report on one-parent families). There was also direct reference to the right of women to equality of treatment and the promise of the setting up of an Equal Opportunities Commission, 'to enquire into areas of discrimination and to report to Government on need for future action'.

Even the Liberals, although they had no specific section on women, referred to their own good record concerning women's rights and added, 'implicit in all our objectives in the field of social policy is a commitment to ensure full and equal rights for women in every sphere. Liberals were the first to initiate legislation against sex discrimination and there will be no let-up in our campaign for equality between the sexes.'

There was a great increase too over the same period in the reports and committees which investigated women's rights and the explanatory literature which was put out by the two major parties. 'A Woman's Place', for example, issued by the Conservative Political Centre in 1969, tried to take account of the growing number of married women working outside as well as inside the home, and 'Work for married women' (CPC, 1969) talked about the changes which would be required to help married women—especially those with professional teaching and medical qualifications—to return to work. At the same time, in the parliamentary party, the Women's National Advisory Council's Parliamentary Subcommittee was pressing for a twelve-point plan to improve the lot of women. It was largely as a result of this rather diffuse agitation that Edward Heath set up the Cripps Committee to look into the legal position of women, and 'determine what changes were desirable . . . to enable women to participate equally with men in the political, economic and social life of the community, and . . . in the law relating to their rights and obligations within the family'. Its report, 'Fair Share for the Fair Sex' (CPC, 1969) dealt with civil and individual rights, family law, property in marriage and taxation.

Also in 1969, Beryl Cooper and Geoffrey Howe, two members of the original Cripps committee, produced a further pamphlet 'Opportunity for Women' (CPC, 1969) which dealt with women in education, employment and public service and stressed the need 'not so much for changes in the law as for changes in general attitudes towards women' (p. 3). The authors then went on to list such recommendations as increasing the opportunities for part-time work, refresher and re-training courses for married women, provision of day nurseries and pre-school play groups on a much larger scale, day release and sandwich courses for girls and a general re-thinking of educational facilities for girls and women. In 1973, Central Office published a pamphlet, 'A Fairer Deal for Women', which showed how far the recommendations of the Cripps Committee had found their way into legislation. The discrimination of affiliation cases for example, where an unmarried mother had to give evidence in person and could only start maintenance proceedings within twelve months of the child's birth, was largely overcome by Dame Joan Vicker's 1972 Affiliation Proceedings (Amendment) Bill. The equal pay recommendations of Cripps were hardly new, and were to be put into practice not by a Conservative but by a Labour government. Again, on some points of legal anti-quarianism, Cripps had recommended changes. Damages for adultery for example were still legally obtainable by a husband from his wife's lover, even if he did not ask the court for a divorce. A wife, of course, had no such right in law against her husband's mistress, since the situation was a hang-over from the time when a woman was legally her husband's property. This provision was abolished by the Law Reform (Miscellaneous Provisions) Act of 1971. Also the law on guardianship until 1973 placed women at a real disadvantage in making decisions about her child's education, for example. The new guardianship Act of that year gave both parents equal rights of guardianship of their children and this allows a woman, where the parents are separated and the child is living with the mother, custody of her child and the right to take decisions on its behalf without a court order having to be sought. Similarly, the Domicile and Matrimonial Proceedings Act came into force in January 1974 and removed another area of implicit discrimination against women who could not until then, even if legally separated, acquire a separate domicile—that is, a legally accepted permanent home—from her husband. The 1974 Act allows not only separate domiciles, but provides that a child living with its mother, may take its mother's domicile, rather than its father's. Once again here women are recognised at law as separate and sovereign individuals, rather than as appendages of men.

Whereas the Conservative Party has tended to woo their women voters, the Labour Party has always assumed their historical commitment to the woman's cause would almost of itself secure the female vote. Whether this is actually the case or not, it is clear that the Labour Party do not put the same effort into producing pamphlets and reports in this area as their major political rivals. They concentrate instead much more on giving women a practical understanding of the role they can play in the Labour Party and particularly in the women's sections of the Party. A perennial publication is the 'Guide to Women's Organisations in the Labour Party' (Transport House), first published fifty years ago and aiming to 'give advice and guidance on the duties of officers within the Women's Movement and on ways in which women can help to promote themselves and their activities'. And indeed the advice is quite practical, explaining everything from how to form a woman's section, to the duties of the Chairman. The impulse is one of self-help, of women being given the framework within which they can get on and promote their own ideas and aims.

Of the same rallying type are the leaflets put out by the party on, for example, 'The Role of the Labour Party in the Women's Movement', which claims that the party has 'always been more sensitive to social injustice than its political rivals and the party attitude to women is no exception to this' (p. 1), and that the Labour Government 'has no intention of playing a passive part in the present time when women are rapidly freeing themselves from the centuries of shackling tradition which have confined them to a subordinate status, and wasted so much of our nation's talent' (p. 2). Another such publication is 'Obstacles to women in Politics and Public Life', which outlined the findings of a report presented to the Organisation Committee of the National Executive Council of the Labour Party. This looks at the financial problems of the non-working wife and the limitations that these may put on her willingness to become politically involved, at the education and training of women and, taking up the point mentioned, but not developed in the Conservatives' 'Opportunity for

Women', considers prejudice and traditional attitudes and the psychological ties that these develop in women.

In 1974, the Labour government produced its White Paper 'Equality for Women', subtitled 'A Policy for Equal Opportunity'. The ideas which it embodies are not new; they are mainly ones which had been put forward and discussed by both major parties since at least the late 60s. Yet it did collect together under one head these much discussed problems and their suggested solutions and produce a structure for legislation which it was hoped would 'encourage a major shift in the attitudes and actions of individual men and women so as to give reality to the ideals of justice and equality' (para. 124). Whether or not this has been to any extent achieved, and whether indeed such a grandiose expectation could ever have been realised by the implementation of a policy which clearly had its limitations and weaknesses even at this stage, is not really to the point here. What is important is that, almost regardless of its substantive effect (and many women—and men—both inside and outside Parliament doubted that it had any more than cosmetic significance), it is a high-water mark of concern with women and their rights and problems, gathering together as it does so many of the arguments and suggestions of the past six or seven years. What is remarkable is that this welter of discussion, recommendation, report and legislation should take place within such a short period of time, when in the twenty-five or so years before that, since the war, very little re-thinking of the female role, far less any radical re-organisation of legal and social structures, had been attempted.

The major parties always claimed to have been supportive of women's rights. Yet the Conservatives' pride in, for example, their introduction of equal pay for teachers and non-industrial civil servants as long ago as 1955 can be rather dented by asking why it took them so long—fifteen years—even to support the extension of the principle into all areas of work. And although the Labour Party did in the end formally introduce and see through the measures on both equal pay and anti-discrimination, they were somewhat tardy for the party claiming a particular sensitivity to women's rights. Here, as in other cases in politics, it was really only when women began themselves to be aware of their position and to agitate about it that the political parties began to see this as a significant political question, worth serious discussion, because worth the votes of half the electorate. And this was scarcely an over-estimation on their part, for as the ideas of the women's movement became more and more mainstream and less and less dismissable as those of a lunatic fringe, they could be accounted only by action. Justice had to be seen to be done, and the first, overdue, act of justice was the equal pay legislation, which is worth looking at in a little detail to discover the parliamentary attitudes which underlie it.

On 9 February 1970, the Equal Pay (No. 2.) Bill was moved by the Rt. Hon. Barbara Castle, who reminded the House that Thelma Cazalet-Keir, as early as 1944 had 'led a successful revolt against the Government on the issue of sex discrimination in teachers' pay, and the great man himself, Winston Churchill, had to come down to the House the next day to make re-imposition of sex-discrimination a vote of confidence'.[3] At any rate now, no party was opposed to the legislation, indeed, both sides of the House went out of their way to claim the honour of having been first to demand equal pay for women, and quite a heated argument developed on this point between, among others, Robert Carr, Christopher Norwood and Eric Heffer.[4]

One of the major points of debate was the value or otherwise of protective legislation for women. The argument in favour of this is generally that such protection is necessary particularly for young women with children who must not be forced to work, for example, unsuitable hours or to do night work. Again pregnant women must be considered and women's lesser physical strength acknowledged by some sort of protection. As against this, many women have for some time now been putting the argument that the demand for equality can only be made a reality where women are as far as possible working alongside men, and that protective legislation, much of which was based on a nineteenth-century view of women and labour, and even on a desire to keep women out of the more lucrative shift work, is simply a barrier to this. Barbara Castle took this line and stressed the anomalies that anyway exist in the law (women in nursing, or running transport or catering at night are generally exempt). She added, 'We women members would scoff at the idea that we were too frail to do all-night sittings. Indeed I have noticed that we usually look fresher than the men at the end of them',[5] and concluded that in general, 'where the women agree, and I am satisfied that there is nothing prejudicial to their welfare, I am always prepared to consider exemptions'.[6]

Much of the House, on both sides, men and women, are prepared to acknowledge the uncertainty of the benefits of protective legislation, most of the Conservatives because they see it as an infringement of personal freedom,[7] and the Labour women and their male supporters because they see it as maintaining the myth of women's weakness and inability to compete directly and work equally with men. Yet at least one Labour woman has indicated reservations about this. Millie Miller, in another debate, was to put the counter-argument strongly when she said, 'Women working in industry are not ready to give up protective legislation until they are satisfied with the more important changes that are necessary in employment protection. Indeed,' she went on, 'many of the protections which apply to working women might well apply to working men to the benefit of our society.'[8]

The debate did bring out not only support, however, but some reservations from members. Mr Ronald Bell made a strong plea for the rights of men to higher pay 'if they produce more'.[9] He agreed with the Bill in as far as it advanced a point of justice, but where was the justice, he wanted to know, in a woman being paid the same wage for less work.[10] His argument however, was dismissed by Mrs Lena Jeger as 'peevish mishmash' and she pointed out that he took his figures (mainly relating to the agricultural industry) from the Report of a Royal Commission which had sat more than a quarter of a century ago.[11]

Qualified support was registered too by Mrs Jill Knight, who reiterated the argument that women must genuinely be prepared to surrender some of their traditional feminine rights if they were to have true equality, and then went on to ask if such surrenders would in fact be worthwhile. She accused Mrs Castle of tending 'to keep a firm grasp on her cake, but to take a large bite at it as well when she said that women will still be entitled to preferential treatment in matters of maternity leave and so on'.[12] She went on to cite the U.S.S.R. as an example of a society where equal pay was taken for granted and women often did 'men's jobs'. But, she hastened to point out, 'such women are demonstrably long on muscle and sadly short on charm',[13] and expressed a hope that 'we in Britain do not sacrifice femininity to the Golden Law of Equality'.[14]

In spite of his strong support for the Bill, Mr Charles Pannell felt constrained to point out that women's true role lay elsewhere than in competition with men. He reminded the House of 'the terrible price in juvenile delinquency and all that sort of thing because some married

women go into factories'.[15] And he went on, 'I have great admiration
for the woman who can realise herself through her growing family
and through looking after her husband'.[16] Miss Mervyn Pike could
not let him get away with this. 'If women who go out to work have
delinquent children, I must claim to be a delinquent . . . But in many . . .
respects women who go out to work bring up families even better,
because they have broader and more tolerant attitudes to life as a
whole.'[17] Mrs Margaret Thatcher, summing up for the Opposition,
talked of the problem of men often being unhappy working for a
woman and in this context charged another contributor to the debate,
Mr Heffer, with being someone, the image of whom 'as a shop steward
working under the authority of a woman foreman, [did not] readily
spring to mind'.[18]

For some, the 1975 Sex Discrimination Bill was simply a sop to the
feminists for International Women's Year. Be this as it may, it did
provide an opportunity for the House once again to debate the 'woman
question' and to give some indications of its attitudes to the question
in the mid-70s. Introduced by the then Home Secretary, Roy Jenkins,
the Bill aimed to put into effect the recommendations of the Government's White Paper, 'Equality for Women'. Although Ian Gilmour
welcomed the Bill for the Opposition, he stressed that it should not
be thought of as any kind of a panacea, for there were 'deeply em-
bedded feelings about what constitutes a woman's place [which]
sabotage both sexes, inuring women to discrimination as much as
allowing men to perpetuate it'.[19]

There were those, however, who were not simply sceptical of the
practical reception of the Bill, but who opposed it in principle. Mr
Enoch Powell began his speech in characteristically dramatic terms:
'There is a German proverb to the effect that against stupidity, the
gods themselves contend in vain; but when the stupidity is fashionable
to boot, the frowning battlements are indeed impregnable.'[20] The
Bill, he said, was founded on an absurd denial, that of the 'infinite
differentiation of jobs and of those best fitted to perform them, [and]
that the differentiation of sex is all-pervasive in relation to different
jobs and functions in society'.[21] This being the case, society 'confers . . .
more or less advantage and benefit [depending] on the way in which
they are performed.'[22] Mrs Renee Short was clearly incensed by the
social impasse implicit in this analysis and wanted to know, 'what
would the Rt. Hon. Gentleman do? . . . leave it as it is?'[23] Mr Powell

agreed that this was exactly what he would do, and totally rejected the 'mania today in legislation for attacking discrimination, oblivious that all life is about discrimination, because all life is about differences. This Bill is a particularly heinous example of the follies into which Governments and Parliaments are led when they give heed to this fashionable but foolish craze'.[24]

Mr Powell's conflation of discrimination and differentiation was echoed by Mr Ronald Bell, who also opposed the Bill. Talking about it in the same terms as the Race Relations Bill (1968), which he also opposed, he said people were being told, 'You may not discriminate', but, he went on, 'Without discrimination there is no life. From the most minute form of animated existence, discrimination is the principle of life.'[25] He was strongly opposed to attempts to use the law 'to control men's minds and to tell them that they must disregard in the workings of their discrimination factors which they believe, rightly or wrongly, to be significant.'[26] He went on to make the strongest case in the debate for the belief that men are different not simply biologically, but 'in general physical and mental characteristics', and this differentiation is to be observed 'not only in man, throughout his history, but throughout animal life . . . The polarisation of function, interest and attitude has been strongly marked at all stages of our development.'[27] In general, Mr Bell claimed that 'There are no legal impediments at all to women doing what they want or becoming what they wish. All the talk about women's rights is wholly misleading, misconceived and beside the point.'[28] Consequently, 'this Bill is not only foolish and ridiculous, but positively wicked and evil.'[29]

This outburst provoked Mr Willie Hamilton, always a fervent supporter of women's rights, to respond that 'Nothing that I can say can drive the Honourable and Learned Member for Beaconsfield [Mr Bell] out of his neolithic cave.'[30] Yet what could one expect, he went on, from a man who had recently described women in Mr Hamilton's hearing, as 'second-class citizens'. When Bell objected, Hamilton called his apologia 'a lie', whereupon the Speaker intervened to protest against this unparliamentary language. Hamilton withdrew the term, but made his point again.[31] It is interesting that such passions should still be aroused, between men, about the status of women.

The women themselves were, of course, not slow to put their own views on what that status should involve. Miss Richardson rejoiced that changing attitudes would help women to get out of the 'housewife and mother' syndrome,[32] while Miss Fookes, on the other hand, claimed that she was 'not one of those who sneer at the contribution that women make to running the home'.[33] She did admit that 'I cannot say that solely running a home would appeal to me', yet she felt that 'women should have the right to do either'.[34] Miss Fookes also believed that the woman parliamentary candidate might gain by the Bill, in that 'it will no longer be possible to have the kind of thinking reflected in . . . a statement made by [the Chairman of] a Conservative Selection Committee less than a decade ago: "This is a big rural community. We could not expect a woman to have the physical stamina to go round at election time and address perhaps eight meetings a night as is done in rural areas" . . . That kind of argument will no longer be accepted or acceptable'.[35]

A number of speakers expressed some disquiet at the way in which girls were still socialised into thinking only in fairly limited career terms and Mr Roderick MacFarquhar thought that the ultimate insult, the final turn of the economic screw, was that having psychologically induced women to accept the home and kitchen as their lot, 'when it comes to cooking for money, when it comes to cooking as a job, it is men who have taken over the dominant role'.[36]

Once again, however, Mrs Jill Knight stood up for the traditional feminine values.

> I am bound to say that I like the small courtesies of life. I like doors to be held open for me. I like to have the feeling that I am occasioned these courtesies because I am a woman. Clause I [of the Bill] says that a man must not treat a woman less favourably. I want to be treated *more* favourably . . . The question is whether the general increase in opportunities—if the Bill turns out to provide them—is worth having if one is to lose all the advantages and comforts of being a woman.[37]

In the light of this, the men might be forgiven for thinking that women seldom seem to know what they want, and when they do, it often distinctly smacks of discrimination against men.

In spite of the great variety of attitudes to women which the debate showed, Shirley Summerskill, summing up for the Government, still felt certain that 'Women . . . are that unique thing, an oppressed majority'.[38] And she went on to substantiate this by revealing that the latest figures showed that women were paid on average half men's wages; that whereas 22% of men got higher education, the figure for women was 8%, and that where 36% of boys were on day-release and 42% got apprenticeships, the comparable figures for girls were 9.2% and 7% respectively. She also castigated the T.U.C. for having, among its 1400 paid officials, only twenty-five women.[39]

It is perhaps worth referring to one other brief parliamentary encounter which exemplifies very starkly certain attitudes to women. During June 1977, the case of a young guardsman sentenced for rape received a good deal of publicity. The soldier had originally been sentenced in March to three years imprisonment for grievous bodily harm and indecent assault (his victim had suffered severe internal injuries and a damaged kidney), but his original sentence was reduced, on appeal, to a six-month suspended one and he was set free.[40] It seemed that the Appeal Court judges were under the impression that if the soldier were given a suspended sentence, he would avoid dismissal from the army and, unwilling to ruin his army career, they accepted his appeal.[41] They were, in the event, wrong and he was discharged from the army, but the furore that their decision caused went far beyond this particular case.

Mr Jack Ashley, the M.P. for Stoke-on-Trent, wrote in strong terms to the Lord Chancellor (Lord Elwyn-Jones) criticising the Court of Appeal's judgement and suggesting that the leniency of the sentence exemplified the 'inexcusable chauvinism shown by some judges in cases of rape' and how they clearly 'regard this crime as of much less importance than offences against property'.[42] The Lord Chancellor denied that this was so and quoted the judgement, in a similar case, of Mr Justice Scarman who said that

> women do have to be seen to be protected by the law. Men who commit sexual offences with the use of violence overwhelming the woman's will must expect to be dealt with in a way which will vindicate the ordinary man and woman's opinion of the gravity of their offences. The mere fact that they are young . . . had taken too much to drink, and that a long prison sentence will do them no good, is part of the tragedy of the matter, but there are times in life when tragedy has to be carried out to the fifth act.[43]

In general, however, feeling ran high that the Court's decision had been a grave mistake,[44] and Mr Ashley decided to try and introduce legislation to secure a statutory minimum sentence for rape, or at least to give the prosecution the right to appeal in cases of rape and other sexual offences. He introduced his measure under the ten-minute rule, on 19 July 1977, concentrating on securing the right of appeal for rape cases only ('because rape is a singular crime requiring particular attention, and because of the attitude of some of the judiciary').[45]

Mr Ashley referred to the guardsman case, where the Court had said that the young man allowed his enthusiasm for sex to overcome his normal good behaviour. But, riposted Mr Ashley, 'the men involved in the Great Train Robbery allowed their enthusiasm for money to overcome their normal good behaviour and were sent to gaol for thirty years'.[46]

Mr Nicholas Fairbairn, himself a lawyer, opposed Mr Ashley's case by initially asserting: 'I think that it is a fantasy in the Hon. Gentleman's mind that there is some outdated hostility to women.'[47] And he went on to suggest that 'rape differs from all other offences in the calendar of crime in that it involves actis criminis that is normal to people and is sought after by people. People do not normally steal, lie or indulge in corruption or fraud, but they do normally seek after sex as a matter which they wish and so it is a very different crime.'[48]

Not only is it the case that rape is a normal reaction, but women themselves are hardly to be trusted in such circumstances and Mr Fairbairn confessed that he always tried to make sure that there were women on the jury when he was defending in rape cases, 'It's not a matter of male chauvinism', he said, 'but women know that women do not always tell the truth'.[49] Finally, reminding the House again that rape 'involves an activity that is normal', Mr Fairbairn made at least his own attitude to women perfectly clear by quoting Ovid: ' "Whether they say yes or no, they all like to be asked. And saying she would never consent, she consented" '.[50] Mr Ashley's Bill got no farther.

It is only too easy, but none the less facile in any survey of attitudes like this, to take a tendentious line in terms of which the various protagonists can be categorised as 'goodies' and 'baddies'. There are some individuals, both men and women, who have been consistently supportive of women's rights. In the last ten years, Harold Wilson, Willie Hamilton and Jack Ashley have been among the most loyal of these. On the other hand, Churchill was not the last major politician to be at the least ambivalent in his attitudes to women in general and in politics in particular. Edith Summerskill recalls being surprised when he congratulated her on her campaign against boxing, believing that he would never be prepared to congratulate a woman member on anything,[51] and Lady Astor asserted that Churchill was one of the men who made her life most uncomfortable when she first came to Westminster. The Viscountess however had the last laugh, for, years later, when she charged him with this, and asked him why he had done so, he responded that he had felt as if he were caught in his bath by a woman and had 'not even a sponge with which to defend myself'. 'Don't be ridiculous, Winston', the Viscountess replied, 'You're not nearly handsome enough to have worries of that kind.'[52]

Yet the predominantly male House of Commons has to deal, not only with the social uncertainty about the status of women, which is reflected in the different attitudes even of the women M.P.s themselves, but also with the volatility and transience of most political preoccupations. It is very difficult to estimate how deep and sincere is the advocacy, even now, of women's rights. As Constance Rover says of the suffragists, even some of the intermittently supportive ones were 'easily deflected by the pull of conflicting party considerations'.[53] And such political considerations are not simply to be dismissed as unworthy in the situation. Willie Hamilton and Jack Ashley, for example, have a view of politics which fundamentally involves the support of the underdog. Their support of women's rights is none the weaker for being largely an extension of this political commitment.

In a rather different way, Harold Wilson also was politically too sensitive to fail to see that women had, by the later 60s to be represented in more than a statutory capacity. And Edward Heath instigated the Committee of Enquiry to examine the law as it related to women (published as 'Fair Share for the Fair Sex') because it was clear by 1968 that some fundamental re-organisation in this area was soon going to be politically expedient. Heath's personal attitude to women in politics is rather less certain, but he does apparently believe that they can make a worthwhile contribution, 'provided they are not just duplicating the male role'.[54] What role is then left them is not clear.

Again, Herbert Morrison's somewhat sexist remark to Lena Jeger on the occasion of her maiden speech was seemingly counterbalanced by his apparent desire to encourage women in the London County Council (L.C.C.). He took a delight in appointing them in areas where his less adventurous colleagues thought they were quite unsuitable. For example, Helen Bentwich went to the Fire Brigade Committee, and Lady Nathan to the Metropolitan Water Board, 'to stir that lot up'.[55] Yet these two attitudes are probably quite of a piece. Morrison was neither an adamant feminist nor an opponent of women's rights. He was primarily a politician and where it was expedient to give the job to a woman, because she was the best available person, or because a woman would make a valuable impact, he would do so. And this is probably as much as women can expect from politicians. They do not support women on principle, but only if supporting women in a specific case exemplifies or advances their own particular principles in politics. And whether these principles themselves involve the consistent fight for the rights of the underdog, or a pragmatic assessment of priorities on a more day to day basis, they are only contingently feministic. It is only when women themselves have been convinced of their own exploitation or disprivilege and have tried concertedly to affect this, that the House of Commons and the political parties have been impressed by their case. And perhaps inevitably; for nobody fights in politics except for those who are themselves convinced they have a grievance to be righted or an interest to be protected. When, over the past fifty or so years, women have from time to time ceased to campaign strongly for their rights these have been largely ignored. Yet when women appear as a more coherent and united group, as they have done since the late 1960s, their claims, if they are continuously pressed, have been greeted as demands of 'logic' and of 'justice'. There can be here no suggestion of a gigantic conspiracy against them, only an indication of the methods by which political priorities are sifted and organised and of the fact that the attitudes of House and parties to women are in the end reflections of the attitudes, the self-confidence and persistence of women themselves.

CHAPTER IX

International Comparisons and the Scandinavian Example

'We need a pincer movement: changes in arrangements and changes in attitudes.' Kerstin Aner (Swedish M.P.)

'If women can get on a list, they can get in.' Norwegian M.P.

This study is primarily concerned with the women members of Parliament in Great Britain. But an understanding of the British experience may well be enhanced by setting it against a wider background and reviewing the position of women's representation in national politics elsewhere in the world.

The most extreme exceptions to the role of women's political underachievement are those cases where they have actually achieved positions of leadership—notably in India, Sri Lanka (Ceylon) and Israel. In India Mrs Ghandi was Prime Minister from 1966 to 1977 and Mrs Bandaranaike has twice been premier of Sri Lanka, between 1959 and 1965 and again from 1970 to 1977. And yet, in neither India nor Sri Lanka do women figure predominantly in the political life of the country. Mrs Ghandi was joined in 1967 by one other woman in the government, but female membership of the Lok Sabha has never been high and has declined since 1962 from 6.4% to 3.3% in 1977. Mrs Ghandi was the daughter of Nehru at whose side she got her initial political experience and it is likely that her family connection (and indeed the fortuitous associations of her married name for many Indians) were a help in her political progress. It must also be accounted, however, that she was active in a country where the transition to representative democracy was taking place with a majority of the population illiterate and politically uneducated, where her position as a member of a high caste, highly educated, was more important than her sex.

In the case of Sirimavo Bandaranaike, although her initial rise to power was the result of the assassination of her husband in 1959, her return to the premiership in 1970 (having been defeated in an election in 1965) cannot be similarly accounted for. Both these women clearly have intense political backgrounds and families, one way or another, and their male relatives may have been for them advantageous connections,[1] but they also have enormous personal ability and political acumen, and they operated in the midst of great social and cultural change which may in itself facilitate the acceptance of atypical leadership.

This latter point may go some way to explaining the political success of the only other woman Prime Minister, Israel's Mrs Golda Meir. Mrs Meir was not a member of a political family nor did she owe her political rise in any way to a husband or father or other male relative. She had become Foreign Minister in the Israeli Government by the time she retired, only to be called back in 1969 to take over as premier on the death in office of the previous Prime Minister. She was by this time a grandmother in her late sixties and the Israelis may have seen in her the family loyalty, strength of purpose, and self-assurance of the Jewish matriarch, which they needed in their leadership at that time of crisis. On the other hand, there is little in the Jewish social and cultural heritage to encourage the elevation of women to equality, far less to supreme power, particularly in questions of politics. It seems likely therefore that the explanation is to be sought more in Israel's Socialist and pioneering inspiration than in its Judaic tradition. The Israeli women work in Kibbutzim as equals with men. The exigencies of almost constant war have meant also that they serve in the armed forces. And yet, as an explanation of Golda Meir's political career, this will not do. Only a very limited number of the population live in Kibbutzim, and in the rest of the country women make up only about one third of the working population.[2] In the Knesset too other women have not made the progress of Mrs Meir. Indeed there were in 1977 only 7.5 % women among the representatives.

Again in all these cases (as in Britain), the overwhelming impression is that women as a group have not made any very important breakthrough into national political life. Rather particular individuals have used their own ability, talents and luck to take advantage of the particular historical, cultural and personal contingencies with which they were faced. The difficulties of cross-cultural comparison perhaps matter less in the case of the rest of Western Europe than they clearly do in the more exotic situations of India, Sri Lanka and even Israel.

In France after all, or Western Germany there is a similar background not only of parliamentary democracy, but of wider cultural and social standards. In some ways, this is fair comment, and it applies also to the Scandinavian democracies, yet the differences of background, of political traditions, of institutional arrangements and so on must never be forgotten, otherwise comparisons can suggest seriously distorted results. For example, it is necessary to know what the systems of election in the different countries are before comparisons can—if they can—be made between them. Again it is necessary to know, for example, that the French Cabinet is often appointed from outside the sphere of party politics altogether, to appreciate that direct comparisons with the British experience are, in this case, not valid.

France

In France, alone of the major Western European countries, the representation of women has almost consistently fallen off since 1945. When French women first got the vote after the war, over 6% of the Assembly were female. By 1956, this figure was down to 2.7% and it had fallen by 1975 to 1.7%, only rising to 3% in 1978.

The fall-off may be largely the result of the inflated post-war high which indicated not an acceptance of women in political life and an encouragement to their further, or at least continued participation, but involved rather the election of the widows of war-time resistance heroes (who stood in place of their husbands, as it were). Significant too was the success of the Communists (twenty-nine Communist women were elected in 1946) at the time and the relative decline of their political power thereafter with the rise of the right-centre parties in which women are less likely to achieve positions of prominence. There may also be the added connection of the Communists being not only more inclined to accept women, but also being heavily involved in the Resistance itself.

It seems likely too that the voting system in operation under the Fourth Republic was more favourable to women than that introduced in 1958 under the Constitution of the Fifth Republic. The argument is that the systems of proportional representation (PR) in existence before 1958 (a party list proportional system in 1945 and 1946, and a weighted system in multi-member constituencies in 1951 and 1956) gave women a better chance of being selected as a part of a list, or on a multi-member basis, but that once the single-member constituency was established, the women's success rate fell dramatically.

Although the general point is well made, that women seem to stand a better chance of being elected in a proportional representation system—and part of the argument of this chapter is that the example of Scandinavia, where such systems operate and where the representation of women is much higher than in any other country, confirms this—the other factors mentioned were clearly important in the French case, for the representative trend for women was already very clearly downward well before 1958. By 1951, for example, it was only 4%, and this fell to 2.7% by 1956. So although the electoral system may have played its part in the slump in the political representation of French women, it was not the only factor at work. Compared with the French example, in Britain there was a small but progressive increase from 3.8% in 1945 to the high of 4.6% in 1964. Since then, the proportion has only been slightly under 4% once, and in 1977 it was back up to 4.4%.

West Germany

In West Germany the French pattern of a declining female representation was, until recently, repeated, although in rather less dramatic form. The chequered history of German democracy since Weimar makes it hard to develop any meaningful comparisons before 1945, although women had the vote in 1918 and were, relatively, quite well represented in the Reichstags of the 20s and from 1949 until 1961 the figure was around 9%. It then dropped throughout the 1960s to something over 6% and only started to rise again to its 1977 level of 7.3% in the early 1970s. As in France, women have not had any spectacular success in office-holding except in a sporadic and individual way. Since 1972 however, the President of the Bundestag has been Frau Annemarie Renger and another woman is one of the Vice-Presidents. Several women are in the administration, but only one, Dr Katharina Focke, is in the Cabinet.

The electoral system again gives some backing to the idea that proportional representation, here a party list, gives women a better chance of political success than a single-member system. This is highlighted in the German case since half the Bundestag is elected by the one method and half by the other. The great majority of women enter by the lists—in the last election the proportion being 1% (single member) to over 6% (via the lists).

Italy

There have however been increases in the proportion of women in politics in other European countries. In Italy, for example, although representation is still not high at 8.4% it appears to be rapidly on the increase. The growth of the women's movement in the last five years has been enormous, given fuel by the 1974 divorce referendum, when not only militant feminists, but housewives and mothers became actively involved in women's issues, and at the same time, in politics. Again in 1977, the failure of the move to legalise abortion, brought women together in force. In fact, very quickly since 1975, Italy has acquired equal rights legislation covering for example women's rights to their maiden name, to co-guardianship of their children and to social insurance. In national politics, women are beginning to stand in greater numbers, and in the present government, the first woman minister, Tina Anselmi, Minister of Labour, has been appointed. What is interesting here is that when women developed the consciousness and the interest in national politics, the electoral framework, the party lists, allowed them in only a year or two to increase their representation to almost twice that of British women.

The Netherlands

In the Netherlands, too, great changes have taken place in this area since the early 1970s. Women's political representation in the Netherlands has been rather uneven. In the 1970s however, it increased rapidly. The 1971 figure of 8% became 13.3% by 1974, and it seems likely that the proportional representation system was an important factor in this development. Since the early 70s there has been a great upsurge of interest in women and their status in society. The Nederlandse Brouwenraad (Dutch Women's Council) was set up and co-ordinates its interests in education, women at work and welfare services, with those of the National Advisory Emancipation Committee, which was established by the Prime Minister in 1974, for a five-year period, to advise the government in this area. A certain amount of positive discrimination is being supported for women particularly in the sphere of government where it is suggested that 'they will have to be trained politically and they should receive preferential treatment in the Civil Service appointments'.[3] Yet it is difficult to see that the Dutch, any more than the Italians, have a society where equality of the sexes is much more radically embraced than in Britain.

Without in any way suggesting therefore that the electoral system has caused the increase in women's representation, it is hard not to conclude that some such framework, allowing women to be considered in far greater numbers than on a single member basis, has been a necessary if not a sufficient condition of that increase. And this would seem to be given backing by the position in America.

U.S.A.

In the U.S.A., as in Britain, the first-past-the-post system of election is used rather than any form of PR. This means that election in America is by a relative majority in single-member constituencies.

Congress is constitutionally the legislature and although women have been represented there since after the First World War, that representation has always been low. In 1948, 1.8% of the House of Representatives was female and this has only gradually increased to the present figure of just over 4%. Only ten women have ever served in the Senate. In the 1953-4 Congress, there were three women Senators, but since then the numbers have fallen off so that in 1977 there were none.[4] Cabinet posts in America are presidential appointments and can be bestowed on people outside the sphere of party politics. Even so, women have not done spectacularly well. Only one woman, Mrs Anne Armstrong, served in the Nixon Cabinet, and she had no departmental responsibility. In the Carter administration, there are two women, Juanita Kreps, Secretary of Commerce, and Patricia Harris, Secretary of Housing and Urban Development.

Although women seem to be represented in the state legislatures in a rather higher proportion than at the Federal level, the figure is distorted by a few states (New Hampshire for example, with 16% in 1973; and Arizona with 15%). In others, the figure is even lower than at the national level (Texas and Alabama, for example, at the same date, both had under 1%).

In view of the strength of the women's movement in America, the home of some of the most radical liberation ideologies of the 60s and early 70s, it seems surprising that so few are involved in national politics (proportionately only half that in Italy, for example). There can, of course, be no single, simple reason for this. It is partly, no doubt, the same kind of chicken and egg problem as elsewhere—because there are so few women involved, women do not think of politics as a serious career option. Again, there is a clear tradition in American politics of electing lawyers to office. The figure is put as high as 40% of American congressmen,[5] while in the early 1970s only 3% of American lawyers were women.[6] The American electoral system, however, putting women at the disadvantage of single-member selection, is probably also a factor in the continuously low level of women's representation there.

In all cases mentioned so far, the pattern of women's political representation is, at best, erratic.

SCANDINAVIA

Only in Scandinavia is a pattern of increasing participation visible, with figures far above those of other Western societies. After the 1977 election, the Norwegian Storting is now composed of 22.5% women. The figure for Sweden is currently 21.4%, for Finland 23.5%, and for Denmark 17%. Why are these figures relatively so high? Since the representative democracies of these countries are not dissimilar to the British model (indeed all of them except Finland have a constitutional monarch as head of state), comparing them with Britain seems a reasonable proposition. There are certainly social, economic and historical differences which cannot be ignored. The size of the countries, for example, means that political comparisons might seem ill-founded. Norway has a population of under four million, Denmark and Finland of just under five million, and Sweden of some eight million. In a sense their national politics look to be more comparable with British local rather than national government. Yet they are sovereign states and their governmental activities do cover the whole range of political involvement. Also, their large geographical size, relative to population, means that the central government does have the same problem of communication as in any other modern state and representatives of the various parts of the country still have to travel to the capitals to take part in government. None of this, however, would seem to affect specifically the rate of representation of women. They are in the same position as political women in Britain in often having constituencies which are far from the capital and having to maintain their contacts with both, as well as looking after their families.

Finland

Women have had the vote in Finland since 1906, the first in Europe to do so. And the year after that, women took their seats in the Finnish Parliament (Eduskunta). By 1970, over 21% of the Parliament were women and this increased in 1975 to 23.5%. This long tradition of female political involvement tends to make the Finns affect surprise when questioned about the issue. Women, they say, are 'quite normal' in Finnish society at all levels and particularly in politics. Even figures for women's current participation in politics are consequentially rather hard to come by. The Finnish Embassy in London, for example, apparently assumes that nobody would be involved in such an inherently sexist enterprise as differentiating in this context between men and women. In the event, nobody had any record of such numbers which had to be obtained direct from Helsinki.

Yet in spite of this assumption of equality, it is clear that the social position of women in Finland is almost as ambivalent as it is elsewhere in Europe, as evidenced by the figures for their participation in nearly all areas of economic and professional life. For example, although women made up in 1971 50.3% of those in the population with university degrees, only 2.3% of university professors were women and 8% of practising doctors.[7] Again, even the high figure for women graduates is rather misleading as there is a great preponderance of arts degrees among women, while in vocational schools, women make up only about 28% of the students.[8]

The National Council of Women in Finland produced, in 1970, a Target Programme for the decade in which were highlighted the successes and failures of women's struggle for equality in that country. While accepting that women did participate in most areas, it concluded 'that the number of women in leading positions in the various walks of life is exceedingly low, [and] that in appointments to many posts and offices, sex still matters more than merits and qualifications'.[9]

Marriage in Finland is based on a principle of equality between the sexes. Since the Marriage Act of 1933, couples have joint legal rights to marital property and joint guardianship of children. The National

Council of Women, however, bemoans the fact that 'despite the equality in principle . . . a remarkable lack of equality prevails in the practical application of the law'. This is put down to 'an insufficient knowledge of legal rights and obligations, an uneven distribution of the work done in and outside the home and of the benefits produced by such work, inadequate social services and antiquated attitudes'.[10]

In spite of this rather harsh appraisal, women in Finland have a higher participation in the work force than anywhere outside Eastern Europe. Also, women's pay is on average, 80% of men's which is a good deal higher than other European countries, with the exception of Sweden and Denmark.[11]

Thus there is, as one finds in the other Scandinavian countries, a legal and social framework in Finland which is fairly advantageous to women, yet which does not make an enormous difference to the representation of women in the professions and in high-level jobs in industry or government when compared with this country. The one important exception is national politics where the Finnish figure is more than five times that of the British. The explanation for this may lie less in the unsurpassed egalitarianism of the Finns than in the advantages to be gained by women from their electoral system.

Members of the (unicameral) Finnish Parliament are chosen by a system of proportional representation.[12] The formal nomination of candidates takes place through voters' associations, but in reality this is determined by the political parties which stand behind the voters' associations. Party lists are drawn up and, given the desire of the party to appeal as widely as possible within the electorate, it is these days increasingly likely that a fair proportion of women will be included in the list. The election result is determined, first by counting the votes cast for each list, and then ranking the candidates by their personal vote. Women tend to do well on the personal vote, but as is clear from the Danish case, they cannot always reap the benefits of this when they represent, as they tend to do, low-population constituencies.

Norway

In the case of Norway, with an immediately post-war figure of 4.6% women members in the Storting, and after a slow start where the figure remained constant until 1957, the upward trend has been fairly direct. In the 1970s, however, the pace of development has increased, and the 1969 figure of 9.3% became 15.4% in 1973 which again jumped by over 7% in 1977.

There have been, over the same period, great changes in attitudes to women, although there is a long history of concern about the role and status of women in Norway. As early as 1813 Camilla Collett, in her novels attacked the middle and upper class ideals of femininity, and Ibsen's *A Doll's House*, published in 1879, showed an equally revolutionary image of women.

Such attitudes are reflected in social and educational provisions. Nursery facilities, for example, have been increased and nurseries now take children from six months to three years during the period when mothers are working. Nursery schools and all-day kindergartens too take children from three to seven years. Such child-care facilities are not thought of in Norwegian society as a kind of second-best alternative to maternal care. They do not therefore assume, as they have done in Britain—at least in the past—the appearance of facilities directed at the 'deprived child' whose mother cannot care for it, but 'have both an educational and social purpose. They are meant to aid the child in harmonious development as well as to meet the needs of working parents'.[13] There has also developed a system of day-home care, whereby children are looked after, under supervision of qualified nursery teachers, in private homes. This has been particularly successful in caring for children under three, 'and for older children who adjust less well to the comparatively large groups in a day-nursery'.[14]

The assumption of authorities and increasingly of parents in Norway seems to be that children must be accepted as the responsibility, as well as the pleasure, of both parents, and where there is only one parent, as in the case of unmarried mothers, there are extensive facilities to help the parent to work and support the child. To this end apartments are built for single-parent families with special baby-rooms and a nursery where the children are cared for while their mothers are at work. Such families also receive special benefits if there is a need to have children looked after outside the state system, and educational grants are also payable to unmarried mothers while they complete vocational training in preparation for becoming self-supporting.

The Norwegian Equal Pay Council has been established since 1959 and it has wide powers to further the principles of equal pay by publicity, by investigating comparative pay rates and encouraging improved employment possibilities for women. Women have, under equal opportunity legislation, the right to seek employment in any area they choose, even in the Church. They also have, and have had for many years, the right to retain their name at marriage, to separate taxation, to half the matrimonial property in the event of divorce and to joint guardianship of children. The 1964 Abortion Law gave rights to termination in certain conditions, and this was extended in 1977 to a right to abortion on request in the early stages of pregnancy.

In spite of this relatively advanced social climate, women are not employed in the professions, or in industry, in very high numbers, although those numbers are rising. Only 7.4% of married women over fifty were in the labour market in 1970, whereas the figure for women from sixteen to fifty was 46% including women with children where the figure was much lower.[15] Women are not particularly well represented in the professions, only 1.7% of university professors being women, less than 1% of hospital doctors (although they made up 11% of other doctors), and 3.6% of secondary school head-teachers.

In general than, although the social climate is now favourable to women in Norway, it has not had the impact on their participation outside the home which might have been expected. Yet in politics their performance is much more impressive. Not only are 22.5% of the Storting female, but five members of the Cabinet are women, one of whom was appointed at the age of thirty-six and one at age thirty-seven. Although there is no rule that members of the Council of State (Cabinet) must come from the political sphere, the women in the Cabinet have always tended to do so and the present female members have all been elected representatives.

The system of election, and the party system in Norway seem to be helpful to women in a way which is at least as direct and important as the liberal climate of public opinion or any legislation to promote equality. The party list is the basis of choice for the electorate and the candidates figure on the list in the order decided by the district convention of the party. Electors vote a party list, but may also indicate preference in choice of candidates by striking out names and substituting others (write-in votes).[16] The method by which the outcome of the balloting is then determined is most complicated. (The modified odd-number method (Lague) has been used since 1953.)

Women have a better chance of selection by this system in that it is likely that a party will be keen to offer a 'balanced' list to the electorate.

Until recently, however, women were disadvantaged in that they were not well represented in the party organisations, or in local government (until 1963, women made up only 10% of the executive councils of local communes). They thus tended not to be known in political circles and to figure, when they did at all, low on the party lists. As votes are allocated proportionally, the lower down the list a candidate comes, the less his or her chance of election. However, since the early 1970s, there have been great changes in attitudes among women themselves and a concerted effort to get women on to party lists—as high as possible—and to increase their representation in local government. So successful was this pressure—which extended to the women's movement encouraging women to support women candidates, that, in the municipal elections of 1971 there was a dramatic rise in the number of women elected, particularly in the urban areas. In Oslo, for example, the proportion of women elected was well over 50%, and in Trondheim women won 46 out of the 85 seats.[17] It is the continuation of this strong involvement that has produced the 1977 general election result.

But why should Norwegian women, who until recently had been behind the other Scandinavian countries in political participation suddenly make this great surge forward? The base had always, of course, been there in that the party organisations and the party lists, and local government with its strong commune basis had always been open to women. The influence of the women's movement is clearly great, and it is suggested, the greater because of the opposition which it met from the women within the Church. In the other countries of Scandinavia, religion does not have such an important role and is thus not a focus of opinion and social attitudes. In Norway however, the State Lutheran Church is still strong and particularly so among women. The concerted opposition to women's movement demands (which seem to have widened out into the demands of the majority of all Norwegian women) came largely from the Church, which was in this way a stimulus to unity and joint action on the part of women, in providing them with a clear opposition in their struggle for political parity. This may seem somewhat dubious in the light of the advanced social attitudes the Church has often displayed in Norway (women have been eligible for the priesthood since 1956). Yet the argument is persuasive if what is being claimed is that Church opposition allowed Norwegian women to unite publicly against an identifiable opponent. This has perhaps given them a strength in their own unity which has not been available to Danish, Swedish or Finnish women living in societies where no such single and identifiable force exists to oppose them, thus leaving them struggling in a way much more diffuse and uncertain, against a prejudice which is not even supposed, in these liberal and egalitarian times, to exist.

Sweden

In Sweden, women's representation in national politics is almost as high as in Norway. In 1945 it was 7.8% and its progress has always been upwards, at first by 2 or 3% each election until it seemed to stabilise around 12–13% in the 50s and 60s. It was 15.4% in 1970 and then went up again to over 19% in 1973 and by a further 2% in 1976 to reach its present level. There are also five women in a Cabinet of fifteen, including the Foreign Minister, Karin Soder.

Like the Norwegians, the Swedes have a long history of involvement with the status of women in society, dating from at least the 1820s, when Fredrika Bremer published her views of women's repressed position in society,[18] although it was not until 1919 that unmarried women and 1921 that married women got the vote. Since then, however, there have been vast changes in attitudes to women, accelerating very greatly in the late 60s and 70s. One of the important influences on Swedish women in their capacity as workers outside the home has been the drop in the number of marriages and the great increase in the divorce rate, which has had an important effect on the numbers of women in the work-force. In 1974 for example, 64% of all women aged 18–66 were employed, as against 54% in 1967.[19]

In 1972, the Swedish Government appointed an Advisory Council on Equality to report direct to the Prime Minister and it has recommended and encouraged changes in laws regarding employment, education, social welfare, marriage and the family, children and women's political role.

Again social attitudes have been given expression in the changing pattern of child-care. The programme for the development of day care places has been very ambitious. In 1965 only 37% of women with young children worked outside the home and by 1968 there were still only 20,000 day care places. By 1975 more than 58% of mothers with pre-school children were working and 70,000 places in day nurseries had been provided. The projection for 1980 is a further 100,000 places and this seems to be high on the government's list of priorities. (However, inflation has hit the project severely and although the numbers of places are still expected to be met it is being suggested that the cost to parents will have to be increased by nearly 100%, thus hitting hardest the least well-off.)

Legislation, since as far back as the 1930s, has gone a long way to giving women equality with men within the family and society. Women have the right to employment in any area (except the Army) and to equality of pay for equal work. They have the right to their own pensions and separate taxation, to abortion on demand, and to joint control of their children.

In education too women have equal rights and there have been attempts recently to encourage girls to pursue more technically based courses and also to see jobs outside the home as a natural, not to say a necessary, step. In order to strengthen this appreciation, Swedish schools have recently begun schemes to arrange periods of apprenticeship in industry for pupils and to give more information about and access to the world of work.[20]

And yet, in almost all cases, the outcome for women's equality has been disappointing. Women are still, as elsewhere, concentrated in service industries (45% of women to 15% of men) as opposed to mining, manufacturing and building where 50% of men were employed but less than 20% of women.[21] Since they tend to work in different fields, there are *de facto* differences between their wage scales which cannot be adequately dealt with by the formula of equal pay for equal work, and in 1974 it was estimated that women received only 85% of men's hourly rate.[22] Again women are many among the low-paid (over 67% of this category) and few among the highest paid (5%).[23]

In the educational sphere too in spite of attempts to reduce differences between boys and girls, girls still make up 63% of students in the general arts and social sciences courses at university, compared with 29% of those in mathematics and pure sciences.[24]

Although social attitudes in Sweden do seem advanced compared with most other Western European societies, Swedish women complain that the reality is not as radical as the impression given by legislation etc. Men are entitled by law, for example, to time off to look after their children—both when the child is born, and if the child is sick—yet they tend not to take this because employers do not approve, and so most fathers in this case put their careers before their family involvements. The legislation is there but the change of attitude is not as fundamental as it might look. Olof Palme, ex-Prime Minister of Sweden recognised this when he told a meeting in Washington, 'The new role of the man implies that he must reduce his contributions in working life—and maybe also in politics— during the period when he has small children. This is what women always had to do alone earlier . . . we could manage this loss in production if we can instead stimulate women to make increased contributions in this area'.[25]

The social situation then is in a state of flux, although women have made some advances. In politics however, the advance has been continuous, again largely as a result of the political system itself, both the electoral method (a party list system) and the whole tenor of Swedish social democracy which is distinctly radical and lacking in the laissez-faire ethos of other European equivalents. Neil Elder stresses the 'radical rationalist spirit' of Swedish democracy which is 'hostile to tradition and the unquestioning acceptance of inherited ways of doing things'.[26] And, he adds, the 'centre of gravity of the Swedish electorate has now been left of centre for a considerable time'. There is also a clear and general acceptance of the claims of minorities, as evidenced by the official view that 'it should be considered repugnant to Swedish traditions . . . to deprive relatively strong currents of minority opinion of representation'.[27]

As in Norway, the party list system gives women a chance to get into the political arena since increasingly parties want to present a balanced list to the electorate,[28] but again until recently, women have not been represented in local government, or in local party organisations to any great extent. In 1958, the figure was 10%, which had grown to 12% by 1966. In 1974, however, over 2000 out of 13,000 members of Sweden's 278 municipal councils were women (i.e. 17%), and 19% of county councillors in 1974 were women.[29] In general, the women's associations and political groups are encouraging women to join their local political parties in order to become known in their area and so stand a better chance of getting on to the party list and at a higher level. It has often been claimed in the past that women were placed low on the list when they made it at all and so stood a poorer chance of election. Now some of the parties (for example the Labour

Party and the Liberal Party) have introduced a self-imposed quota system, whereby women are not only brought in higher up the list, but are also placed alternately with men. Kerstin Aner, a Liberal M.P., says that this kind of action does not preclude any more formal legislation or education to change attitudes to women. Rather what is needed is a 'pincer movement' where changes in attitudes are aided and encouraged by some kind of positive discrimination (she suggests a 40% quota system) for women.

One area through which the political representation of women may be expanding in Sweden is the trade union movement. In 1967, 26% of the Swedish Confederation of Trade Unions (LO) were women. In 1973, the proportion was 33%. In spite of this, the proportion of women in official positions in unions is still small and the LO Congress in 1971 had only 38 women delegates out of 300. However, the proportion of women officers does seem to be on the increase, among chairmen of local branches, for example. Whatever women's showing in Union activity, they do seem to be acquiring an increasing share of the parliamentary seats which although not sponsored by the unions in the British style are associated with unions and often filled by their officers. In the present Labour Party, for example, Barbro Engman and Gertrud Sigurdsen are examples of women who have come up through their unions as organisers and have got into politics by way of this experience, utilising the strong links between the Labour Party and the unions. As more women are involved in union organisation it seems likely that more of them will become politically involved in a similar way.

Denmark

In Denmark, the proportion of women in politics is not quite so high as in Finland, Norway or Sweden, yet it is still significantly above that of the rest of Western Europe. By the early 50s the figure was 8% and it rose slowly but steadily through the 60s to 11% in 1968. In 1971, it increased at a stroke to 17% and then fell back slightly in 1973 and 1975, before regaining that level in 1977.

Danish women have always had considerable equality within the framework of marriage. Since legislation in 1925, marriage has been seen as a partnership within which the spouses have equal privileges and duties. Danish husbands do not have the sole duty of supporting their wives. Wives too are expected to contribute to the maintenance of the family. Women have the right to retain their maiden name, and children may take their mother's name. Since 1973 too Danish women have the right to abortion on request, up to twelfth week of pregnancy.

In 1965, the Prime Minister appointed the Commission on the Position of Women in Society, with a mandate 'to examine the position of women in society and . . . to put forward suitable proposals . . . to create actual equality for women in all areas of the life of society'.[30]

One of the recommendations of the final report of the Commission was that a permanent body be set up to 'treat all possible questions concerning equality or discrimination between people' and in particular to be 'concerned with questions relating to the position of women in the labour market'. In 1975, the Council on Equality was created with a president and seven members drawn from the trade unions, employers' federation and women's organisations. The Council reports direct to the Prime Minister, and according to Mrs Dahlerup, the President, has had considerable success in pursuing and rectifying cases of discrimination.

The number of women in the labour market has increased dramatically in recent years, and the greatest increase has been among married women. In 1965, only 33% of married women worked: by 1970 this figure was 65%. By 1977, the figure projected in 1972 for 1987— 69.6%—had already been reached.[31] But women still work largely in traditional women's sections of the labour market and few have executive or senior jobs in commerce and industry.[32] Again, in principle equal pay has been accepted since 1960 when Denmark ratified the Geneva Convention to that effect. However, the Federation of Danish Trades Unions acknowledge that women are paid lower wages than men—on average they get 83% of men's wages—but as elsewhere this is often largely due to women being involved in work which is traditionally low-paid.

Educationally, at the school stages at least, girls are equally represented with boys. They are less likely however to go on to further education (two thirds of boys and one third of girls did so in 1972). Women at university too, tend to remain within the arts and humanities courses, and only 35% of them completed their studies in 1972 compared with 65% of men.[33] A recent report on women doctors suggested that although they do tend to use their training, it is generally in a lower capacity than their male equivalents. Not only do many work part-time, but they do not seek promotion, indeed may openly acknowledge that they prefer a less responsible position.

In national politics, once again the existence of a system of proportional representation seems to be of some help to women. To be seen to represent as wide a section of the population as possible is clearly an electoral advantage to a party, and these days, parties have to appeal to women as well as men. The rules of election are convoluted, involving not only votes for the party, but personal votes for candidates.[34] It is claimed by the women M.P.s that they are allocated the constituencies with small populations, and they can therefore acquire only small numbers of personal votes. The whole situation is complicated by the fact that at least three different forms of candidate nomination exist, but in all cases personal votes are very important and it can upset the list if a candidate gets a particularly large personal vote. Women candidates tend to get a comparatively large personal vote, but they claim that they cannot exploit this fully if they are contesting a small constituency.

The overwhelming impression in the case of Scandinavia is of societies where women are indeed ahead of many other European countries in their demands for equality and in the substantive legal and social provision for equal opportunity. On its own, however, this consciousness cannot explain the relative political success of women there. It is rather the combination of the social awareness and official recognition of women's claims, and the electoral system itself, which has facilitated the Scandinavian achievement in this sphere. All the countries so far considered use a party list system. This is, of course, not the only form of PR and it is thought by some to give too much power to parties, in that electors can generally only show preferences on a list already composed by the party itself. Indeed, when English-speaking countries have adopted proportional representation, they have almost all chosen the single transferable vote (STV) form. This involves voting for numbered preferences so that the elector's vote is transferable. If the candidate for whom he votes has either more votes than he needs for election or so few votes that he cannot be elected, the vote will be transferred to the elector's next choice. It is thus possible to indicate not only a party preference but a preference for candidates pledged to certain policies, or for women or social minority candidates.

This was the form of proportional representation used to elect the university members between 1918 and the abolition of the seats in 1945. It has already been mentioned that Eleanor Rathbone, as one of the members for the Combined English Universities, probably gained by the system. As both a woman and an Independent she would have stood little chance in a first-past-the-post contest, yet she had a comfortable majority for many years and is the only woman ever to sit in the House without party affiliation.

STV is the method used in Ireland to elect the Dail, and also the Northern Irish Assembly and Convention. The position of women in Irish society can hardly be said to be advanced. The Church tends to restrict their role and to limit demands even for discussion on contraception, abortion and divorce, often indicators of social attitudes to women. Yet, in spite of this, women in the Republic have a political representation of nearly 5 %, rather higher than that of British women who might well consider themselves both more advanced, and more accounted in their own society.

The use of STV would also seem to have had an influence on the elections for the Convention and Assembly in the North. Here, although for example no women candidates stood in the last elections for the mainly Catholic S.D.L.P., 5.1 % of those elected to both bodies were women.[35] Neither STV nor any other form of PR will automatically and of itself increase the number of women M.P.s, but there seems to be a good case for saying that proportional systems may remove obstacles in the way of those who seek election and of those who support them.

Without the development of a supportive social climate, women's claims for political representation may never be considered, and indeed such demands may never even be strongly made by women themselves. Such has, until very recently, been the case in, for example, Italy. In such cases, even when PR is in existence, there is little social pressure for women to be included on lists, and so little incentive for parties to promote them. When the climate begins to change, however, and the claims for women's equality begin to be seen as more than the outlandish demand of a few extremists, the existence of PR can promote the rapid assimilation of women into national politics. This would seem to be what has happened in Italy since 1970. The women's movement there moved from being exclusively a young, middle-class, urban, politically radical and extremely small group in the early 70s to almost a mass-movement, motivated originally by the 1974 divorce referendum. In the space of only one election, women's representation has gone from under 3% to nearly 8.5%. In a single-member system, such a dramatic change would be highly unlikely.

The lack of a PR system is an important factor, it seems, in keeping women in Britain and America so under-represented in politics, in spite of the fact that there the women's movements are strong, and social attitudes and official recognition of women's rights are relatively advanced. Seen against this background, it is not really surprising that British women have been represented at the same low level of about 4% or under in every Parliament since 1945. Regardless of widespread changes since then in attitudes to women and in women's own self-perception, the mechanics of selection and election are, as they stand, uncompromisingly against them.

CHAPTER X

Prospects

'To please, to be useful to us, to make us love and esteem them, to educate us when young and take care of us when grown up, to advise, to console us, to render our lives easy and agreeable – these are the duties of women at all times, and what they should be taught in their infancy.' Rousseau

'I do not wish [women] to have power over men but over themselves.' Mary Wollstonecraft

Without exception, every M.P. I asked, male or female, was in favour of more women in national politics. They were less sure, however, about how to encourage this. Doing nothing but simply pointing to the existence of formal equality has meant little difference in the level of women's political participation at least since the war. And indeed doing nothing may cease to be a viable political option before long, as women become more aware of themselves as a potent electoral force, demanding at least as much wooing as the Welsh, or the Scots, the trade unionists, or the immigrants.

The possibilities for change range from the quite practical re-organisation of social, and indeed parliamentary life to less clear-cut developments in consciousness and attitudes. The two are not, of course, entirely distinct. Re-organisation of institutions may be both a result of changing attitudes, and itself a force for change. Of itself, the encouragement of, for example, flexible working hours and more nursery facilities would not bring more women into politics, but the impression it would convey, of the social acceptance of working women, and in particular working mothers, would be an important step in this direction. Changes in educational frameworks too could encourage the acceptance of girls and boys as individuals, without the sex-stereotyping which is still predominantly the pattern in families, schools and colleges. This might allow people to find a role, less by constraint than by choice, which could liberate the man who wanted to be a midwife, or take care of his children, as much as the woman who wanted to be Chancellor of the Exchequer. And lest this be dismissed as brave new world, it should be pointed out that the Danes have gone a long way to making such role reversal a real possibility and the men who choose to stay at home now figure in the official statistics.

Such changes in educational priorities would have to be wide; they would also, it seems have to be specific. Girls are, according to recent research,[1] quite clearly less politically informed, as well as less involved, than boys. Yet the remedy here may not be more intensive civics tuition or compulsory O-level British Government for all girls, but simply the conveyance to them of the idea that they are responsible members of society who must think in terms of making their way and supporting themselves, and who should see themselves as equally efficacious and competent as their male peers.

And this is not simply a massive propaganda exercise. It is the presentation of what is largely now, and will probably increasingly become, the case. That is, that more women will cease to see themselves as in any way the passive dependants of the active, competent male. The increasing divorce rate alone has meant that many thousands of women who were brought up to believe that once married, they would be cared for for life, have had to learn the hard way that they are individuals and must ultimately, and often painfully, take responsibility for themselves. For women brought up in this realisation, politics is much more immediately important than for their grandmothers or even their mothers—wrapped as they were in the cocoon of an almost inevitably lasting marriage. It is not the case that women in the past had no ability to form political convictions or develop political views of their own; it is rather that politics did not impinge, as they saw it, very directly on their lives. It related to the external world, the world outside the home, and that was men's territory. Politics will only have universal significance for women when they are, metaphorically at any rate, turned out of the house. And that means when because of the frequency of divorce, and indeed the not unconnected changing view of family life, marriage ceases to be conceived of as a job, a meal-ticket, a real economic option for women.

And society moves inevitably, it seems, in that direction. 'To be free of the dangers of conception and to be able to earn one's own bread are typically male attributes', says Kerstin Aner.[2] And, she continues, the human being who is now most respected is 'the independent male . . . not tied to his biological function, nor tied to his mate in order to survive. To this status women can now aspire.' Whether precisely this would be, or will become most women's aspiration is perhaps contentious. Yet the very fact that we can speculate about it, shows how uncertain women's present status and consciousness is, and perhaps it is this very uncertainty—the 'divine discontent' as Mrs Aner calls it—that will take women, no longer secure in their role as wife and mother, out into the world to find their individuality.

In this context, social and legal changes are at least as important for the attitudes which they embody as for their substantive content. The inadequacies of the Equal Pay Bill and the even greater failings of the anti-discrimination legislation are perhaps not in the end as significant as the formal social acceptance of the injustice and inequality which prompted such legislation.

In the same way, the importance for women of unionisation may be more than a very direct training ground for, and path to, national politics. As the Swedish example shows, women can, once they get into union leadership, begin to exploit this connection. But perhaps more important, along the way, they can become politicised. Only recently have women begun to become aware of the strength of organisation and of unity. Again, this gives them a first taste of being more in control of their own economic destinies, as contraception allows them control of their biological destinies. And this realisation is not confined to women in the Labour Party, the traditional supporters of women's rights, but was being discussed for example by Conservative women at their Annual Conference in May 1977. In the past, women were not a very coherent group: they were shut off from each other in their homes, unlikely to develop much political awareness and unable to get any real political experience. As they come out of the home in greater numbers, the political awareness will develop (as politics becomes perceived as part of the reality of their lives), and the political experience of economic power will increasingly enhance their self-confidence.

It has been suggested that instead of building up a national system of day nurseries, a long-term and costly operation, parents should be encouraged to have their children cared for 'privately', by individual child-minders, in the home of the child, or the minder. To this end, it is said parents ought to be compensated by tax allowance for the expenses of child care. At present, a woman who goes out to work, cannot officially claim any tax exemptions or rebates on the domestic help she employs, either to have her household maintained or her children cared for. There is the wife's earned income allowance, but this is not in any way comparable to a domestic or household allowance. In America, for example, where the general policy has been to provide only minimal state nursery facilities, such tax allowances have been available since 1972.

Whichever policy is thought to be more appropriate, it is clear that in Britain neither is adequately pursued, with the result that many parents cannot afford to have their children properly looked after. The most obvious and appalling result of this has been the growth in the number of overworked, unregistered baby-minders, which as a substitute for a national policy in this area is lamentable. Not only is it unacceptable in terms of the care and concern these children are due from society, but it leaves the parents, and this most often means the mothers, in great uncertainty. They may well be aware of the inadequacy of the substitute care their child is receiving and have little or no choice in the matter, and they are certainly aware of the strains imposed by the equivocation of a society which on the one hand encourages them to join the work force but on the other makes no adequate provision for the care of pre-school children. The resolution of this basic social confusion, the somewhat vague acceptance of the worthwhile nature of the extension of women's interests and involvements outside the home, while providing almost nothing in the way of enabling conditions for this, would do more for women's self-confidence than almost any other single factor. It would as I have said be an indication of society's approval of the working woman and an acknowledgement that domestic responsibilities cannot be her's alone.

It has been argued that the only way by which woman can aspire to equality in societies which have for so long regarded them as unequal, is by some kind of positive discrimination. For some time at least, it is claimed, women will have to have the leeway of centuries made up to them by giving them more chance than men, whether in education or business or politics. There are many examples of such thinking. Bernard Shaw was convinced that the only way women would get into public life in adequate numbers was by having a 'coupled vote', whereby electors voted for both a man and a woman.[3] Kerstin Aner, a Swedish Liberal M.P., believes that women must be given a minimum of perhaps 40% of political seats for equality to begin to be a reality. Maureen Colquhoun's abortive 1975 Bill attempted to introduce the same kind of principle into British public life, largely via Boards and Commissions. And in a rather more modified form, Mrs Castle accepts the same idea in suggesting that women ought to figure at selection conferences at least in proportion to their numbers on the electoral roll.

The idea has appeal. Not that it is naively suggested that formal equality is the same thing as genuine acceptance, but that genuine acceptance may depend to some extent on women being seen to be represented in much more than a token way. An alternative view is held, however, by Karen Dahlerup, President of the Danish Council on Equality, who argues that it is only by changing the law and the social perception of women directly that equality can become a reality. She tells of the successes of her Council in, for example, persuading the Danish housing authorities that it was unnecessary to name the man of the house as tenant, and simply to refer to the 'leaseholder'. Similarly, on her instigation, social security offices will now accept a woman's own national insurance number rather than insisting on that of a husband or male supporter. Mrs Dahlerup believes that neither active discrimination, nor even sexist attitudes is the greatest enemy of equality, but simply the thoughtless acceptance of the status quo, and this would not change with the promotion of purely formal equality. She believes that the little legalistic, even trivial changes, like the above, are necessary in order to change attitudes and unless these change women's claimed equality will only result in them taking on commitments outside the home, on top of the domestic burden which they will still be expected to carry. If equality is not to be a travesty, by which women are bound to under-achieve, because of the range of their commitments and the diffusion of their energies, men must take their share of domestic involvements and responsibility for child care, and women must be accounted legally and socially—and not just formally—as equal to men. Otherwise, women, with their apparent equality, may simply attempt too much and leave themselves open to the charge that they are not up to the demands of equality when they are given it.

Substantive changes in the hours, organisation and facilities of Parliament itself would probably be a useful development for all M.P.s. Yet a supermarket in the Palace of Westminster, or a ladies' hairdresser, or even child-care facilities are hardly going to make the difference between a woman's getting politically involved and not. Even changes, which many M.P.s think long overdue, in the hours of business of the House are unlikely to affect women a great deal more than men. Politics is, after all, not a nine-to-five job and nobody who is politically committed expects it to be so. A change in the voting system itself, however, is a rather different matter. The introduction of some form of proportional representation would probably help not only the minority parties, but aspiring political women as well.

The arguments against proportional representation of course are well-known, the main one being that it results in the splitting of the vote among several minority parties and the election in most cases of minority or coalition governments, which within the British tradition have always been thought of as weak governments. Yet perhaps over the past few years, British politics itself has become less bipartisan. Richard Rose shows that whereas in 1951 the two major parties had between them 96.8% of the vote, by 1970 this was 89.4% and by October 1974, it was down to 75.1%.[4] The emergence of the nationalists as an important force, for example, the various calls for a 'coalition of the centre', the minority position of the Labour Government since the spring of 1977, all serve to emphasise this. Again, the precedent would seem to be set in the suggestion for a regional list system for the direct elections to the European Parliament, endorsed at the time by both the Prime Minister and the Foreign Secretary. Although in the end finally rejected by the House, it has brought to the fore again the whole issue of electoral processes and reform.

It is scarcely an exaggeration to say that what keeps women out of national politics is largely the technicalities of getting in. Discrimination direct or indirect can be diluted if not destroyed by playing for numbers. In a first-past-the-post system, electors, particularly selection committees, are often predisposed to choose a man. In a proportional system, there is positive advantage to be gained from presenting a balanced choice which must, as Enid Lakeman points out, include its quota of women, if only 'so as to appeal to as many different kinds of electors as possible'.[5]

The suggestion here is not that women would inevitably want to stand in vast numbers if PR were introduced. Clearly not everybody, man or woman, is interested in politics. But women do often seem to exclude themselves from this particular form of activity by their belief that they are not intelligent, articulate or informed enough to get involved, at the national level at any rate. These beliefs about inadequacy are themselves shored up by the obvious fact of women's under-representation in the area. Thus develops Catch 22, where the beliefs inhibit the exploration of involvement, like political involvements, which could themselves undermine the beliefs. In this sense the fifth column in the fight for equality is often women's own self-perception. As one American writer has it 'it is hard to fight an enemy who has outposts in your head'.[6] In the political context, the circle of under-achievement and expectation of under-achievement will only be broken if more women stand and get into Parliament, for if more get in, more would be willing to stand. And in the long run, giving girls this sense of their own potential would be educationally more important than present attempts to substitute meccano sets for dolls' prams. From this point of view, minor tinkerings—supermarkets and hairdressers—are clearly inadequate, and quite fundamental levels of technical and even constitutional reorganisation may be necessary. Attitudes, of course, will not change all at once, either the attitudes of women themselves, or the attitudes of others to them. It is still the case that the standards, personal as well as public, which are demanded of a woman are rather different from those expected of a man, as the case of Maureen Colquhoun, rejected by her constituency party, would appear to underline. Although Ms Colquhoun's local party organisation claimed to have several grounds for dissatisfaction with her, it seems clear that her own avowed sexual attitudes and practices were the real basis of their disapproval.[7] In view of the fact that a male M.P.[8] faced a similar attack from his constituency party at about the same time, and survived, while Ms Colquhoun did not, a double standard would appear to be in operation. This at any rate was the construction put on it by *The Guardian*,[9] and even *The Scotsman* described the situation as part of 'the diet of petty prejudice which has long been the plat de jour of British political life'.[10]

Another dish on that menu is the assumption by many men in Parliament that women are not serious political opponents, and although most are politically astute enough to realise that making such a point overtly would be inadvisable, they are not above emphasising when they can a woman's femininity, and implicitly, inadequacy in the rough and tumble of the tough, masculine world of politics. Such is the impression that Mr Callaghan, for example, seems to want to give in his parliamentary skirmishes with Mrs Thatcher.[11] Furthermore, in the electoral battle, men still appear to assume that, although a woman may not in the ordinary way actually lose the party votes, in a position of potential power, she will not be favourably regarded by the majority of the electorate—including the women. It was this belief which led the present Labour Party leadership to greet Mrs Thatcher's election to the Conservative leadership with such glee. According to Lady Falkender, they apparently believed, as they slapped each other on the backs, that their electoral chances were enormously enhanced by this. The assumption was that a woman in command was patently a political albatross for their opponents. In this case, they clearly had to modify their opinion when only a day or so later, the polls were showing substantial sections of their own supporters (female) predisposed to support Mrs Thatcher in a general election.

Throughout this study, the implicit assumption has been that politics is a worthwhile form of activity, that the efforts and sacrifices of participation are rewarded at least by the sense of doing something important and central to the continuity and even improvement of society. Yet there has been in the past few years a general devaluation of politics in the public view. The membership of the main political parties is declining. Since 1952, the official figures show a falling away of support for the Labour Party, and between 1975 and 1976 there was a drop in membership of nearly 17,000. Although the Conservative Party does not publish exact figures, surveys by outside bodies indicate that it too had its membership peak in the early 1950s, which has now dropped by about half.

This need indicate nothing so drastic as a retreat from politics itself, but simply a disenchantment with the existing orthodoxy of the major parties' frameworks. However, it may go deeper than this. In the early 60s, Jean Mann was suggesting that the best people, and especially the best women, were often just not attracted by the political life in which she pessimistically saw 'no scope for individual contribution, no prospects beyond that of a backbencher, and the salary ... can easily be picked up for less effort in other professions'.[12] This belief is perhaps confirmed, if for other reasons, by the reactions of at least some very able and indeed politically interested women at the moment. Lady Falkender, for example, says that she had no desire to stand for Parliament herself, largely because of her dislike of the public relations component in politics, the histrionic aspect of political persuasion. In the same vein, Lady Wootton is on record recently stating her distrust of the 'so phoney' political art of speechifying, which she says disinclined her to pursue such a career herself.[13] In a rather different context, Ghita Ionescu offered a more profound critique of the political world as one of shrinking power, where the trade unions, national and multi-national corporations, the regions, the international community, and especially the E.E.C., all circumscribed to a greater or lesser extent the autonomy of Parliament.[14] The Social Contract between government and unions, Ionescu suggests, will result in a 'mixed representative-corporate process of policy-making'. 'All these "contracts" and "treaties" ', he continues (and, he might have added, suggested referenda), 'spell out a limitation of the previous total sovereignty of British Representative Government'.

The question is raised too of the governability of a society as complex as modern Britain. This uncertainty may reflect on the image of Parliament which loses prestige when it is seen as, far from supreme, dependent on Trade Unions or events overseas which may drastically undermine its policies.

Yet in the end, at any rate as an explanation of the very limited participation of women in politics, these ideas will not do. Through the late 60s and 70s, the number of women putting themselves forward as candidates has steadily increased, reflecting the increasing interest of women in this area. The number may be small in absolute terms, but this is the case for women in almost any sphere of comparable level and status in our society. And the explanation for this is not primarily to be sought in any general political malaise but rather largely in the status and self-image of women themselves. And the two are intimately connected. The social ambivalence about women's status and role makes for uncertainty in women's own sense of themselves. While as a society we may talk glibly and vaguely about the worthwhile extension of women's interests outside the family, we provide almost nothing in the way of enabling conditions for this. And enabling conditions—day nurseries, flexible working hours, tax concessions, or whatever, are important not only in giving substantive help, but also psychological support, by demonstrating society's approval here. After all, in politics, more than other activities, symbols are often as important as substance.

In the political sphere this syndrome is particularly acute. Again, the vague agreement that 'more women' would be 'a good thing' goes hand-in-hand with the undisguised acknowledgement that, within the present system of selection and election, women are permanently disadvantaged. And in politics, nothing is an issue until it has been shown to be electorally significant. Women, as more than one male M.P. told me, could force things, even at the selection level, if they used their numbers and insisted on, for example, far more women being represented at selection conferences. But they do not; often it seems female party workers are the ones who are most insistent on and supportive of a man. And women will be relegated to the sidelines and the support systems in party, as in factory and office, while they themselves predominantly accept this as their appropriate role.

As I have indicated, in the case of women in politics, changes in the electoral system would almost certainly and immediately increase fairly dramatically the number of women in the Commons. It would also indicate a serious social commitment to women's equality, rather than the merely banal reiteration of the current liberal shibboleths on the subject. And it might even, on the way, invest our much maligned parliamentary democracy with greater credibility and prestige, if it were seen to represent more fairly, in the very central organ of government itself, the female half of the population.

Postscript 1979

The General Election of May 1979 was held as this book was going to press. It seemed appropriate, however, to incorporate briefly the results, especially in view of their significance for women. At one level, that significance is of course historic: Margaret Thatcher became the first woman Prime Minister. Ironically, she did so at an election which produced fewer women MPs than any since 1951.

In 1979, 206 women stood as candidates of whom only nineteen were returned, eight Conservatives and eleven Labour members.[1] A considerably greater number of women stood therefore than ever before for the smallest return in nearly thirty years. The reasons for this are not very hard to find, and would seem to confirm many of the arguments of this book. To begin with, as ever, women tended to be standing for the marginal seats, both those already in the Commons and those aspiring to be so. At the dissolution, there were eighteen Labour women, seven Conservatives and two Scottish Nationalists, a total of twenty-seven women, at least twelve of whom might have been thought to be in vulnerable seats with majorities of under 2000. There were also four women retiring (Mrs Castle, Mrs Butler, Mrs Jeger and Miss Harvie Anderson—three Labour and one Conservative), all of whom had comfortable majorities and all of whose places were taken by men, who, in each case, held the seat. In the event, the large swings to the Conservatives (in the south at any rate) meant that the Labour women with the small majorities were among the first to go.[2] The swing away from the Labour Party was so large in some places that it toppled as well-known a member as Shirley Williams with her apparently secure majority of over 9000.

Although the Labour Party ran more women at this election than ever before (fifty-three of them) they were unable to prosper when their party was being so heavily defeated, and only one new Labour woman (Sheila Wright) emerged to replace the eight either defeated or retired. The swing to the Conservatives did not however usher in a new wave of Tory women to back the new Prime Minister. For only thirty-one Conservative women stood and, apart from the six re-elected, a mere two managed to take advantage of their party's fortunes to win a seat. Of these, only one has never sat in the House before, Sheila Faith who took Belper. The other was Peggy Fenner, 'Prices Peg' of the 1970 Heath administration, who recaptured Rochester and Chatham where she had been defeated in 1974.

The Liberals as usual ran a high proportion of women candidates (forty-nine in all), but none was returned. The Scottish Nationalists suffered in the virtual destruction of the party as a parliamentary force and both Winnie Ewing and Margaret Bain, with her tiny 1974 majority of 22, were defeated. The trend already referred to of women having a greater representation among candidates when the party is less success-ful or secure,[3] is borne out in the continuing fall in S.N.P. women can-didates in 1979 (six out of seventy-two) and it will be interesting to see whether, if the party survives as an electoral force, its decreased strength will lead to more women again representing it in the future. The idea that women do seem to have greater representation among the minor parties is confirmed by the 1979 figures. Seventy-three stood for the minor parties and in all cases their representation was proportionately considerably higher than in the major parties. The Conservatives ran only rather over 4% women, the Labour Party 8% and the Liberals 7%. The Communists however show 10%, the Worker's Revolution-ary Party over 11% and the Ecologists 15%.[4] The National Front ran thirty-three (11%) women, that is two more than the Conservatives who, of course, had over-all nearly 300 more candidates.

The conclusion to be drawn from all this would seem to be that in spite of Mrs Thatcher's personal triumph, women can expect to remain much where they have been since the war in politics. They have once again increased their representation among candidates, only to achieve an even greater fall in the numbers of members elected. Representation is again proportionately greatest for them in the minor parties, and higher in the Labour than in the Conservative Party. Again, as has been repeatedly pointed out in the course of the book, an exceptional woman may be successful, but this is not cumulative. As Margaret Bondfield can hardly be said to have opened the way to women in the Cabinet—it was after all sixteen years before another woman was to be there—so Margaret Thatcher may well retain her new record for very many years to come. And this expectation can only be reinforced by the loss to the Labour Party of Shirley Williams, and the announcement by the new

Prime Minister of a Cabinet bereft, save for herself, of women members.

In spite of all this, there may be a couple of points on the credit side. One of the themes of this book has been the clear need for more women to be in visible positions of power so that girls increasingly develop a sense of their own potential in such areas. A Prime Minister wields power and dispenses patronage in a perhaps uniquely visible and dramatic way and Margaret Thatcher's position cannot in this sense be lost on women, or indeed men, from now on. It is also the case that, if the election of 1979 showed anything, it was that the assumption that a woman leader would inevitably lose the party significant support, proved to be unfounded. Need it be too much to hope that, from now on, those responsible for candidate selection will bear this in mind rather than aiming for an apparently largely non-existent male chauvinist vote?

In the end, however, one individual's achievement of the top honours can hardly produce a social revolution. Probably few people have in any case doubted for some time that women could, practically and intellectually, do any top job; the question was more whether they had the ambition, incentive and self-confidence to try, and the luck to make it. In politics, one had and she did. Yet fundamentally what is needed is numbers not uniqueness, models more diffused, less rarified— in short sixty or seventy women in the House which would seem unlikely, for all the reasons already given, without changes in the electoral system.[5] In the meantime the election of 1979 has been for women in politics one large step forward and a number of smaller ones backwards, and its impact more dramatic than substantive.

Women Members of Parliament 1918–1979

(with party, constituency and date of first election)

ADAMSON	Mrs J. L.	(Lab.)	1938	Dartford
ANDERSON	Rt Hon Betty Harvie	(Con.)	1959	Renfrewshire E.
APSELY	Lady	(Con.)	1943	Bristol Central
ASTOR	Viscountess	(Con.)	1919	Plymouth, Sutton
ATHOLL	Duchess of	(Con.)	1923	Perth and Kinross
BACON	Rt Hon Alice (later Baroness)	(Lab.)	1945	Leeds S.E.
BAIN	Mrs Margaret	(Scot. Nat.)	1974	Dunbartonshire E.
BENTHAM	Dr E.	(Lab.)	1929	Islington E.
BONDFIELD	Rt Hon Margaret	(Lab.)	1923 1926	Northampton Wallsend
BOOTHROYD	Miss Betty	(Lab.)	1973	West Bromich W.
BRADDOCK	Mrs E. M.	(Lab.)	1945	Liverpool Exchange
BURTON	Miss E. (later Baroness)	(Lab.)	1950	Coventry S.
BUTLER	Mrs Joyce	(Lab.)	1955	Wood Green
CASTLE	Rt Hon Barbara	(Lab.)	1945	Blackburn
CAZALET-KEIR	Mrs (Miss T. Cazalet)	(Con.)	1931	Islington E.
CHALKER	Mrs Lynda	(Con.)	1974	Wallasey
COLMAN	Miss G. M.	(Lab.)	1945	Tyneside
COLQUHUON	Mrs Maureen	(Lab.)	1974	Northampton N.
COPELAND	Mrs I.	(Con.)	1931	Stoke-on-Trent
CORBET	Mrs F.	(Lab.)	1945	Camberwell (Peckham)
CULLEN	Mrs A.	(Lab.)	1948	Glasgow, Gorbals
DALTON	Mrs Hugh	(Lab.)	1929	Bishop Auckland
DAVIDSON	Viscountess (later Baroness Northchurch, D.B.E.)	(Con.)	1937	Hemel Hempstead

DEVLIN	Miss B.	(Ind.		
		Unity)	1969	Mid-Ulster
DUNWOODY	Mrs G. P.	(Lab.)	1966	Exeter
			1974	Crewe
EMMET	The Hon Mrs E.			
	(later Baroness)	(Con.)	1955	E. Grinstead
EWING	Mrs W.	(Scot.	1967	Hamilton
		Nat.)	1974	Moray and Nairn
FAITH	Mrs Sheila	(Con.)	1979	Belper
FENNER	Mrs Peggy	(Con.)	1970	Rochester and
				Chatham
FISHER	Mrs Doris	(Lab.)	1970	Birmingham,
	(later Baroness)			Ladywood
FOOKES	Miss Janet	(Con.)	1970	Plymouth, Drake
FORD	Mrs P.	(Con.)	1953	Down N.
GAMMANS	Lady	(Con.)	1957	Hornsey
GANLEY	Mrs C. S.	(Lab.)	1945	Battersea S.
GOULD	Mrs B. A.	(Lab.)	1945	Hendon N.
GRAVES	Miss M.	(Con.)	1931	Hackney S.
HALL	Miss Joan	(Con.)	1970	Keighley
HAMILTON	Mrs M. A.	(Lab.)	1929	Blackburn
HARDIE	Mrs A.	(Lab.)	1937	Glasgow,
				Springburn
HART	Rt Hon Judith	(Lab.)	1959	Lanark
HAYMAN	Mrs Helene	(Lab.)	1974	Welwyn and
				Hatfield
HERBISON	Rt Hon Margaret	(Lab.)	1945	Lanark N.
HILL	Mrs Eveline	(Con.)	1950	Manchester,
				Wythenshawe
HOLT	Miss Mary	(Con.)	1970	Preston N.
HORNSBY-SMITH	Rt Hon Dame	(Con.)	1950	Chislehurst
	Patricia			
HORSBRUGH	Miss Florence	(Con.)	1931	Dundee
			1950	Manchester,
				Moss-side
IVEAGH	Countess of	(Con.)	1927	Southend
JACKSON	Miss Margaret	(Lab.)	1974	Lincoln
JEGER	Mrs Lena	(Lab.)	1953	Holborn and
				St Pancras
JEWSON	Miss D. (Mrs Camp-			
	bell Stephen)	(Lab.)	1923	Norwich
KELLET-BOWMAN	Mrs Elaine	(Con.)	1970	Lancaster

KERR	Mrs A. P.	(Lab.)	1964	Rochester and Chatham
KNIGHT	Mrs Jill	(Con.)	1966	Birmingham, Edgbaston
LAWRENCE	Miss S.	(Lab.)	1923	East Ham
LEE	Rt Hon Jennie (Mrs Aneurin Bevan, later Baroness)	(Lab.)	1929 1945	Lanark N. Cannock
LESTOR	Miss Joan	(Lab.)	1966	Eton and Slough
LLOYD-GEORGE	Lady Megan	(Lib.) (Lab.)	1939 1957	Anglesey Cramarthen
MCALLISTAIR	Mrs Mary	(Lab.)	1958	Glasgow, Kelvingrove
MACDONALD	Mrs Margo	(Scot. Nat.)	1973	Glasgow, Govan
MCDONALD	Dr Oonagh	(Lab.)	1976	Thurrock
MCKAY	Mrs Margaret	(Lab.)	1964	Clapham
MCLAUGHLIN	Mrs Patricia	(Con.)	1955	Belfast West
MANN	Mrs J.	(Lab.)	1945	Coatbridge and Airdrie
MANNING	Mrs L.	(Lab.)	1931 1945	Islington E. Epping
MARKIEVICZ	Countess (did not take seat)	(Sinn Fein)	1918	Dublin, St Patrick's
MAYNARD	Miss Joan	(Lab.)	1974	Sheffield, Brightside
MIDDLETON	Mrs Lucy	(Lab.)	1945	Plymouth, Sutton
MILLER	Mrs Millie	(Lab.)	1974	Redbridge, Ilford N.
MONKS	Mrs Constance	(Con.)	1970	Chorley
MOSLEY	Lady Cynthia	(Lab.)	1929	Stoke-on-Trent
NICHOL	Mrs M. E.	(Lab.)	1945	Bradford N.
NOEL-BUXTON	Lady	(Lab.)	1930 1945	Norfolk N. Norwich
OPPENHEIM	Mrs Sally	(Con.)	1970	Gloucester
PATON	Mrs F.	(Lab.)	1945	Rushcliffe
PHILIPSON	Mrs M.	(Con.)	1923	Berwick-on-Tweed
PHILLIPS	Dr Marion	(Lab.)	1929	Sunderland
PICKFORD	The Hon Mary	(Con.)	1931	Hammersmith N.

PICTON-				
TURBERVILL	Miss E.	(Lab.)	1929	The Wrekin
PIKE	Miss Mervyn			
	(later Baroness)	(Con.)	1956	Melton
PITT	Dame Edith	(Con.)	1953	Birmingham,
				Edgbaston
QUENNELL	Miss Joan	(Con.)	1960	Petersfield
RATHBONE	Miss E.	(Ind.)	1929	Combined
				English
				Universities
REES	Mrs Dorothy	(Lab.)	1950	Barry
RICHARDSON	Miss Josephine	(Lab.)	1974	Barking
RIDEALGH	Mrs M.	(Lab.)	1945	Ilford N.
RUNCIMAN	Viscountess	(Lib.)	1928	St Ives
RUNGE	Mrs N.	(Con.)	1931	Rotherhithe
SHAW	Mrs C. M.	(Lab.)	1945	Ayr
SHAW	Mrs H. B.	(Con.)	1931	Bothwell
SHORT	Mrs R.	(Lab.)	1964	Wolverhampton
				E.
SLATER	Mrs Harriet	(Lab.)	1953	Stoke-on-Trent N.
SUMMERSKILL	Dr Shirley	(Lab.)	1964	Halifax
SUMMERSKILL	Rt Hon Edith	(Lab.)	1938	Fulham W.
	(later Baroness)		1955	Warrington
TATE	Mrs H. B.	(Con.)	1931	Willesden W.
			1935	Frome
TAYLOR	Mrs Ann	(Lab.)	1974	Bolton W.
TERRINGTON	Lady	(Lib.)	1923	Wycombe
THATCHER	Rt Hon Margaret	(Con.)	1959	Finchley
TWEEDSMUIR	Lady			
	(later Baroness)	(Con.)	1946	Aberdeen S.
VICKERS	Dame Joan	(Con.)	1955	Plymouth,
	(later Baroness)			Devonport
WARD	Dame Irene	(Con.)	1931	Wallsend
	(later Baroness)		1950	Tynemouth
WARD	Mrs S. W.	(Con.)	1931	Cannock
WHITE	Mrs Eirene			
	(later Baroness)	(Lab.)	1950	Flint E.
WILKINSON	Rt Hon Ellen	(Lab.)	1924	Middlesbrough
			1935	Jarrow
WILLIAMS	Mrs Shirley	(Lab.)	1964	Hitchin
			1974	Hertford and
				Stevenage

WILLS	Mrs E. A.	(Lab.)	1945	Birmingham, Duddeston
WINTRINGHAM	Mrs M.	(Lib.)	1921	Louth
WISE	Mrs Audrey	(Lab.)	1974	Coventry S.W.
WRIGHT	Mrs Beatrice (Mrs Rathbone)	(Con.)	1941	Bodmin
WRIGHT	Mrs Sheila	(Lab.)	1979	Birmingham, Handsworth

Appendix 2

Number of Women Candidates and Elected Members since 1918

	Number standing	As a %	Number elected	As a %
1918	17	1.0	1	0.1
1922	33	2.3	2	0.3
1923	34	2.4	8	1.3
1924	41	2.9	4	0.7
1929	69	4.0	14	2.3
1931	62	4.8	15	2.4
1935	67	5.0	9	1.5
1945	87	5.2	24	3.8
1950	126	6.8	21	3.4
1951	77	5.6	17	2.7
1955	92	6.5	24	3.8
1959	81	5.3	25	4.0
1964	90	5.1	29	4.6
1966	81	4.7	26	4.1
1970	99	5.4	26	4.1
1974 (Feb.)	143	6.7	23	3.6
1974 (Oct.)	161	7.2	27	4.3
1979	206	8.0	19	2.9

SOURCES. *Times Guide to the House of Commons*
Dods, *Parliamentary Companion*
Butler and Sloman, *British Political Facts, 1918–1975*
Craig, *British Election Results, 1918–1975*

Appendix 3

Women Cabinet Ministers

Margaret Bondfield	(Lab.)	(1929–31)	Minister of Labour
Ellen Wilkinson	(Lab.)	(1945–7)	Minister of Education
Florence Horsbrugh	(Con.)	(1953–4)	Minister of Education
Barbara Castle	(Lab.)	(1964–5)	Minister of Overseas Development
		(1965–8)	Minister of Transport
		(1968–70)	First Secretary of State and Secretary of State for Employment and Productivity
		(1974–6)	Secretary of State for Social Services
Judith Hart	(Lab.)	(1968–9)	Paymaster General
Margaret Thatcher	(Con.)	(1970–74)	Secretary of State for Education and Science
Shirley Williams	(Lab.)	(1974–6)	Secretary of State for Prices and Consumer Protection
		(1976–9)	Secretary of State for Education and Science

Appendix 4

Women's 'Firsts' in National Politics

First woman M.P. (and first Conservative woman)	Lady Astor (C.)	(1919)
First Liberal woman M.P.	Mrs Wintringham (Lib.)	(1921)
First Labour woman M.P.	Susan Lawrence[1] (Lab.)	(1923)
First woman to introduce successful Private Member's Bill	Lady Astor (C.)	(1923)
First women Minister	Margaret Bondfield (Lab.)	(1924)

First woman Parliamentary Private Secretary	Susan Lawrence (Lab.)	(1924)
First women Tellers	Dorothy Jewson (Lab.) Duchess of Atholl (C.)	(1924)
First woman to join her husband in the House	Hilda Runciman[2] (Lib.)	(1928)
First woman Cabinet Minister (and Privy Councillor)	Margaret Bondfield (Lab.)	(1929)
First (and only) Independent woman M.P.	Eleanor Rathbone (Ind.)	(1929)
First woman Chairman of the Labour Party	Susan Lawrence (Lab.)	(1929–30)
First woman to move the Address in reply to the Speech from the Throne	Florence Horsbrugh (C.)	(1936)
First woman on the Speaker's panel of Chairmen of Committees (and as such first woman to preside over the whole House)	Florence Paton (Lab.)	(1946)
First woman elected to the 1922 Committee of the Conservative Party	Lady Davidson (C.)	(1948)
First woman Whip	Harriet Slater (Lab.)	(1964)
First woman Deputy Chairman of Ways and Means (and first to sit in the Speaker's Chair)	Betty Harvie Anderson (C.)	(1970)
First woman Party Leader	Margaret Thatcher (C.)	(1975)
First woman Prime Minister	Margaret Thatcher (C.)	(1979)

NOTE. As can be seen, the honours are very evenly split between Labour and Conservative women. Indeed leaving aside purely party appointments, the two major parties have between them created women's 'firsts' in almost exactly equal numbers.

[1] Miss Lawrence's result was declared first, but Margaret Bondfield and Dorothy Jewson were also returned in 1923.

[2] While on the more 'domestic' front, the first woman to marry while an M.P. was Thelma Cazalet (thereafter Cazalet-Keir) in 1939, and the first woman to have a baby while a member was Mrs Wright, in 1943.

Appendix 5

Private Members' Bills Which Became Law Introduced by Women

House of Commons

C Intoxicating Liquors (Sales to Persons under 18) Act 1923 – Astor
C Nursing Homes (Registration) Act 1927 – Philipson
C Illegitimate Children (Scotland) Act 1931 – Atholl
L Sentence of Death (Expectant Mothers) Act 1931 – Picton-Turbervill
C Methylated Spirits (Sale by Retail) Act 1937 – Horsbrugh
C Poor Law (Amendment) Act 1938 – Ward
L Hire Purchase Act 1938 – Wilkinson
C Adoption of Children Act 1939 – Horsbrugh
L Criminal Law Amendment Act 1951 – Castle
L Disposal of Uncollected Goods Act 1952 – Burton
C Rights of Entry (Gas and Electricity Boards) Act 1953 – Ward
C Protection of Birds Act 1954 – Tweedsmuir
C Protection of Animals (Anaesthetics) Act 1955 – Davidson
C Drainage Rates Act 1958 – Pike
C Public Bodies (Admission to Meetings) Act 1960 – Thatcher
C Nurses (Amendment Act) 1961 – Ward
C Penalties for Drunkenness Act 1962 – Ward
C Public Lavatories (Turnstiles) Act 1963 – McLaughlin
C Animals (Restriction of Importation) Act 1964 – Harvie Anderson
C Young Persons (Employment) Act 1964 – Vickers
C Nurses Act 1964 – Vickers
L British Nationality Act 1965 – Jeger
C Design Copyright Act 1968 – Knight
C Affiliation Proceedings (Amendment) Act 1972 – Vickers
L Domestic Violence and Matrimonial Proceedings Act 1976 – Richardson

NOTE. Two Private Members' Bills, Lady Astor's Intoxicating Liquor Bill and Lady Tweedsmuir's Protection of Birds Bill, were piloted through the House of Lords by their husbands, and Mrs Thatcher's Public Bodies legislation by another woman—Lady Elliot of Harwood.

Nineteen Conservative M.P.'s Bills have been successful compared to six Labour. Dame Irene Ward (Baroness Ward) was responsible for no less than four Private Members' Bills and Florence Horsbrugh (Baroness Horsbrugh) and Dame Joan Vickers (Baroness Vickers) for two each.

Appendix 6

Dates of Enfranchisement of Women

1881	Isle of Man
1893	New Zealand
1893–1909	States of Australia
1869–1918	20 States and 1 Territory of the U.S.A.
1906	Finland
1907	Norway
1915	Denmark
1915	Iceland
1917	U.S.S.R.
1918/1928[1]	Great Britain
1919/1921[2]	Sweden
1918	Germany
1919	Netherlands
1945	France
1945	Italy
1948	Israel

[1] 1918, Women over 30; 1928, women over 21.
[2] 1919, Unmarried women; 1921, all women.

Appendix 7

Percentages of Women in Parliament in Various Countries (October, 1977)

Denmark	17.0
Finland	23.5
France	1.7
India	3.3
Israel	7.5
Italy	8.4
Netherlands	13.3
Norway	22.5
Sweden	21.4
U.K.	4.4
U.S.A.	4.1
West Germany	7.3

Party List Proportional Representation

Denmark	Norway
Finland	Sweden
Italy	West Germany
Netherlands	

Single Member Systems

First past post: U.K.
                U.S.A.
Second ballot: France

NOTE. Some of the figures supplied by the Embassies are for the last election. The figures therefore might be slightly different if there has been a by-election since then. In any event the final figure would only show a small increase or decrease. The general trend remains clear.

SOURCES. Embassies of each country, and in the case of America, Statistical Abstracts from the Library of the American Embassy, and of Finland, the Finnish State Calendar.

Bibliography

The most useful general works of reference, which I have used constantly throughout this study, are, in addition to *Hansard: The Times Guide to the House of Commons*, issued by the Times Publishing Company for every election since 1929; *Dod's Parliamentary Companion*; *Vacher's Parliamentary Companion*; *Who's Who*, and *Who was Who*; and the *Dictionary of National Biography*. Andrew Roth's books *The Business Background of M.P.s* (Parliamentary Profiles, 1975) and *The M.P.s Chart* (Parliamentary Profiles, 1977) are useful sources of information often not available in the other reference works.

For brevity's sake I have listed here only books specifically mentioned in the text.

Aner, K., *Sexism in the Year 2000*, IDOC Bulletin, Geneva, 1965.

Bax, Belfort, *Essays in Socialism*, Grant Richards, London, 1907.

Bondfield, M., *A Life's Work*, Hutchinson, London, 1950.

Bowlby, J., *Maternal Care and Mental Health*, W.H.O. Bulletin, 1951.

Brittain, V., *Lady into Woman*, Dakers, London, 1953.

Brookes, P., *Women at Westminster*, Peter Davis, London, 1967.

Charzat, G., *Les françaises sont-elles des citoyennes?*, Denoel Gouthier, Paris, 1972.

Cole, M., *The Story of Fabian Socialism*, Heinemann, London, 1961.

Currell, M., *Political Woman*, Croom Helm, London, 1964.

Dawkins, R., *The Selfish Gene*, Oxford University Press, Oxford, 1977.

Donoughue, B. and Jones, G., *Herbert Morrison*, Weidenfeld and Nicolson, London, 1973.

Elder, N., *Government in Sweden*, Pergamon, London, 1970.

Eulau, H. and Sprague, J., *Lawyers in Politics, a study of professional convergence*, Bobbs Merrill, New York, 1961.

Gavron, H., *The Captive Wife: Conflicts of housebound mothers*, Routledge and Kegan Paul, London, 1966. Penguin Books, Harmondsworth, 1968.

Goot, M. and Reid, E., *Women and Voting Studies*, Sage Publications, London, 1975.

Goldberg, S., *The Inevitability of Patriarchy*, Maurice Temple Smith, London, 1977.

Hobbs, M., *Born to Struggle*, Quartet Books, London, 1973.

HMSO, *Report on the Social Insurance and Allied Services*, Cmnd 6404, 1942 (Beveridge Report).

HMSO, *Report of the Central Advisory Council for Education*, 1959 (Crowther Report).

HMSO, *Half our Future, Report of the Council for Education*, 1963 (Newsom Report).

HMSO, *Children and Their Primary Schools*, 1967 (Plowden Report).

HMSO, *Report of the Royal Commission on Local Government in England and Wales*, 1969 (Radcliffe-Maud Report).

HMSO, *Women and Work: Sex Differences and Society*, Manpower Paper, No. 11, 1974.

HMSO, *Equality for Women*, Cmnd 5724, 1974.

Jaquette, J., *Women in Politics*, John Wiley, New York, 1974.

Jenkins, R., *Asquith*, Collins, London, 1964.

Jephcott, P., *et al.*, *Married Women Working*, Allen and Unwin, London, 1962.

Klein, V., *The Feminine Character: History of an Ideology*, Routledge and Kegan Paul, London, 1946.

Lakeman, E., *How Democracies Vote*, Faber and Faber, London, 1974.

Mackie, L. and Pattullo, P., *Women at Work*, Tavistock Publications, London, 1977.

McKenzie, R. and Silver, A., *Angels in Marble*, Heinemann, London, 1968.

Mann, J., *Women in Parliament*, Odhams, London, 1962.

Middleton, L. (ed.), *Women in the Labour Movement*, Croom Helm, London, 1977.

Milburn, J., *Women as Citizens*, Sage Publications, London, 1976.

Miller, K., *Government and Politics in Denmark*, Houghton Mifflin, Boston, 1968.

Oakley, A., *Sex, Gender and Society*, Maurice Temple Smith, London, 1972.

Paterson, P., *The Selectorate*, MacGibbon and Kee, 1967.

Radice, L., *Reforming the House of Commons*, Fabian Tract 448, 1977.

Ranney, A., *Pathways to Parliament*, Macmillan, London, 1965.

Rapoport, R. and Rapoport, R., *Dual Career Families*, Penguin, Harmondsworth, 1971.

Roper, E. (ed.), *The Prison Letters of Constance Markievicz*, Longmans Green, London, 1934.

Rose, R. (ed.), *Electoral Behaviour*, Collier Macmillan, London, 1974.

Rover, C., *Women's Suffrage and Party Politics in Britain, 1856–1914*, Routledge and Kegan Paul, London, 1967.

Rustow, D., *The Politics of Compromise*, Princeton University Press, Princeton, 1955.

Sandberg, E., *Equality is the Goal*, Report of the Advisory Council on Equality, The Swedish Institute, Stockholm, 1975.

Selid, B., *Women in Norway*, Norwegian Joint Committee on International Social Policy, Oslo, 1970.

Smith, T., *Anti-Politics: Consensus, Reform and Protest in Britain*, Charles Knight, London, 1972.

Storing, J., *Norwegian Democracy*, Allen and Unwin, London, 1963.

Strachey, Ray, *The Cause*, Bell and Sons, London, 1928.

Stradling, R., *The Political Awareness of the School-leaver*, Hansard Society, London, 1977.

Summerskill, E., *A Woman's World*, Heinemann, London, 1967.

Sykes, C., *Nancy, The Life of Lady Astor*, Collins, London, 1972.

Tornud, K., *The Electoral System of Finland*, Hugh Evelyn, London, 1968.

Verba, S., *Small Groups and Political Behaviour*, Princeton University Press, Princeton, 1961.

Wassan van Schaveren, P., 'Planning the Emancipation of Women', in *Planning and Development in the Netherlands*, vol. VIII, no. 1, 1976, pp. 4–16.

Wedgwood-Benn, A., *The New Politics: A Socialist Reconnaissance*, Fabian Society Pamphlet No. 402, 1970.

Wilkinson, E., *Peeps at Politicians*, Allan and Co., London, 1931.

Wilson, E., *Socio-biology: The New Synthesis*, Harvard University Press, New Haven, 1975.

Wilson, H., *The Governance of Britain*, Weidenfeld and Nicolson, and Michael Joseph, London, 1976.

Notes

CHAPTER I

1 The by-election caused by the death of Hugh Delargy brought to Parliament Dr Oonagh McDonald as member for Thurrock.

2 Edith Summerskill, *A Woman's World*, p. 61.

3 And of these by far the majority are in the 'female' areas of geriatrics, paediatrics and obstetrics (*Women in Medicine*, DHSS, 1975). This report also makes clear that there are no women on the Councils of the Colleges of Physicians or Surgeons, and only two out of 44 on the General Practitioners' Council.

4 And this belief is correct in that in 1976, women's average wage was less than 70% that of men.

5 Department of Employment Statistics—1975 figures (last available).

6 On the whole question of women's attitudes to their social role and the stereotyping of society's images in this respect, see H. Gavron, *The Captive Wife: conflicts of housebound mothers*, pp. 125–131, also A. Oakley, *Sex Gender and Society*, pp. 128ff.

7 For example, in 1975, only 71 out of 2330 T.U. officials were female—and these in the female-dominated Unions. On overtime, Department of Employment Statistics for 1976 showed that overtime for male manual workers accounted for over 13% of all earnings, while the figure for female workers was only just over 2%.

8 On this see for example, R. Rapoport and R. Rapoport, *Dual Career Families*; P. Jephcott et al., *Married Women Working*; A. Oakley, op. cit.

9 The comment has been ascribed to both Ellen Wilkinson and Eleanor Rathbone.

10 The Labour Party A-list, i.e. those candidates sponsored by Unions, contained only 3 women, as of June 1977 (Transport House figures).

11 *Women and Work: Sex differences and Society.*

12 J. Bowlby, *Maternal Care and Mental Health* (Report prepared on behalf of the World Health Organisation).

13 *The Inevitability of Patriarchy.*

14 E. Wilson, *Sociobiology: The New Synthesis.*

15 R. Dawkins, *The Selfish Gene*. Dawkins' argument involves the suggestion that the urge to reproduction is not personal (i.e. not for the sake of the individual personality or whatever) but genetic (i.e. for the perpetuating of the individual gene). Women with only one ovum (at a time, at least) are genetically determined much more obsessively to protect that carrier of genes than men who have millions of sperms (potential gene carriers).

16 For a fuller account of this change in women's attitudes and men's reactions—see the discussion on the Abortion Bills (Chapter V).

17 See Chapter III.
18 Audrey Wise tells of being asked at a selection conference if she thought she would be able to give enough time to her husband and children if she became an M.P. She managed to turn this to advantage not only by making a proper virtue of her family experience, but by suggesting the Committee ask the same of the other three candidates—all male and all married with children.
19 Quoted in C. Sykes, *Nancy: The Life of Lady Astor*, p. 200.
20 On a recent poll, over 80% of voters, both men and women, said that, faced with a woman candidate, they would not discriminate against her on grounds of sex. (N.O.P. poll published in the *Daily Mail*, 11 July 1978. I am grateful to Michael English, editor of the *Daily Mail*, for permission to quote from the survey and to John Fidler of N.O.P. for letting me see unpublished sections.)
21 See Lisanne Radice, *Reforming the House of Commons*, pp. 14–15.
22 H. Eulau and J. D. Sprague, *Lawyers and Politics: A Study of Professional Convergence*.
23 The Royal Commission on Local Government in England and Wales, (Radcliffe-Maud), 1969, HMSO, gives 12% Council members as female.

CHAPTER II

1 Vera Brittain, *Ladies into Women*, p. 50.
2 By the Representation of the People Act of that year, and then only applying to women over 30 years of age. This Act left the validity of the candidacy of women in Parliamentary Elections unclear however and it needed a further Act—The Parliament (Qualification of Women) Act—to make this unambiguous.
3 *The Times*, 23 October 1918.
4 E. Roper, ed., *The Prison Letters of Constance Markievicz*, p. 188.
5 See Chapter III.
6 Mrs Miller died in office at the end of October 1977, when this study was already completed. She is included in the figures throughout.
7 Austin Ranney, *Pathways to Parliament*, p. 138.
8 *Women at Westminster*, pp. 243–4.
9 The figures are somewhat difficult to determine, but Liberal Party Head-quarters said that in July 1977, 24 out of 322 candidates already selected to fight constituencies at the next election were women. On the list of candidates available for selection only 6 out of 139 were women.
10 In 1970, 10 women were candidates out of a total of 65. By October 1974, the number had fallen to 8 out of 71. (Figures from the S.N.P. Press Office.)
11 Hansard, 3 November 1936, vol. 317, col. 14.
12 The death of Millie Miller took the number down again to twenty-seven.
13 This 'memo' can now be seen (in facsimile) in the Fawcett Library.
14 In 1972, 2 out of 100 on the A-list were women. In 1977, the number was 3. (Figures supplied by Transport House.)

15 'An Opponent's Viewpoint', written for Michael Astor.
16 See Chapter V.
17 See Chapter VI.

CHAPTER III

1 A *Guardian* article (of 29 November 1976) attempted to trace the process of selection of the Labour candidate for Stechford (left vacant when Roy Jenkins took up his duties in the E.E.C. Commission) and came to the conclusion that the principal factors affecting the selection of the candidate at least in this case, were 'inertia and luck'—inertia, mainly on the part of the bodies who might have proposed candidates, but did not, and luck on the part of the candidates who for no very apparent reasons were selected.
2 *Woman in Parliament*, p. 117.
3 There have only been four Liberal women M.P.s, the last being Lady Megan Lloyd George who served as Member for Anglesey from 1929–51. (When she returned to Parliament in 1957, it was as *Labour* member for Carmarthen.)
4 P. Paterson, *The Selectorate*, p. 45.
5 David Wood writing in *The Times*, 15 August 1977.
6 *Angels in Marble*, p. 88.
7 See M. Goot and E. Reid, *Women and Voting Studies*, passim.
8 See R. Rose, *Electoral Behaviour*, pp. 521–2.
9 See, for example, Agenda of the Labour Party Conference 1972; Agenda of the Conservative Party Conference 1968, 1972, 1973; Agenda of the Liberal Party Conference, 1968, 1973.
10 Margaret Bondfield, *A Life's Work*, p. 245.
11 In fact women have followed other women on a few occasions, but only once has a woman handed over to another woman of her own party—when Mrs Jill Knight took over Birmingham Edgbaston in 1966 from Dame Edith Pitt, some of whose personal support she undoubtedly inherited. Mrs Knight had herself, of course, a long record of service to her party.
12 'Women in Trade Unions Today' (Ch. 8 of *Women in the Labour Movement*, ed. L. Middleton).
13 See Chapter X.

CHAPTER IV

1 Quoted in her obituary notice in *The Times* of 31 January 1946.
2 1972 figures: Department of Education Statistics.
3 The actual numbers of women are, of course, throughout very small, which in many cases limits the significance of the percentages.
4 *Reforming the House of Commons*, Fabian Tract 448.
5 'Are all our M.P.'s pulling their weight?' *The Guardian*, 23 December 1976. The one woman was Joan Maynard who wrote to me, when I asked her about this point, 'I do not think the number of Parliamentary Committees or the number of questions asked is indicative of whether or not the M.P.

is doing a good job—May I say the N.E.C. does take up a lot of time—I also think I do more meetings outside Parliament than most M.P.s'.

6 *The Guardian*, 1 March 1977. This is not to suggest that a male minister in similar circumstances would have been unaffected, but only that women do seem to take longer to acquire confidence, and also to lose it more easily. (See e.g. Mrs Thatcher's comment in the next paragraph.)

7 *The Times*, 9 May 1977.

8 Domestic Violence and Matrimonial Proceedings Act (1976).

9 *A Woman's World*, p. 62.

10 This went on to the Statute Book as the Public Bodies (Admission to Meetings) Act. It was the first Bill also to be piloted through the House of Lords by another woman, Lady Elliot of Harwood.

CHAPTER V

1 See J. Jaquette, *Women in Politics*.

2 *The Feminine Character: History of an Ideology*. For the general force of peer group pressure, see S. Verba, *Small Groups and Political Behaviour*.

3 This view is very clearly behind the argument of a letter I had from Lady Wootton (15 May 1977). She rejected the idea of an enquiry into political *women* on the basis that she was 'in politics as a *person* . . . I admit that women have some interests unique to them in sexual and maternal matters but these are not my specialisms, and I wish to function as a *person* in public life . . .' (the emphases are Lady Wootton's).

4 See Hansard, 19 July 1961, vol. 644, col. 1256.

5 On the occasion of the rejection by the women of the composition of the Select Committee on Abortion (1976). This is done by interjecting with 'Object' when this is announced.

6 *Woman in Parliament*, p. 232.

CHAPTER VI

1 *Political Woman*, p. 23.

2 Following Susan Lawrence in 1930, Jenny Adamson was Chairman in 1936, Barbara Gould in 1940, Ellen Wilkinson in 1945, Alice Bacon in 1951, Edith Summerskill in 1955, Margaret Herbison in 1957, Barbara Castle in 1959, Jennie Lee in 1968, Eirene White in 1969, and Joan Lestor in 1977.

3 Hansard, 3 November 1936, vol. 317, col. 13.

4 Mann, op. cit., p. 18.

5 A. Wedgwood-Benn, *The New Politics* (Fabian Pamphlet), p. 19.

6 *Anti-politics, Consensus, Reform and Protest in Britain*, p. 171.

7 15 August 1977.

CHAPTER VII

1 *Asquith*, p. 247.

2 *Letters of the Earl of Oxford and Asquith to a Friend* (ed. D. MacCarthy),

1st Series, 1915–22. Quoted in C. Rover, *Women's Suffrage and Party Politics in Britain*, p. 157.

3 This was the popular name for the Prisoner's Temporary Discharge for Ill-health Act, which allowed the release of hunger-striking prisoners and their subsequent re-imprisonment, so as to avoid the deaths of suffragettes from starvation.

4 *The Story of Fabian Socialism*, p. 127.

5 A reference to women's participation in local government.

6 Hansard, 23 October 1918, vol. 110, col. 842.

7 Herself a veteran of the suffrage campaign as Mrs Fawcett's second-in-command in the National Union of Women's Suffrage Societies and subsequently the Independent Candidate for Brentford and Chiswick in the 1918 election.

8 *The Cause*, p. 369.

9 Hansard, 29 February 1924, vol. 170, col. 871.

10 Ibid.

11 Ibid., col. 878.

12 Ibid., col. 938.

13 Ibid., col. 934.

14 Ibid., col. 873.

15 Ibid.

16 Ibid., col. 874.

17 Hence much of the argument of the debate revolved around the advisability of giving the vote to those with no permanent abode. The Duchess of Atholl for example stirred up a hornet's nest when she opposed the claims of tinkers (cols. 873–4) to the vote.

18 Ibid., cols. 918–19.

19 Hansard, 29 March 1928, vol. 215, col. 1370.

20 Ibid., col. 1371.

21 Ibid., col. 1379.

22 Ibid.

23 Ibid.

24 Ibid., col. 1386.

25 Ibid., cols. 1390–1.

26 Ibid., col. 1391.

27 Ibid., col. 1391.

28 Ibid., cols. 1392–3.

29 Ibid., col. 1395.

30 Hansard, 27 November 1931, vol. 260, col. 699.

31 National Health Insurance and Contributory Pensions Bill, Hansard, 11 May 1932, vol. 265.

32 Ibid., col. 1974.

33 Report on the Social Insurance and Allied Services, 1942, p. 40.

34 Hansard, 20 March 1941, vol. 370, col. 316.

35 Ibid.

36 Ibid., col. 317.

37 Ibid., col. 321.
38 Ibid., col. 326.
39 Ibid., col. 327.
40 Ibid., cols. 350–1.
41 Ibid., col. 398.
42 See e.g. Maureen Colquhoun's Bill, 'Balance of the Sexes', Hansard, 16 May 1975, vol. 892, cols. 930–66.
43 The one exception in this context was Mrs Agnes Hardie who was a pacifist and who opposed female conscription tooth and nail. 'A woman who is training and bringing up children', she said, 'is doing a far more important job for the future generations . . . than filling shells with which to kill some other woman's son' (ibid., col. 353).
44 Op. cit., col. 375.
45 Ibid., col. 375.
46 Ibid., col. 375.
47 Ibid., cols. 347–8.
48 Ibid., cols. 393–4.
49 Hansard, 5 March 1942, vol. 378, col. 838.
50 Ibid., col. 848.
51 Ibid., col. 843.
52 Ibid., col. 852.
53 Ibid., col. 860.
54 Ibid., cols. 862–3.
55 Ibid., col. 884.
56 Hansard, 5 March 1942, vol. 378, col. 841.
57 Hansard, 20 March 1941, vol. 370, col. 395.
58 Op. cit., col. 841.
59 Op. cit., col. 386.
60 Ibid., col. 347.
61 Op. cit., p. 52.
62 Ibid., p. 49.
63 Ibid.
64 Op. cit., p. 52.

CHAPTER VIII

1 Hansard, 20 March 1962, vol. 656, col. 216.
2 'Equality for Women'.
3 Hansard, 9 February 1970, vol. 795, col. 914. Mrs Castle did not finish the story, for when Churchill met Mrs Cazalet-Keir soon afterwards, he remonstrated genially, 'Thelma, Thelma, you are trying to put an elephant into a perambulator!'
4 Ibid., cols. 929–31.
5 Hansard, op. cit., col. 922.
6 Ibid.

7 Ian Gilmour for example gives a classic exposition of this position in another debate—see Hansard, 26 March 1975, vol. 889, col. 528.
8 Hansard, 26 March, 1975, vol. 889, col. 546.
9 Hansard, 9 February 1970, vol. 795, col. 956.
10 Hansard, vol. 795, cols. 957–67.
11 Ibid., col. 968.
12 Ibid., col. 972.
13 Ibid., col. 974.
14 Ibid.
15 Ibid., col. 945.
16 Ibid.
17 Ibid., col. 946.
18 Ibid., col. 1025.
19 Hansard, 26 March 1975, vol. 889, col. 527. Mr Gilmour was also quick to point out some of the practical inequalities of the Bill which, as he showed, were recognised by Labour supporters too. In this context, he quoted a contribution to *Labour Weekly* (9 August 1974) in which the Labour prospective candidate for Crosby had complained that 'the midwives who wish to keep their profession for women only are to lose this right, but the big Trade Unions who wish to keep the 19th Century based laws which stop women working night work and restrict the hours of over-time are to keep theirs.' (Ibid., col. 529.)
20 Ibid., cols. 539–40.
21 Ibid., col. 541.
22 Ibid.
23 Ibid., col. 543.
24 Ibid., col. 544. Mr Powell's opposition in this area had been consistently maintained since at least 1973. This is clear from a speech, which he kindly sent to me, made to the Ilford Chamber of Commerce (25 September 1973) when he argued in substantially the same terms about equality for women.
25 Ibid., col. 588.
26 Ibid., col. 590.
27 Ibid., col. 591.
28 Ibid., col. 588.
29 Ibid., col. 593.
30 Ibid., col. 594.
31 Ibid., col. 594.
32 Ibid., col. 556.
33 Ibid., col. 557.
34 Ibid.
35 Ibid., col. 559. Miss Fookes was probably optimistic here, as it's hard to see what difference the Bill could make unless the candidate were explicitly told that her femininity was the reason for her rejection. It is much more likely, however, that this sort of argument would be made in Committee, in private, and could thus hardly form the basis of a claim to the Equal Opportunities Commission.

36　Ibid., col. 574.

37　Ibid., cols. 582–3.

38　Ibid., col. 609. Although Dr Summerskill is a strong supporter of women's rights, she has no time for the demand for 'positive discrimination' or statutory representation of women in whatever capacity and is on record to this effect elsewhere (Hansard, 16 May 1975, vol. 892, col. 938).

39　Ibid., col. 610.

40　See Reports in *The Guardian*, 23 June 1977, and *The Times*, 21 June 1977. (See also full transcript of the judgement, *The Times*, 22 June 1977.)

41　See Report in *The Times*, 29 June 1977.

42　*The Guardian*, 25 June 1977.

43　*The Times*, 29 June 1977.

44　See for example Michael Zander writing in *The Guardian* (23 June 1977), and the untypically passionate *Times* editorial of 21 June 1977.

45　Hansard, 19 July 1977, vol. 935, col. 1396.

46　Ibid., col. 1397.

47　Ibid., col. 1399.

48　Ibid., col. 1399. It is interesting that a similar comment was made by an American judge in a rape case in Wisconsin, when he suggested that rape might be 'a normal reaction', especially in a society which was sexually permissive. (Reported in the *Herald Tribune*, 27 August 1977.) The judge, Archie Simonson, was forced to stand for re-election and was heavily defeated (*Guardian*, 9 October 1977).

49　Ibid., col. 1400.

50　Ibid., col. 1401. Mr Fairbairn confirms that this is indeed his belief but that under the ten-minute rule, the time-constraint made his speech 'merely a telegram'.

51　*A Woman's World*, p. 139.

52　Quoted by, among others, Edith Summerskill, ibid., p. 60.

53　Rover, op. cit., p. 136.

54　Interview in *The Observer*, 16 January 1966. When I asked Mr Heath for clarification on this point, he felt unable to help. (Letter from Edward Heath, 11 January 1978.)

55　Donoughue and Jones, *Herbert Morrison, Portrait of a Politician*, p. 193.

CHAPTER IX

1　But which in the end ironically may have worked out against the two of them. Both Mrs Ghandi and Mrs Bandaranaike were accused of attempting to develop a dynasty, via their sons, Sanjay Ghandi and Anura Bandaranaike. (See Dilip Hiro in *The Sunday Times*, 17 July 1977.)

2　The Israeli Embassy: 'Manpower in Israel' (abstract of the Census—1974).

3　Paula Wassan-van Schaveren, 'Planning the Emancipation of Women', in *Planning and Development in the Netherlands*, vol. VIII, no. 1, 1976, pp. 4–16.

4 In 1978, following the death of her husband Hubert Humphrey, Muriel Humphrey took his seat in the Senate.
5 See e.g. J. D. Barber, *The Lawmakers*, Yale University Press, 1967.
6 Milburn, op. cit., p. 19.
7 Suomen Valtiokalenteri (Finnish State Calendar), 1971.
8 The National Council of Women in Finland—Target Programme for the 1970s (Helsinki, 1970), p. 5.
9 Ibid., p. 3.
10 Ibid., p. 4.
11 See Milburn, op cit., p. 33.
12 For a detailed account of this see K. Tornudd, *The Electoral System of Finland*.
13 Betty Selid, *Women in Norway*, p. 104.
14 Ibid., p. 105.
15 Central Bureau of Statistics (Division of Employment Statistics), Oslo.
16 For a detailed account of the process see J. A. Storing, *Norwegian Democracy*, pp. 59–72.
17 See *The Times*, 10 September 1971. Also E. Lakeman, 'Much better, but not best', *Representation*, No. 46, January 1972, pp. 7–9.
18 The Fredrika Bremer Institute is now the largest non-political organisation for women in Sweden and constantly presses for greater participation for women in Swedish society.
19 Elisabet Sandberg, 'Equality is the Goal', The Swedish Institute, Report of the Advisory Council on Equality, 1975.
20 Sandberg, op. cit., p. 45.
21 *Women in Swedish Society* (Swedish Institute FS82c/Ohj, 1976).
22 This is still higher than any other European country. See Milburn, op. cit., p. 33.
23 Ibid.
24 Sandberg, op. cit., p. 41.
25 *Hertha*, no. 2, 1975, p. 19.
26 *Government in Sweden*, p. 189. This willingness to accept even quite radical constitutional change is perhaps exemplified by the 1978 legislation which allows the Crown to pass to the Sovereign's eldest child, male or female, and not only via the male line.
27 Statens Offentliga Utredningar, 1963: 17, p. 68 (in Elder, op. cit., p. 19).
28 For a description of the electoral system see Elder, op. cit., pp. 18–20. Also on the impact of proportional representation D. A. Rustow, *The Politics of Compromise*, pp. 72–6.
29 Sandberg, op. cit., p. 76. Women are normally better represented in urban areas than in rural ones. In this case, the increase in female municipal councillors is greater than it looks, since during the period since 1966, the municipalities were amalgamated into larger units so that the total number of those elected has dropped sharply.
30 Quoted in 'The position of Women in Society' (Final report of the Com-

mission appointed by the Prime Minister concerning the position of women in society, Copenhagen, 1974).
31 Figures from the Office of the Council on Equality, Copenhagen.
32 Less than 1 % (Council on Equality figures).
33 All figures from the Council on Equality.
34 For a description of the electoral system, see K. E. Miller, *Government and Politics in Denmark*, pp. 95–126.
35 See *New Society*, vol. 39, no. 752, p. 452, 3 March 1977.

CHAPTER X

1 Robert Stradling, *The Political Awareness of the School Leaver.*
2 *Sexism in the Year 2000*, p. 105.
3 Shaw put forward this idea in a letter to Eirene Lloyd Jones, the Labour candidate for Flint, which was quoted in the *Manchester Guardian* of 5 July 1945.
4 'The Voting Surveyed', *The Times Guide to the House of Commons*, October 1974, p. 31.
5 *How Democracies Vote*, p. 137.
6 Sally Kempton, quoted in Jaquette, *Women in Politics*, p. 157.
7 See *The Times*, 16 September 1977 and *The Guardian*, 16 September 1977.
8 Nicholas Scott, M.P. for Chelsea.
9 *The Guardian*, 5 October 1977.
10 *The Scotsman*, 30 September 1977. An alternative reading might of course be that Ms Colquhoun's fault was not in her sexual proclivities, but in her politically naive belief that it was possible to publicise this without some such repercussion.
11 See Ronald Butt, 'Why should a woman be more like a man?', *The Sunday Times*, 30 October 1977. Also Alan Watkins in *The Observer*, 11 December 1977.
12 Op. cit., p. 58.
13 *The Guardian*, 14 December 1977.
14 'The shrinking world of Bagehot', *Government and Opposition*, vol. 10, no. 1, 1975, pp. 1–11.

POSTSCRIPT

1 See Appendix 2.
2 The women defeated in this way were Ms Colquhoun, Miss Jackson, Mrs Hayman and Mrs Wise.
3 See p. 33 and notes.
4 The small number of women involved here, as elsewhere in the study, limits the significance of the figures. This is inevitable where a difference of one woman may make a difference of several percentage points.
5 See Chapter X.

CHAPTER X

POSTSCRIPT

Index